HIPPOCRENE BEGINNER'S SERIES

BEGINNER'S
GA

James MacLaren

HIPPOCRENE BOOKS, INC.
New York

Hippocrene paperback edition, 1999.

Fourth printing, 2006.

Originally published as:

Introduction to Gaelic for Beginners	1911
Gaelic Self-Taught	1914
MacLaren's Gaelic Self-Taught	1923
New Revised Fourth Edition	1935
Reprinted 1941, 1944, 1948, 1957, 1960, 1963, 1967	

For information, address:
HIPPOCRENE BOOKS, INC.
171 Madison Avenue
New York, NY 10016

ISBN 0-7818-0726-3

Printed in the United States of America.

PREFACE.

IT was my original intention merely to correct and revise Mr. James White MacLean's "Introduction to Gaelic," but as the revision progressed I found that I was practically re-writing the whole work so that the portion of it I was leaving intact had also to be re-written, regraded and arranged to suit the revised matter. The volume I present to the student is therefore an entirely new work.

I have endeavoured to keep the phonetic sounds as simple as possible ; some of the finer ones may have been omitted, but these may be left to be acquired as the student progresses. I have considered it inadvisable to follow the pronunciation of any one district. Varying dialects will be found in Sutherland, Inverness, Lewis, Skye, Mull and Islay, and I have endeavoured to find a standard between them. On the whole a very fair idea of the pronunciation is given and the work of the teacher is thus in the case of learners of the language very much simplified. The various lessons and exercises are judiciously and effectively graded and the difficulties which invariably meet learners of Gaelic rendered easy by simple, helpful explanations and illustrations of the peculiarities of Gaelic idiom as compared with English, which should go far to make the study of the language not a little attractive.

A teacher who can speak the language should not confine himself to the lessons alone. He should introduce familiar objects by simple short questions and answers suggested by or containing some words in the lessons. Such phrases may be written on the blackboard to be copied by the pupils into their books. But to teach the pupil **to speak** should be the main object, as a living language is synonymous with a spoken language. Pronounce every word of Gaelic in the vocabularies, exercises, etc., and make the pupils in turn read out the Gaelic sentences. At the same time I have tried to make the lessons throughout as clear and as simple as possible, remembering that a large number of my readers will have no teacher. Beginners should be cautious of using some Gaelic words in any way outside their use as they occur in the lessons.

I have again avoided as far as possible the unnecessary use of the accent or duration mark and the apostrophe. In this I have followed the suggestions given from time to time by authorities on Gaelic. As instances where I consider it necessary to use an accent however, such words as **bata, bàta ; bas, bàs ; cas, càs,** could be given. I have retained the apostrophe in the negative **cha'n** ; but it, too, is being avoided more and more, and the form **chan** is getting generally adopted. Complete Gaelic-English and English-Gaelic vocabularies have been added to this edition.

In the preparation of this little book I have to acknowledge my indebtedness to each and all of our Gaelic grammars and grammarians ; all having contributed in some way, more or less ; in some cases by a suggestion and others by a quotation. I have also to acknowledge much help received from the study of Irish grammars. In the revisal of manuscript and assistance in proof reading I am much indebted to one of our rising Gaelic writers, Mr. Hector Macdougall, without whose help, readily given, it is questionable if I would have attempted this volume. My acknowledgements are also due to Mr. John MacDonald, M.A., for some time teacher of Gaelic in Glasgow High School, for valuable help and assistance.

Suas leis a' Ghàidhlig.

JAMES MACLAREN.

PREFACE TO THE FOURTH EDITION

It gives me great pleasure to see another edition of my little Grammar being required. I have taken advantage in this new and fourth edition to make a few changes and some typographical corrections which were known to me and others which my most diligent students have been good enough to bring to my notice. To each of them I tender thanks and wish them good progress in their studies. It is a great pleasure to know that my little book has made the study of Gaelic quite an interesting one and that it has filled a felt want with both teachers and pupils. I am sorry space does not permit of my quoting from correspondence received from students the world over. One who has eight languages at his command is delighted with " Gaelic Self Taught." He knows of nothing to equal its simplicity in the other languages which he has taught and studied.—James MacLaren

ABBREVIATIONS.

Most of these, such as *adj*. for *adjective* are not given, as they cannot but be understood ; others are :—

d, dat.	dative.	m.	masculine.
f, fem.	feminine.	nm.	noun masculine.
g, gen.	genitive.	f, nf.	noun feminine.
cf.	compare.	n, nom.	nominative.

CONTENTS.

Gaelic Self-Taught.

An Introduction to Gaelic.

1. The difficulties to be surmounted in studying and pronouncing the Gaelic are not at all so formidable or so numerous as they may at first sight appear to a person who is unacquainted with the structure of the language. The combination of vowels and quiescent consonants which present themselves in many words, impress the minds of individuals who have spent little or no time in examining the importance and nature of these combinations with the idea that the task of learning the language is impracticable. This is by no means the case, for it is quite easy by a little study and perseverance to acquire a good reading and speaking knowledge of this venerable old language.

2. The first thing that strikes us is the habitual use for the purposes of nominal and verbal flexions, of that modification of the internal vowel, traces of which we find in the English nouns "man, men," "mouse, mice," etc., and the causative verbs, "fell," "graze," and "glaze," from "fall," "grass," and "glass." In Gaelic this change appears most frequently in the cases of nouns where another vowel is inserted, and the flexion is made by changing the vowel into a diphthong or two vowels that flow so sweetly into one another as almost to become a diphthong. Thus in the numerous class of nouns the genitive singular and nominative plural are formed by changing **a** into **ai** as in **dan** "a song," **dain** "of a song," **dain** "songs"; so **brog** "a shoe" becomes in the genitive singular **broige**; **carn** "a heap" becomes **cuirn**; **long** "a ship," **luinge**; **fiadh** "a deer," **feidh**, etc. In a few cases contrariwise the

B

double-vowel or diphthong of the nominative singular becomes a single vowel in the genitive as in **ceann** " a head," **cinn** ; **lion** " a net," **lin** ; **athair** " a father," **athar**, etc. In the comparison of adjectives the same principle reigns— **ban** " fair," **baine** " fairer," etc. ; and a considerable number of verbs change **ai** into **a, caidil** " sleep," **cadal** ; **caill** " lose," **call**, etc.

3. But the most characteristic device for nominal and verbal flexion is what goes by the name of aspiration. This is simply a breathing represented by the letter **h**, which modifies the letter into a softer sound and sometimes smooths it away altogether. Thus **b** when aspirated becomes a **v**, the letter **s** when aspirated becomes obliterated altogether, and this obliteration is carried still further in the case of **f**, as in **fios**, where the addition of the **h** produces **fhios**, in which **fh** is silent, leaving **ios**, pronounced *eess*.

4. Until the student understands the application of Gaelic aspiration and inflexion, he cannot make use of any Gaelic vocabulary or dictionary. By rules simple and beautiful, the aspirate **h** is so managed as to silence or euphonise the consonants wherever their initial sound would injure the easy flow or graceful cadence of a word, a verse, or sentence. The knowledge of the power and proper use of the aspirate is therefore the most important requirement of the Gaelic student.

5. This aspiration or breathing sign **h** is not included as a letter in the Gaelic alphabet, and though the sound of **h** is common in Gaelic words, there is not a single word in the language which commences with it.

6. The application of **h** in Gaelic has the effect of aspiration as we know it in English, Latin, and Greek, when used as a prefix to a vowel. In this position it has the same sound as the English aspirate **h** in " hold " and " him." In Gaelic it is generally followed with a hyphen and written thus : **a h-uan** " her lamb."

7. For certain purposes the nine consonants **b c d f g m p t** and also **s** when preceding **l n r**, cease to have their ordinary sound and acquire a new sound or become

silent. To indicate this change an **h** is affixed to them, and they are then said to be aspirated, though it is only in some cases that this term "aspiration" is to be taken in its common meaning of "breathing," as in "house." The mere affixing of the **h** is called aspiration although some of the effects of the combination do not appear like what is usually associated with "breathing" (par. 36).

8. In modern Gaelic grammar aspiration denotes the change that an initial consonant may undergo in the various syntactical relations of the word. It is an adjunct and aid to inflexion ; it is used to denote or help in denoting gender, number, case and tense. Thus in **bean mhath** "a good wife," where **math** appears as **mhath**, the aspiration shows that **bean** is feminine ; in **cinn mhoir** it shows that **cinn** from **ceann** is genitive masculine ; in **do'n cheann**, the aspirated **c** helps to mark the dative ; and in **bhuail e** "he struck," the aspiration differentiates the past tense from the imperative or dependent future **buail.** In short, aspiration in Gaelic is a sign of prime importance.

9. Aspiration may take place at the beginning, middle, or end of a word. This change is caused either by the natural sound of the word in which any of these aspirated or mutable consonants enter, requiring it by their position in a sentence ; by their relation or connection with other words which have an influence on their sound. When certain words precede, the following consonant must always be aspirated. The principle of this curious change is evidently euphonic, for it takes place principally after vowels and liquids. Etymology teaches us that when a consonant is aspirated the cause is generally traced to the fact that it is flanked on both sides by a vowel ; that it has a vowel before and after it, the latter if final having dropped away in the course of time. Thus the Latin word **mater** "mother" is in Gaelic **mathair** pronounced *ma'ür* ; the original hard **t** being softened away almost entirely by the aspiration.*

---

* In the modern language final vowels do not always cause aspiration. It will always puzzle a student to understand why **a** "his" should aspirate, while **a** "her" should not aspirate. The absence of the aspiration is a sign of gender. **a cheann** "his head " ; **a ceann** "her head."

10. Two words closely connected syntactically become practically compound words and are so treated in Gaelic. Hence, if the first of such a couple of words ended in a vowel, the initial of the second, if aspirable, is aspirated. Thus : **mo thigh** signifies " my house " ; **mo** ends in a vowel, being in fact a genitive case ; pronounced rapidly with **tigh** the **t** of the latter became vowel-flanked and was worn away to the aspirate form, **th** being pronounced **h**. A great many feminine nouns in Gaelic belonged to the **a** declension which answers to the Latin first declension. These nouns ended in the vowel **a** ; now, if an adjective came to qualify such a noun, the two became a rough compound word, and the initial of the adjective being practically vowel-flanked suffered aspiration. Thus we have **bean mhath** for **bena matis** " a good wife." The genitive of nouns of the **o** declension (chiefly masculine) which answers to the Latin second declension, and the nominative plural also, ended in the vowel **i** ; hence the adjective is aspirated after these cases, and the final **i** is in this way remembered though it has disappeared long ere now. The dative of all nouns ended in a vowel ; accordingly the adjective after every dative singular is aspirated. Prepositions ending now or originally in a vowel aspirate the word they govern. Thus **do thigh** is for **do tegos** " to a house." The preposition **air** is now a decayed form descended from three original prepositions, these were **are, vor** and **iarn,** and only the first caused aspiration, the one which ended in a vowel. Hence arises the fact that **air** sometimes aspirates and sometimes does not. Thus we have **air chois** " afoot " parallel with **air cul** " behind." In the cases where the article causes aspiration this can also be traced to an original organic vowel ending which it had in these cases.

11. The use of the aspirated sounds of the consonants arose from the fact that, while in other languages inflexions of nouns, adjectives, pronouns, and verbs are made by terminal changes, Gaelic does not admit of many terminal changes, and thus some changes are made in the body of words and others at the beginning. In **mor** and **beag** the **m** and **b** have their normal sound, but the genitives of both

begin with the sound of **v** as if they had been spelled **vor** and **veag.** Spelling them thus would have made a radical change in the initial consonants and would have sadly destroyed the orthography of the language and rendered etymology difficult. By retaining the initial consonant unvaried and by indicating the change to its second sound by the application of the **h**, Scots Gaelic has preserved its orthography. Compare the effect of the mutation of the consonant in Welsh by departing from this system. In Welsh the radical initial is changed so considerably and so often, that it is hardly recognised as the same word.

Scots Gaelic.	Welsh.	English.
ceann	pen	*a head*
do cheann	dy ben	*thy head*
mo cheann	fy mhen	*my head*
a ceann	ei phen	*her head*
caraid	cyfaill	*a friend*
do charaid	dy gyfaill	*thy friend*
mo charaid	fy nghyfaill	*my friend*
a caraid	ei chyfaill	*her friend*

12. But the great difficulty in Gaelic with most people lies in the pronunciation. Here the main thing to be noted is that as in our English words " though," " plough," etc., the final consonant having first been aspirated at last falls off altogether, similarly as a general rule does final **gh** and **dh** in Gaelic. In learning to read and speak Gaelic we require to acquire the habit of softening or slurring an aspirated consonant, as we do in the English words "might," " light," " fight " ; merely extend this to a larger family and the speaking of Gaelic becomes easy. Thus in the middle of **saoghal** and **sabhal** the two medial consonants are omitted and the spoken letters remain **saol** and **sawl** ; and in the same way **b m g c** at the commencement of a word are softened into **bh mh gh** and **ch**, whose pronunciation is as uniform to the ear as to the eye.

13. Gaelic is a soft vocalic and mellifluous language, in which harsh and hard sounds are avoided, softened, or assimilated. This general assimilation is a mutual smoothing down not only of an initial consonant, but also of the terminal consonant of the preceding word. It will be observed, for instance, that when the noun after the article

is aspirated, the article itself loses the final **n** ; the second word influencing the first as much as the first influences the second ; a mutual accommodation which is not found necessary when the article is followed by a dental, as it is a sound more easy of approach from the final **n**. Initial labials again, when not aspirated, change the **n** of the article to **m** for the same reason. This process of assimilating one word with another is an important one in Gaelic pronunciation. Similarly with vowels, an unstressed final vowel is elided before a stressed initial vowel in a word following, as : **m'athair** for **mo athair**, **d'iarr** for **do iarr**, **b'fhearr** for **bu fhearr**, **'nan** for **ann an**, **'san** for **anns an**, **gu'n d'fhalbh** for **gu an do fhalbh**, **leam** for **le mi**, **gill' og** for **gille og.**

14. Eclipsis is also a form of assimilation, an expedient governing euphony and facility of utterance, an effort at economy* in articulation, consisting of the suppression under certain circumstances of the sound of an initial mutable consonant for that of a cognate or homo-organic letter which, though not shown in the written language, is nevertheless a not uncommon feature in the spoken language in some districts of Scotland.

Instances of eclipsis as it is heard in some districts :—

b by **m**—	orain nam beann	(*orain na meann*)
	mullach nam beann	(*mullach na meann*)
d by **n**—	moch an de	(*moch ŭn-ā*)
	an do ghabh thu e ?	(*na ghav oo ā*)
	ar Dia	(*ur nea*)
t by **d**—	gu'n d' thainig thu	(*gun danik oo*)
	ar tir	(*ar deer*)
c by **g**—	an cu, nan con,	(*ungcu, nungon*)
	an ceart uair	(*un gerst oor*)
s by **t**—	an t-slat	(*un tllatt*)
f by **bh**—	am bheil (bhfeil)	(*um vāl*)
	a bhos (a bhfos)	(*ŭ vos*)

15. The consonants are twelve in number, and these have almost unvarying sounds, determined by their proximity to either broad or small vowels, or to the aspirate **h**. Let the sound of these letters be once learned and their place in the syllable observed, their pronunciation will not present difficulty to any student. The chief difficulty

---

* Often a laziness in the vocal organs not to be encouraged : cf. "in a nour" for "in an hour" in English.

found is the difference in sound values certain letters have from their English sound. The sounds approximate more nearly their continental sound values. In the same way vowel sounds are still more simple.

16. As will be seen, our scheme of pronunciation is a simple one and does not attempt the extreme niceties of phonological exactitude which are the aim of more elaborate schemes, but its simplicity will be found of considerable advantage. A simplified scheme involves of course some amount of compromise ; to express a greater number of vowel sounds than those indicated would have obliged the reader to refer continually to an intricate table of diacritic marks* which would have reduced its general utility. In the table the sounds chosen are standard and common to the English language, and are to be found in any dictionary. Previous gleaners in the field of Gaelic phonetics gave many localisms† as a guide to pronunciation, but as the readers of this little grammar will be scattered world-wide it is useless for us to follow suit. We have endeavoured to give some idea of the Gaelic sounds in the language which the student speaks, instead of invoking the aid of some unknown foreign tongue. A Gaelic sound can only be imitated perfectly in English if that sound occurs in English, and it stands to reason that sounds which never occur in English can only approximately be rendered in English syllables. We have many sounds peculiar to Gaelic, and it has to be

---

* How many of our readers can speak and pronounce Greek. Yet we are told in many Gaelic grammars that " **ch** broad," is to be pronounced as a certain Greek letter is in Scotland, and that " **ch** small," is to have the pronunciation it gets in England ; another gives " **ch** as in German " ; then we find that a certain **a** is to have the pronunciation of " **a** in ' that ' as pronounced by a lowlander but not as by an Englishman." Helps like these convey nothing to me, far less will they help a man in London, Vancouver, or Melbourne.

† Compare some of M'Alpine's phonetic spellings ; these three chosen at random look worse than the original Gaelic. **innean** ($^2\bar{e}nn''$-$\ddot{a}\breve{e}n'$) ; **meadhon-oidhche** ($m\acute{e}n'$-$\ddot{u}v^2$-$chy\ddot{a}$) ; **buaidh** ($b\breve{u}\ddot{a}\breve{e}'$-$gh'$) with the same under a more simplified scheme (een-$y\ddot{u}n$) ; ($mee\ddot{u}n$-$oich$ $\ddot{u}$) and (boo y). Some of M'Alpine's English key words, too, are based on a purely local pronunciation, and not as generally accepted.

admitted that a number of these can be acquired more accurately if heard *viva-voce.* Our imitated pronunciation is intended for self-taught students only, but with it a certain steady progress is sure to be made. The student will then be able to approach some Gaelic-speaking Highlander for further aid—there is no outpost of empire but where he will be found. A summer holiday spent in one of our Gaelic-speaking districts would be very helpful after a course such as outlined in this little work.

LESSON I.

THE GAELIC ALPHABET.

17. In the Gaelic alphabet there are eighteen characters of which five are vowels, **a o u e i**; and twelve are consonants **b c d f g l m n p r s t**; and the breathing or aspirate **h**.

18. The vowels are divided into broad and small—
Broad: **a o u**; Small or narrow: **e i**.

19. The consonants may be classified according to the organs of speech by which they are sounded.

Palatals:	**c g**	Linguals:	**l n r**
Labials:	**b f m p**	Sibilant:	**s**
Dentals:	**d t**		

20. Certain of the consonants have a second sound, caused by aspiration. **h** is the mark of aspiration.

Plain,	**b**	**c**	**d**	**f**	**g**	**l**	**m**	**n**	**p**	**r**	**s**	**t**
Aspir.	bh	ch	dh	fh	gh	—	mh	—	ph	—	sh	th
Sound,	*v*	*ch*	*ugh**	—	*ugh**	—	*v*	—	*f*	—	*h*	*h*

21. Note **l n r** and **s** when followed by **g m p t** do not have an aspirated form shown in writing or print, but where the other consonants aspirate these also have a slightly aspirated sound.

22. There are two accents : the grave and the acute. Either of these indicates a long vowel with a special sound.

---

* Sound of **dh** and **gh** : page 13; pars. 40-41, page 15.

We use them in this little work sparingly, chiefly where they are necessary to distinguish between words that are the same in spelling but have different meanings. **bàta** "a boat," **bata** "a stick."

23. Two or three vowels coming together with the sound of one passing into the other are called diphthongs and and triphthongs.

Diphthongs : **ai, ao ; ea, ei, eo, eu ; ia, io, iu ; oi, ua, ui.**
Triphthongs : **aoi, eoi, iai, iui, uai.**

24. The use of the letter **i** in some of the diphthongs and triphthongs is to qualify the sound of the consonant which follows it, and has no distinct sound of itself. **Ao, eu**, though classed among the diphthongs have but one simple sound which is always long.

THE VOWEL SOUNDS.

25. The Gaelic vowels sound very similar to the Continental vowels, as follows :—

A (*ah*) ; **E** (*ay*) ; **I** (*ee*) ; **O** (*oh*) ; **U** (*oo*).

Each vowel has a long and a short sound, especially when the quantity of the vowel may determine the meaning of the word. In contact with **m, mh**, or **n**, vowels become nasalised.

26. Key to the phonetic vowel sounds.

	English.			Gaelic Examples.
â	represents **a** in " far "	(*fâr*) ;		**bàs** (*bás*) death.
				cail (*kâl*) vigour.
a	,,	**a** ,, " fat "	(*fat*) ;	**bas** (*bas*) a palm.
				fan (*fan*) stay.
ā	,,	**a** ,, " fate "	(*fāt*) ;	**bheil** (*vāl*) am.
				aige (*ākü*) at him.
au	,,	**au** ,, " Paul "		**anns** (*auns*) in.
				corr (*kaur*) odd.
e	,,	**e** ,, " met "		**lean** (*len*) follow.
				le with.
ee	,,	**ee** ,, " tree "		**tri** (*tree*) three.
				cir (*keer*) comb.

B*

y represents **ee** in " feet " (*fyt*)·

o	,,	**o**	,,	" hot "	
ō	,,	**o**	,,	" more "	(*mōr*) ;
oo	,,	**oo**	,,	" moor "	
ow	,,	**ow**	,,	" town "	
ü	,,	**u**	,,	" but "	(*büt*) ;
ŏ	,,	**o**	,,	" word "	(*Irish*);*
nn	,,	**ni**	,,	" onion "	

min (*myn*) meal.
smig (*smyk*) chin.
ploc (*plochk*) turf.
mor (*mōr*) big.
tom (*tom*) a hillock
cu (*koo*) a dog.
cur (*koor*) putting.
toll (*towll*) hole.
fonn (*fownn*) a tune
goil (*gül*) boil.
a (*üh*) his, who.
gun (*gün*) without
laoch (*llŏch*).
binn (*bynn*) sweet
seinn (*shāynn*)
singing

27. A vowel may be obscure, that is it may have a shorter sound than an ordinary short vowel. In English we have the **a** in " pillar," the **o** and **e** in " cover," the **i** in " cousin," the **u** in " fur," as obscure sounds which sound very much alike. In Gaelic these vowels have also an obscure sound like this. They will be shown in the pronunciation with two dots over them thus *ü*.˙

28. The following are examples of this obscure vowel sound :—

a and e final : **aba** (*abü*) ; **feile** (*fālü*) ; **lugha** (*llüghü*).

a and ea short before **dh, gh,** and unaccented **ch** :
cogadh (*kokügh*) ; **ordugh** (*ortügh*) ; **ciontach** (*kyntüch*).

a and u in the article and in most of the particles :
am faigheadh (*üm fayügh*) ; **ag radh** (*üg ra*).
gun (*gün*) ; **lamhan** (*llavün*) ; **dh'iarr** (*yee-ür*).

ai and oi before the linguals **l, n, r** :
tairbhe (*türvü*) ; **piobair** (*peepür*).

A correspondent vowel sound : **airm** (*ürüm*) ; **earb** (*arüp*).
The plural termination of nouns : **lamhan** (*llavün*) ; **faidhean** (*fây-ün*).

---

* This **ŏ** (=**ao**) is an obscure sound rather longer than the very short obscure **u**. It is a sound not heard in English. it is similar to œu in French **sœur** (*sŏr*); German modified **ŏ** in **Söhne** (*sŏ-nü*); **e** as pronounced by an Irishman in **word**; or as we hear **bird** sometimes sounded in English (*bŏrd*).

29. SOUNDS OF THE PRINCIPAL DIPHTHONGS.

ai, eu, ei, like **ã** in " fate " ; **air** (*ār*) ; **speur** (*spār*) ; **fein** (*fān*).*

ea, like **ã** in " fate " ; **dean** (*jān*); sometimes **yã, neamh** (*nyāv*).

ea, sometimes **yâ** ; **eala** (*yâllü*) ; **fearr** (*fyârr*).

ea, ei, sometimes like **e** in " met " ; **leat** (*let*) ; **geir** (*ger*) ;

io, ia ; long **i** (o and a almost silent) ; **piob** (*peep*) ; **cian** (*keen*) ; **ciall** (*keeül*) ; **fios** (*feess*).

ua, uai, ui ; long **u** like **oo** in " moor " ; the other vowels almost complementary ; **luath** (*looüh*) ; **fuaim** (*fooym*) **cuin** (*koon*) ; **luib** (*llooyp*) ; **cluas** (*kloous*).

eo, iu ; the initial vowels very short ; **deoch** (*joch*) ; **ciurr** (*kewr*) ; **fliuch** (*flooch*).

ao ; obscure **a,** silent **o** ; **naomh** (*növ*) ; **taobh** (*töv*) ; **caol** (*köll*) ; **maor** (*mör*) ; **gaoth** (*gö*).

oi ; as **oi** in " boil " ; **oidhche** (*oichü*) ; **coilltean** (*koil-chün*).

30. SOUNDS OF THE TRIPHTHONGS.

aoi, as **caoidh** (*koo-y*) lament.
    laoigh (*lloo-y*) calves.

eoi, as **treoir** (*treo-yr*) strength.
    geoidh (*keeo-y*) geese.

iai, as **ciaire** (*kee-ar-ü*) darker.
    fiaire (*fee-ar-ü*) more crooked.

iui, as **ciuin** (*kee-oon*) meek.
    fliuiche (*flooch-ü*) wetter.

uai, as **fuaim** (*fooym*) sound.
    cruaidh (*krooü-y*) hard.

31. A vowel is never doubled in the same syllable of a Gaelic word like **ee** or **oo** in English, and there is no silent final vowels like English **e** in " where " (*whār*) ; " came " (*kām*)* ; " give " (*giv*).

32. When two vowels belonging to two different syllables of the same word come in contact with each other, the common practice is to separate them by inserting a pair of silent consonants between them, thus : **bi-th-eam** pronounced (*bee-üm*) let me be ; **cnothan** (*kro-ün*) nuts.

* The vowel sound of *ã* in " fate " is a compound sound. In English we hear the same sound in the following combinations : they (*thã*) ; there (*thãr*) ; gaol (*jãl*) ; · clay (*clã*) ; rein (*rãn*) ; rain (*rãn*) ; reign (*rãn*) ; pear (*pãr*) ; pair (*pãr*) ; pare (*pãr*) ; eight (*ãt*).

33. Vowel sounds coming together in this manner are regulated by a rule which is seldom broken. The rule is

Leathan ri leathan, agus caol ri caol.

" Broad to broad, and small to small."

34. In words of more than one syllable, the last vowel of the first syllable, and the first vowel of the next syllable must be of the same quality ; *i.e.*, if the last vowel of a syllable be *broad*, the first vowel of the next syllable must be *broad* also ; but if *small*, a *small* vowel follows.

35. In conformity with this rule, a broad or small vowel is introduced, as the case may be, although it serves no purpose in respect of derivation or pronunciation. Thus, **sùilean** is the plural of **sùil** : **an** is the plural termination, and the introduction of the **e** makes no difference in the sound, but is inserted in conformity with the above rule. Again, all regular verbs form their future by adding **idh** to the root. Take the verb **tog**, lift, add **idh** to form the future tense, and you get **togidh**, which is a breach of the rule, as the consonant **g** is preceded by the broad vowel **o**, and followed by the small vowel **i** ; an **a** must be added to keep to the rule, and the correct spelling of the future form is **togaidh** (*ttog-y*).

36.   Sounds of the Consonants.

b   b is like **b** in " boat " with an inclination to a **p** sound.

bh   bh at the beginning and end of a word is like **v** in "vale."
     bha (*va*) was ; **gabh** (*gav*) take ; **siribh** (*shyryv*).
     bh in the middle of a word is sometimes like **w** or **u**, but it is generally silent : **leabhar** (*llyoür*) a book ; **dubhar** (*doo-ür*) shade ; **gobhar** a goat, pronounced *gour*, hence **Ardgour**

c   c always hard like **c** in " call " and **k** in " keep." Never like **s**. **caoidh** (*koo-y*) lament.
     When final after vowels **a o u**, like **chk** : **mac** (*machk*)

ch   ch has no English sound equivalent, beside a broad vowel has a strong guttural sound as the Scots word " loch " (*lawch*) or in " clachan." Beside a small vowel like the Scots " nicht " for " night "
     ch   When initial as the English aspirate **h** in " hew ": Never like **ch** in " cheer "

d   **d** before a small vowel, is a mixture of the **d** in " duke " and **j** in " Jew "; before a broad vowel, like **d** in " consider," or almost the same sound as **t**, only softer. **deoch** (*joch*) drink ; **dana** (*danü*) songs. **d** terminal after **ch** :—**chd** ; like a **k**, **seachd** (*shachk*) seven.

dh   **dh** followed by **a, o, u** is like **ghy**, it has a strong thick guttural explosive sound (see **gh**).

    dh before a small vowel has a **y** sound : **Mo Dhia** (*mo yeeü*) my God ; in the middle and at the end of some words it is silent : **radh** (*ra*) saying ; **minidh** (*meen-y*) awl ; **fanaidh** (*fann-y*) will stay.

f   **f** is the same as in English. **fliuiche** (*flooch-ü*) wetter.

fh   **fh** always silent **fhear** (*err*), **fhad** (*att*) ; except in the words **fhein, fhuair**, and **fhathast**, which are pronounced *hān, hoo-ür* and *ha-üst* respectively.

g   **g** before a broad vowel like **g** in " galley " : **gabh** (*gav*) take.

    g before a small vowel like **g** in " gear " : **gile** (*geel-ü*).

    g preceded by or between small vowels like a **k** or the hard **c** of " can " : **slige** (*slykü*).

gh   **gh** before and after broad vowels like **ch** but more guttural, like **rgh** in " burgh " as sounded by one having a burr. An explosive gutteral not heard in English (par. 40).

    gh before a small vowel has the sound of **y** in English " yes " **gheibh** (*yōv*).

    gh in the middle and at the end of a word has no power other than that of lengthening the sound of the preceding vowel, just as **gh** in English words " high " and " neighbour " and " thought," i.e., **righ** (*ree*) a king ; **dheighinn** (*yāynn*).

h   in Gaelic **h** is the sign of aspiration only.

l   **l** almost as in English. Beside a small vowel like **ll** in English " million." **leabhar** (*llyoür*) a book

m   **m** as in English. **min** (*myn*) meal.

mh   **mh** is always like a **v** with a nasal touch : **mharbh** (*varv*) killed ; **ramh** (*rav*) an oar.

    mh in the middle of a word is generally silent, imparting a nasal sound to the preceding vowel : **comhradh** (*co-rü*) dialogue.

n   n as in English. **minidh** (*meen-y*) awl

n after **c g m t** sounds like **r** nasal : **cnap** (*krap*) ; **cno** (*kro*) a nut ; **gnuth** (*groo*) grim ; **mnaoi** (*mraoi*) of a woman.

n final before an initial **c** or **g** of a word following interpolates a nasal **g** sound : **an cu** (*ungkoo*) the dog ; **nan con** (*nüng kon*) of the dogs ; '**nan cadal** (*nang kat-tül*) in their sleep.

nn   nn after **i** like the **ny** in " Bunyan " : **gn** in *signora*.

p   p as in English.

ph   ph always like **f** as in English : **phill** (*fyll*) returned.

r   r as in English, though generally with more of a roll.

rt   rt as **rst** or **rsht** : **mart** (*marst*) a cow.

s   s is always sounded like **sh** whenever it comes before or after the small vowels : **sinne** (*shynn-ü*) ; there is one exception to the rule, the assertive verb **is**, like **iss** in the word " hiss " and not **ish**.

s before or after the broad vowels is like **ss** in the word " pass," like **s** in " soon." The demonstrative pronouns are exceptions to this rule, **so** and **sud** being pronounced *show* and *shoot*.

s following **t-** of the definite article is completely eclipsed and lost in pronunciation. In this particular way **s** is unique, all other aspirable consonants are aspirated in this position : **an t-slat** (*un tllat*) the rod.

sh   s when aspirated, **sh**, the **s** is completely eclipsed and is not sounded, the aspirate **h** alone being heard, like **h** in " has " ; **shin** (*heen*) stretched.

t   t before broad vowels like **tt** in " matter " : **tog** (*ttok*) lift.

t preceding small vowels like **ch** in " cheer " : **tim** (*cheem*) time.

th   th is like **h** in " him," the aspirate **h** eclipsing the consonant **t** : **thug** (*hook*) brought ; in the middle and end of a word it is generally silent : **sith** (*shee*) peace ; **leathan** (*llyā-ün*) broad.

37. The combination of lingual consonants with labials and also **g** and **ch** is noted in that they interpolate an added vowel sound between them and one generally correspondent to the preceding vowel. Thus, the combinations **lb**, **lch**, **lg**, **lm**, **lp**, and so on, interpolate this distinct drawl vowel between them. **falbh** (*falüv*) ; **Alba** (*alabü*) ; **tilg** (*tchy lyk*) etc. Similarly between the same groups of consonants when they come next each other in compound words, **ban-mhaighstir** (*banavāshtchyr*) (par. 19).

38. The dentals **d** and **t**, and also **s** when followed by **g t p m** (i.e., **sg**, **st**, **sp**, **sm**) are not aspirated when they follow other words ending in a dental or lingual, **an dorus**, the door.

39. Diminutives in **an** sound it *an*, but plurals in **a, an**, or **ean** sound *ü* and *ün*: **cnocan** (*krokan*) a little hillock ; **dana** (*danü*) songs ; **brogan** (*brogün*) shoes ; **preasa** (*prās-sü*) bushes.

40. The broad sound of **dh gh** : it is not easy to learn this sound except by ear, but the following will be helpful in an endeavour to pronounce it. The **gh** in **ugh** is about the nearest we can get in English. This **dh** and **gh**—a highly explosive guttural—is produced by pressing the point of the tongue on the lower or upper gum and then forcing the breath against the roof of the mouth, without allowing the tongue to touch the back part of the mouth, or as if a short or inaudible **u** were sounded before the **dh** or **gh**. The sound of **g** in **auger** (a carpenter's tool) is also near our sound.

41. **y** final is used in the phonetics as representing the **y** sound heard final in " mighty " (*mit-y*) ; " gaudy " (*god-y*) ; " steady " (*sted-y*). Gaelic ex. **cuiridh** (*koor-y*) ; **dachaldh** (*tach-y*) ; bithibh (*bpeeh-yv*) ; bithidh (*bpeeh-y*)

42. In some of the phonetic key words it must be observed that the almost sameness of sound is all that is intended to be expressed, for the sound may be rather longer or rather shorter than that of the key word.

LESSON II.

VERB "TO BE"; PRESENT INDEPENDENT TENSE.

43. The Gaelic verb always precedes the noun or pronoun and is not declined, being the same for all persons and numbers.

tha mi (*ha mee*)	I am.	**tha sinn** (*ha sheen*)	we are.
tha thu (*ha oo*)	thou art.	**tha sibh** (*ha sheev*)	you are.
tha e (*ha ā*)	he is.	**tha iad** (*ha eeüt*)	they are.
tha i (*ha ee*)	she is.		

44. Memorise the following vocabulary :—

an la (*ün llâ*) the day.
an duine (*ün doo-nü*) the man.
an gille (*ün geel ü*) the boy
luath (*llooü*) swift, quick.
fuar (*fooür*) cold.
fliuch (*flooch*) wet.
blath (*bplâh*) warm.

deas (*jess*) read.,
an so (*ün sho*) here.
an sin (*ün sheen*) there.
an sud (*ün shoott*) yonder
sgith (*skee*) tired.
a nis (*ü nysh*) now.

45. When we make a statement about the subject of the sentence, the predicative adjective or adverb comes last in the sentence as in English.

Tha an gille fliuch,   *the boy is wet.*

46. Read in Gaelic and translate the following :—
1. Tha an la fuar.   2. Tha an duine fliuch.   3. Tha e an sin a nis.
4. Tha an gille an so.   5. Tha mi sgith.   6. Tha sinn deas.   7. Tha an la blath.   8. Tha e fliuch a nis.   9. Tha iad an sud.   10. Tha thu deas.   11. Tha an duine luath.   12. Tha an gille an sud.   13. Tha mi fuar.   14. Tha an duine deas a nis.   15. Tha an gille fliuch.   16. Tha sinn fuar.   17. Tha iad sgith.

47. Translate the following into Gaelic :—
1. The man is wet.   2. I am ready.   3. He is tired.   4. We are warm now.   5. They are wet.   6. You are tired.   7. She is here.   8. The boy is swift.   9. He is here now.   10. He is ready.   11. The day is wet.   12. The man is here.   13. The boy is tired.   14. They are there now.   15. They are cold.   16. He is ready now.   17. You are quick.   18. We are cold now.   19. The day is warm.

48. As **tha** "is" always precedes its nominative, **tha an la fuar** literally means "is the day cold" as if asking a question. This position of the verb need not lead to confusion as we never use **tha** in that way. The meaning of **tha** never varies, it is always the sign of an affirmative sentence, and in translation follows its nominative.

LESSON III.

49. VERB "TO BE"; PARADIGM OF THE PRESENT TENSE.

Independent **tha** (*ha*)		*Dependent* **bheil** (*vāl*)
tha mi (*ha mee*)		I am.
am bheil mi ? (*üm vāl mee*)		am I ?
cha 'n eil mi (*chan yāl mee*),		I am not.
nach eil mi ? (*nach āl mee*)		am I not ?
ma tha mi (*mü ha mee*)		if I am.
mur eil mi (*mür āl mee*)		if I am not.
ged a tha mi. (*ket ü ha mee*)		though I am.
ged nach eil mi (*ket nach āl mee*)		though I am not.
gu 'm bheil mi (*küm vāl mee*)		that I am.
nach eil mi (*nach āl mee*)		that I am not.

50. As the verb is the same for each person in both numbers it is unnecessary to print the same words six times over. The learner has only to repeat the pronouns in their order after every temporal change of the verb.

51. It will be noticed that **nach** occurs twice with different meanings, but no ambiguity should occur, as, when it is the interrogative particle, it comes at the beginning of a sentence or clause, and when the relative negative it is in the middle and follows its antecedent.

52. " I am tired " simply is in Gaelic **tha mi sgith** ; but " he says that I am tired—he is saying that I am tired " is rendered into Gaelic by **tha e ag radh gu'm bheil mi sgith**, it is not **tha e ag radh a tha mi sgith.** **Tha** is only used in the direct present to make a definite and independent statement about the subject and **bheil** is employed when the verbs " am, art, is, etc.," follow another verb upon which they are dependent, or when a question is asked or something is denied.

53. **Bheil** being the form used after the particles is always aspirated **am bheil mi sgith ?** " am I tired ? " **Cha'n eil** is used for **cha bheil, bh** is thrown out for euphony's sake and an organic **n** is retained between **cha** and **eil** to prevent a hiatus.

54. The sign of the participle is **ag**, which becomes **a'** before all consonants except **radh**. The participle follows the subject.

55. When we wish to answer " yes " or " no," we repeat the verb in the same tense as is used in the questioning sentence. The noun or pronoun is not required.

> Am bheil an gille fliuch ? *is the boy wet ?*
> Tha. Cha'n eil. *he is = yes. he is not = no.*

56. Memorise these vocabularies as we have not space to repeat previous lists.

mall (*maull*) slow.
crubach (*kroobüch*) lame.
dachaidh (*tach-y*) home.
a' dol (*ü daul*) going.
a' tighinn (*ü cheeün*) coming.
ach (*âch*) but.
agus (*â-ghus*) **is** (*is*) and.
an cu (*koo*) the dog

ag radh (*üg ra*) saying.
fathast (*fâhust*) yet.
do'n bhaile (*ton valü*) to the town.
an t-each (*ün tchyäch*) the horse.
og (*ogk*) young.
an diugh (*ün joo*) to-day.
mise (*meeshü*) *pron.* I, me.
thusa (*oosü*) *pron.* thou, you

57. Read in Gaelic and translate into English :—

1. Am bheil an la fuar ? 2. Cha'n eil an la fuar, tha e blath. 3. Ged a tha e blath tha e fliuch. 4. Tha an t-each crubach ma tha e mall. 5. Nach eil an duine an sin a nis ? 6. Cha'n eil, tha e an so a nis. 7. Mur eil an gille fuar tha e fliuch. 8. Tha an gille an so an diugh. 9. Tha an gille sgith, ach cha'n eil e fuar. 10. Tha e ag radh gu'm bheil e og, ach tha mise ag radh nach eil e. 11. Am bheil thu a' dol dachaidh a nis ? 12. Cha'n eil, tha mi a' dol do'n bhaile. 13. Am bheil iad a' dol do'n bhaile ? Tha. 14. Tha i a' tighinn dachaidh a nis. 15. Nach eil an la blath ? Tha.

58. Now translate into Gaelic :—

1. You are going to the town to-day. 2. Are you not ready yet ? 3. No, he is ready, but I am not. 4. The horse is lame to-day. 5. It is not here yet. 6. The boy is young. 7. If the man is not wet he is cold. 8. The day is warm. 9. The horse is swift, but the dog is slow. 10. Is the man not coming home ? 11. No, he is going to the town. 12. You are not coming to the town to-day. 13. The boy is cold and wet. 14. If the man is not there the boy is here. 15. Though the boy is not young. 16. If the horse is not tired it is lame. 17. She says (is saying) that the man is coming here, but they say (are saying) that he is not. 18. Are you not going home now ?

LESSON IV.

59.   VERB "TO BE"; PAST INDEPENDENT FORM.

bha mi (*va mee*)	I was.	**bha sinn** (*va sheen*)	we were.
bha thu (*va oo*)	thou wert.	**bha sibh** (*va sheev*)	you were.
bha e, i (*va ā, ee*)	he, she was.	**bha iad** (*va eeŭt*)	they were.

60. For the English article " a " we have no equivalent in Gaelic. There is only one article in Gaelic—that which corresponds to the English " the "; as :—

Duine, *a man.*   An duine, *the man.*

61. **Tha** and **bha** before an indefinite noun can take the meaning in English of " there is," " there are," " there was," etc., as :—

Tha duine aig an dorus (*torus*)   *there is a man at the door.*
Cha 'n eil duine aig an dorus,   *there is not a man at the door.*
Bha gille aig an dorus,   *there was a boy at the door.*

62.   *Vocabulary.*

co ? (*ko*) who ?
cu (*koo*) a dog.
na coin (*nŭ ko-yn*) the dogs.
na daoine (*nŭ dŏy-nŭ*) the men.
aig an tigh (*āk ŭn tâ y*) at the house, at home.
an raoir (*ŭn rŏ-yr*) last night

na gillean (*nŭ keelyŭn*) the boys
'nuair (*nooŭr*) when
an de (*un jā*) yesterday.
aig (*āk*) at.
ann (*aunn*) in; there.

63. Read in Gaelic and translate into English :—

1. Co bha a' dol an sin ?   2. Cha'n eil mi a' dol a nis.   3. Bha mi an sin an raoir.   4. Co bha aig an dorus ?   5. Bha na daoine an sin. 6. Bha na gillean a' tighinn dachaidh.   7. Bha an t-each mall ach bha e crubach.   8. Bha na coin a' dol dachaidh.   9. 'Nuair a bha sibh an sin bha mi sgith.   10. Bha sinn an sin an de.   11. Co bha aig a' bhaile ?   12. Bha iad aig a' bhaile.   13. Bha an cu aig an dorus.   14. Bha na coin an so an raoir.   15. Bha iad an sin an de. 16. Am bheil i an so a nis ?   17. Bha i an so nuair a bha thu-sa an so. 18. Bha i fuar.   19. Co bha an so an de ?   20. Bha e aig an tigh.

64. Now translate into Gaelic :—

1. The horse was going to the town.   2. The boys were at the door last night.   3. There is a man coming to the town.   4. He was coming yesterday.   5. I was there last night.   6. The dogs were going home. 7. There was a dog at the door.   8. It was at the door to-day. 9. When it was here it was wet.   10. They were tired last night. 11. He was going home yesterday.   12. I was coming home when I was tired.   13. The horse was lame.   14. The dogs were here yesterday.   15. A dog was here, but the dogs were at home last night.   16. Who was here yesterday ?   17. A man was at the door. 18. He was ready.

LESSON V.

65. VERB " TO BE " ; PARADIGM OF THE PAST TENSE.

Independent **bha** (*va*)   was, wert, or were.
Dependent   **robh** (*ro*)   was, wert, or were.

bha mi (*va mee*)	I was.
an robh mi ? (*ün ro mee*)	was I ?
cha robh mi (*cha ro mee*)	I was not.
nach robh mi ? (*nach ro mee*)	was I not ?
ma bha mi (*mü va mee*)	if I was,
na'n robh mi (*nün ro mee*)	if I was, If I had been
mur an robh mi (*mur ün ro mee*)	if I was not.
ged a bha mi (*ket ü va mee*)	though I was.
ged nach robh mi (*ket nach ro mee*)	though I was not.
gu'n robh mi (*kün ro mee*)	that I was.
nach robh mi (*nach ro mee*)	that I was not.

66. All Gaelic verbs have a special form for use after the relative pronoun ; but in the present and past tenses notice that we use the independent forms of the verb **bi**, i.e., **tha** and **bha** to follow the relative pronoun **a**, and the conditional particles **ged** and **ma**. In the future of the verb **bi** we have a special form for use after these as will be shown.

67. When the relative pronoun is nominative it precedes the verb and no other pronoun is necessary after it.

An duine a tha an so,   *the man who is here.*

68. To make our statement more emphatic, we add what we term an emphatic suffix to the pronouns.   Thus we have

mi	thu	e	i	sinn	sibh	iad
mise	**thusa**	**esan**	**ise**	**sinne**	**sibhse**	**iadsan**

(*meeshü*) (*oosü*) (*essün*)(*eeshü*)(*sheennyü*)(*sheev-sü*) (*eeutt sun*)
Ma tha thusa a' dol, tha mise a dol,   *if you are going, I am going.*

69. **Nuair**, literally **an uair a**, " the time that " = " the hour which " = " when," and really an adverbial phrase, generally written **nuair a** or simply **nuair**.   The relative **a**, " that," being ofteri omitted, as it often is in English.

70.   *Vocabulary.*

leisg adj. (*llāshk*) lazy.
caillte adj. (*kâyl tchü*) lost.
thubhairt irr. v. (*hoo ürtch*) said.
anns a' phairc (*auns ü fâ yrk*) in the park.
anns a' choille (*auns ü choil yü*) in the wood.

71. Read in Gaelic and translate into English :—

1. An robh an duine aig an dorus ? 2. Cha robh e aig an dorus. 3. An robh an t-each anns a' phairc ? 4. Cha robh. 5. Bha mi sgith. 6. An robh na gillean anns a' bhaile ? 7. Cha robh iad anns a' bhaile. 8. Bha na coin mall. 9. Bha na coin luath ach bha iad ‚crubach. 10. Nach robh iad anns a' phairc ? 11. Bha iad anns a' choille. 12. Nuair a bha iad an so an raoir bha mi sgith. 13. Nach robh iad sgith ? 14. Cha robh, ach bha iad fliuch. 15. Bha na coin caillte anns a' choille an de. 16. Thubhairt e gu'n robh e caillte anns a' bhaile an raoir. 17. Mur an robh iad an sud an diugh, bha mise an sin an de 18. Na'n robh mi mall, bha mi sgith. 19. Tha sinn a' tighinn a nis. 20. Nach robh sinn an sin ? 21. Cha robh. 22. Thubhairt e gu'n robh e a' dol dachaidh.

72. Now translate English into Gaelic :—

1. Was the horse in the park ? 2. No, the horse was in the wood. 3. Were the men at the door ? 4. They were not at the door. 5. A man was at the door last night. 6. Was he wet ? 7. He said that he was not wet. 8. They were in the wood last night. 9. The horse was there to-day. 10. If it was there to-day it was not there last night. 11. The dogs were swift though they were lame. 12. The day was wet. 13. We were tired last night. 14. He said if we were going home he was going to the town. 15. Was he not slow ? 16. No, he was quick. 17. The dog was lost in the wood last night. 18. He says that the dog was lost in the town yesterday. 19. If I was lazy he was slow. 20. We were cold in the park to-day. 21. Who was in the park yesterday ? 22. I was not there.

LESSON VI.

73.   VERB " TO BE " ;   SUBJUNCTIVE TENSE,
INDEPENDENT FORM.

Singular.

1st	**bhithinn** or **bhiom**	(*vee-ynn* or *veeüm*)	I would be.
2nd.	**bhitheadh tu**	(*vee-ügh too*)	thou wouldst be.
3rd.	**bhitheadh e**	(*vee-ügh ā*)	he would be

Plural.

1st.	**bhitheamaid** or **bhiomaid**	(*veeümātch*)	we would be.
2nd.	**bhitheadh sibh**	(*vee-ügh sheev*)	you would be.
3rd.	**bhitheadh iad**	(*vee-ügh eeüt*)	they would be.

74. The Subjunctive is the only tense in which any change takes place, and this in the first person singular and plural, in which the pronouns have become amalgamated with the verb.   Also termed the imperfect, customary, or habitual past.

  Bhithinn   *I would be, or I used to be.*

75.   *Vocabulary.*

briste adj. (*brees-tchü*) broken. **an sgian** f. (*ün skecün*) the knife.
an-moch adj. (*ünümoch*) late. **an uinneag** f. (*oonyack*) the window.

76. Read in Gaelic and translate into English :—

1. Bhitheadh tu sgith. 2. Bhitheadh tu an-moch an raoir. 3.
Bhitheamaid a' tighinn dachaidh a nis. 4. Bhitheadh iad mall.
5. Bhithinn an sin a nis ach bha mise an-moch. 6. Bhitheadh na
daoine a' dol do'n bhaile. 7. Bhitheadh an t-each crubach. 8.
Bhitheadh na coin caillte. 9. Bhitheadh iad fliuch. 10. Bhitheadh
e fliuch anns a' choille. 11. Bhitheadh an sgian caillte. 12. Bhitheadh an uinneag briste. 13. Bhitheadh i caillte anns an tigh. 14.
Bhitheadh e an-moch a' dol do'n bhaile an diugh. 15. Bhithinn an
sin na 'n robh thu-sa ann.

77. Now translate into Gaelic :—

1. I used to be quick but I am tired now. 2. You would be late in
coming home last night. 3. The men would be home yesterday.
4. The dogs would be lame. 5. The horse would be slow coming
home. 6. They would be tired. 7. I would be at home yesterday
but I was at the town last night. 8. The knife would be broken.
9. It would be lost in the house. 10. The window would be wet.
11. It would be broken. 12. The boys would be in the wood to-day.
13. They would be wet. 14. I would be there if you were. 15. He
would be in the park in the evening.

LESSON VII.

78.   Verb " to be " ; Paradigm of Subjunctive
Tense.

Independent **bhitheadh** or **bhiodh** (*vee-ügh*) would be.
Dependent, **bitheadh** or **biodh** (*bee-ügh*)   would be.

am bithinn (*üm bee-ynn*)	would I be ?
am bitheamaid (*üm beeümātch*)	would we be ?
am bitheadh e (*üm beeügh ā*)	would he be ?
cha bhithinn (*cha vee-ynn*)	I would not be.
cha bhitheamaid (*cha veeümātch*)	we would not be.
cha bhitheadh e (*cha veeügh ā*)	he would not be.
nach bitheadh e ? (*nach beeügh ā*)	would he not be ?
na'm bitheadh e (*nam beeügh ā*)	if he would be. had been
mur bitheadh e (*mür beeügh ā*)	if he would not be.
ged a bhitheadh e (*ket ü veeügh ā*)	though he would be.
ged nach bitheadh e	though he would not be.
gu'm bitheadh e (*küm beeügh ā*)	that he would be.
nach bitheadh e (*nach beeügh ā*)	that he would not be.

79. In these dependent forms of the subjunctive notice that the verb is not aspirated after the particles **am, an, nach, na'm, na'n, mur, gu'm, gu'n, ged nach**, but that the initial of the verb is aspirated after **cha** and **ged a.** All verbs whose initial letter is an aspirable one are affected in this way in the subjunctive.

80. *Vocabulary.*

sgoil f. (*sgoll*) school. **anns an sgoil** at school.
anns an fheasgar (*auns ün es-gür*) in the evening.
anns a' bhàta (*auns ü vátü*) in the boat.
am maireach (*üm márüch*) to-morrow.
an earar (*ün yär ür*) the day after to-morrow.
sin (*sheen*) that, those

81. Read in Gaelic and translate into English :—

1. Cha bhitheamaid sgith na'm bitheadh i a' dol. 2. Na'm bitheadh i deas bhithinn sa.* 3. Cha bhitheadh an sgian briste. 4. Bha an sgian briste ach tha i caillte a nis. 5. Bhitheadh an duine aig an tigh anns an fheasgar. 6. Bhitheadh iad anns a' choille an de. 7. Nuair a bha iad og bhitheadh iad anns an sgoil. 8. Nach bitheadh e anns a' bhaile am maireach ? 9. Thubhairt e nach bitheadh e an sin am maireach ach gu 'm bitheadh e an earar. 10. Am bithinn blath anns a' bhaile ? 11. Bhitheadh tu blath anns a' bhaile. 12. Nach bithinn fuar anns a' phairc ? 13. Cha bhitheadh tu fuar anns a' phairc. 14. Nach bitheadh esan sgith anns a' choille ? 15. Bhitheadh e sgith anns a' choille. 16. Mur bithinn fuar, bhithinn blath. 17. Bhitheadh an uinneag briste. 18. Na'n robh mi an sin cha bhitheadh i briste.

82. Now translate into Gaelic :—

1. Though the dogs would be there they would be tired. 2. It would be cold. 3. We would be going there though the men would be late. 4. I would not be tired if she would be there. 5. If I were there I would be warm. 6. He said he would be late to-morrow. 7. The window would be broken. 8. It would not be broken if you had been there. 9. He said they would be going to the town to-morrow. 10. Would they be going to the town in the evening ? 11. Would it be warm in the town ? 12. That man would be at the house last night. 13. When they were young they would be at school. 14. Would the knife not be broken ? 15. It would be lost in the wood. 16. They would be in the wood last night. 17. Would I not be cold in the park ? 18. You would not be cold in the park. 19. Would it not be wet in the wood ? 20. He would be wet in the wood. 21. He said he would be ready and that he would be in the boat. 22. They said they would be at home to-morrow.

---

* After some of these verbal forms the emphatic particle is sometimes used : cf. faighinn-sa ; gheibheadh thus*a*.

LESSON VIII.

83. Verb "to be"; Future Independent Tense.

1. **bithidh mi,** I shall or will be   **bithidh sinn,** we shall be.
2. **bithidh thu,** thou shalt be.   **bithidh sibh,** you shall be.
3. **bithidh e, i** he, etc., shall be.   **bithidh iad,** they shall be.
(Pronounced *pee-hee-mee*).

84. The English auxiliaries "shall" and "will" when used to express future action are not translated into Gaelic ; the Gaelic verb itself assumes a form suited to that meaning.

85. The past tense may be termed the narrative and the future the philosophical—the former describes what once happened and the latter describes what always happens.

86.   *Vocabulary.*

an tuathanach nm. (*ün tooanüch*) the farmer.
an ciobair nm. (*ün keepür*) the shepherd.
na h-eich so (*nü hãch sho*) these horses.
am bàta nm. (*üm bpãtü*) the boat.
dorcha (*dtorüchü*) dark.
air ball (*ãr paul*) immediately.
an nochd (*ün-nochk*) to-night.

87. Read in Gaelic and translate into English :—

1. Cha robh an tuathanach an so an raoir 2. Ach bithidh e añ so an diugh. 3. Bithidh na h-eich so sgith. 4. Bithidh an ciobair an sin. 5. Bithidh am bàta an so air ball. 6. Bithidh e dorcha air ball. 7. Cha robh na h-eich sin an sin an de. 8. Bithidh na gillean leisg. 9. Bithidh mi a' dol dachaidh a nis. 10. Bithidh e a' dol do 'n bhaile. 11. Bithidh thu sgith a nis. 12. Bithidh mi fuar an diugh. 13. Bithidh na h eich so og. 14. Bithidh e anns a' bhàta anns an fheasgar 15. Bithidh sinn a' dol do 'n tigh am maireach. 16. Bithidh iad an sin an diugh.

88. Translate into Gaelic :—

1. The shepherd will be here immediately. 2. The farmer was here yesterday and he will be here to-day. 3. These horses will be tired. 4. They will be coming home late. 5. They will be there now. 6. We shall be coming to the town in the evening. 7. You will be going to the town. 8. It will be dark immediately. 9. The boat was here last night and it will be coming to-day. 10. It will be here yet. 11. These horses will be going home now. 12. The boys will be lazy. 13. It will be cold to-day. 14. The farmer will be coming home immediately. 15. He is here now. 16. We will be going to the house to-morrow. 17. You will be going there to-night.

LESSON IX.

89. Verb " to be " ; Paradigm of the Future Tense.

Independent Future, **bithidh** (*peehee*).
Dependent Future, **bi** (*pee*).
Relative future, **bhitheas** (*veehüs*).

bithidh mi (*peehee mee*)	I will be.
am bi mi ? (*üm pee mee*)	will I be ?
cha bhi mi (*cha vee mee*)	I will not be.
nach bi mi ? (*nach pee mee*)	will I not be.
ma bhitheas mi (*mü veehüs mee*)	If I will be.
mur bi mi (*mür pee mee*)	If I will not be.
ged a bhitheas mi (*ket ü veehüs mee*)	though I will be.
ged nach bi mi (*ket nach pee mee*)	though I will not be.
gu'm bi mi (*küm pee mee*)	that I will be
nach bi mi (*nach pee mee*)	that I will not be.

The Relative Pronoun as Nominative.

90. The relative future is generally used only in the third person, except where an emphatic statement of existence is made, when we may say **'s mi a bhitheas** " I will be (indeed)." Literally the form **a bhitheas** means " who will be," and **a bhitheas e** " who he will be." For simple " he will be " the form is **bithidh e.** The relative pronoun **a** in all cases and tenses precedes the verb which it always aspirates. **Bhios** is a contracted form of **bhitheas.**

Am fear a bhitheas an so, *the man who will be here.*
An gille a bhitheas an sin, *the boy who will be there.*

91. *Vocabulary.*

oidhche (*oichu*) night.
am feasgar (*üm fes-gür*) the evening.
thig *irr v.*, come, comes
thainig, *v.*, came, *past of* **thig**

leis (*lläsh*) with him, his.
anns (*auns*) in (*before the*).
gle (*klä*) very (aspirates the adj.).

92. These demonstratives are placed after the definite noun.

so (*sho*) this, these (near at hand—here).
sin (*sheen*) that, those (further away—there).
ud (*oodt*) yon (much further away—yonder).

Bha am fear sin an sin an raoir, *that man was there last night.*
(lit. : *the man there was there last night*).

93. Read in Gaelic and translate into English :—

1. Ged a bhitheas e aig a' bhaile an diugh, bithidh e anns a' bhàta. anns an fheasgar. 2. An duine a bhitheas an-moch. 3. Am bi thu

anns a' bhaile ?   4. Am bi e gle sgith ?   5. Bithidh e gle sgith agus bithidh e gle leisg.   6. Am bi mi anns a' bhaile an nochd ?   7. Bithidh mi anns a' bhaile am feasgar so.   8. Nach bi e anns a' choille ?   9. Cha bhi e anns a' choille.   10. Thubhairt mi gu 'm bi e an so am maireach.   11. Tha thu ag radh nach bi e an so.   12. Bithidh an tuathanach sin an sin am maireach ach bithidh an ciobair an sin an earar.   13. Ma bhitheas e an sin am maireach cha bhi mi an so.   14. Bithidh an oidhche gle dhorcha.   15. Cha bhi.   16. Tha an duine a bhitheas a' dol leis an so.   17. Bithidh an gille so an sin.   18. Nach bi na gillean anns a' bhàta am feasgar so ?   19. Thubhairt iad gu'm bitheadh iad an sin an nochd.   20. Mur bi iad deas air ball bithidh sinn an-moch.

94. Translate into Gaelic :—

1. I said he will be late.   2. Will he be here to-night ?   3. He will not be here this*afternoon, but he will be here this evening.   4. I will not be with him.   5. Will he not be in the town to-day ?   6. The man who will be in the town to-morrow.   7. I will be coming with him.   8. I will not be there to-morrow.   9. If the boy will be going with him they will be very late.   10. The boy will not be very quick. 11. He will be in the wood immediately.   12. Who will be with him ? 13. The man will be ready immediately.   14. The man who will be ready will not be lazy.   15. He will be very tired when he comes home.   16. These boys will not be coming home to-day.   17. They said that they will be in the town to-morrow.   18. Though they will be in the boat to-day I will not be there.   19. If it will be wet in the evening, we will not be going to the town.   20. I will be ready to-morrow.   21. Will you be going to the town the day after to-morrow ?   22. Yes.

* Meadhon la, *midday—noon*, an deidh *after*.

LESSON X.

95.   VERB " TO BE " ;   IMPERATIVE MOOD.

Singular.

1st Per.	**bitheam** (*bee-üm*)	let me be.
2nd ,,	**bi** (*bee*)	be thou.
3rd ,,	**bitheadh e** (*bee-ügh ā*)	let him be.

Plural.

1st Per.	**bitheamaid** (*bee-ümātch*)	let us be.
2nd ,,	**bithibh** (*bee-yv*)	be ye.
3rd ,,	**bitheadh iad** (*bee-ügh eeüt*)	let them be.

96. The formation of the persons in the imperative of this verb is accòrding to the rules governing all Gaelic verbs.   The 2nd person sing. of the imperative being termed **the** root of the verb.   In the regular verbs all tenses can

be formed from the root either by affixing a termination, by prefixing a particle, or by aspiration (Lesson XL.)

97. The 2nd person sing. and plural is the order of command ; no pronoun is necessary unless for further emphasis, when the emphatic pronoun **thu-sa** can be used, **bi thu-sa**.

98. The 1st and 3rd persons express a desire, whether purpose or request. The pronoun must be expressed in the 3rd person.

99. An imperative negative can be made by placing the imperative particle **na** in front of any verb in the imperative mood. This particle is reserved for, and can only be used to form, this imperative negative or imperative prohibition, as :—**buail mi**, strike me ; **na buail mi**, strike me not. It does not cause aspiration. No other particles are used with the imperative.

100. The 3rd person imperative is very often used to translate the word " whether."

Bitheadh e 'na righ no 'na fhlath,   *whether he be a king or a prince let him be a king or a prince.*

101.   *Vocabulary.*

lag-chridheach (*lakchreeüch*) faint-hearted.
treun (*trān*) adj. brave.   **duinte** (*dtoontchü*) adj. shut.
samhach (*savüch*) adj. quiet.   **fosgailte** (*foskyltchü*) adj. open.

102. Read in Gaelic and translate into English :—

1. Na bi lag-chridheach. 2. Bitheamaid anns a' choille an nochd. 3. Bitheadh an duine treun. 4. Bitheadh an dorus duinte. 5. Na bitheadh an uinneag fosgailte. 6. Bitheamaid deas. 7. Na bitheadh iad anns a' bhaile an diugh. 8. Bitheamaid anns a' bhaile an nochd. 9. Na bitheadh e leisg. 10. Bitheadh an uinneag duinte. 11. Bitheadh e a' dol dachaidh a nis. 12. Na bitheadh e an-moch a nis. 13. Na bitheadh an uinneag briste. 14. Na bitheadh an sgian caillte. 15. Bitheam a' dol a nis. 16. Na bitheadh na gillean anns a' choille am feasgàr so. 17. Bitheadh iad treun. 18. Bitheamaid leis an earar.

103. Translate into Gaelic :—

1. Let us be in the wood to-night. 2. Let the man be brave. 3. Don't let him be faint-hearted. 4. Be brave. 5. Let them be with him in the wood to-morrow. 6. Don't let the boys be quiet. 7. You be quiet. 8. Let us be brave. 9. Don't let him be late to-night. 10. Let us be in the town to-night. 11. Don't let the window be broken. 12. Let the window be open immediately. 13. Don't

let the door be shut. 14. Let us be ready this evening. 15. Let the door be shut now. 16. Don't let the knife be lost. 17. Don't be faint-hearted. 18. Let us be brave to-night. 19. Let me be with him to-morrow. 20. Don't let us be cold. 21. Be quiet.

LESSON XI.

104. VERB " TO BE " ; RECAPITULATORY.
GENERAL EXERCISE ON THE VERB **bi.**

Vocabulary.

an lathair (*ün llāür*) present. near
an dràsd (*ün drast*) presently, just now
bo, na ba (*bpa*) a cow, the cows.
air a' mhonadh (*ār ü vonügh*) on the hill.
anns an fhang (*auns ün ank*) in the pen.
na feidh (*fā-y*) (the) deer (plural).
na caoraich (*nü kŏ-rych*) the sheep (plural).
anns a' mhaduinn (*vattynn*) in the morning.
anns an achadh (*auns ün achügh*) in the field.

no or.

maide, *nm.*, a stick.

105. Read in Gaelic and translate into English :—

1. Tha na caoraich anns an fhang. 2. An robh iad air a' mhonadh an raoir ? 3. Cha robh ach tha iad anns an fhang an drasd. 4. Bha na ba caillte an de. 5. Bha na feidh air a' mhonadh am feasgar so. 6. 'Nuair a thainig e do 'n bhàta bha e sgith. 7. 'Nuair a bha iad og bhitheadh iad anns a' bhaile. 8. Tha na gillean an so an diugh ach cha robh iad an so an de. 9. Bhitheamaid a' tighinn dachaidh an raoir. 10. Bhitheadh an uinneag briste. 11. Tha an dorus duinte. 12. Bhitheadh iad an-moch an raoir. 13. Bitheamaid treun. 14. Tha na h-eich so an so a nis. 15. Am bheil an cu aig an dorus? 16. Tha e aig a' bhàta. 17. Tha na ba anns an fhang ach bha iad air a' mhonadh an sud an de. 18. Bitheamaid anns a' bhaile anns a' mhaduinn am maireach. 19. Ma bhitheas e aig an tigh an nochd bithidh mise an sin an dràsd.

106: Translate into Gaelic :—

1. When I was in the wood yesterday the boy was not present. 2. He will be here to-night or to-morrow. 3. The farmer was in the town when I was there in the morning. 4. Is the window not broken? No. 5. The dog is not in this field, it is on the hill. 6. There are deer on the hill. 7. Were the men not here last night ? 8. No, they were in the boat. 9. Though you will not be ready I will be. 10. The deer were not in this field, they were on the hill. 11. These boys were not in the boat. 12. When we were there they were not present. 13. They will be there to-morrow. 14. If the sheep are not in the pen they will be in the field. 15. The shepherd was on the hill. 16. Don't let that stick be lost. 17. Will the window be open in the morning ? 18. When the shepherd was there the farmer was in the town.

LESSON XII.

IDIOMS.

107. An Idiom is an expression that has acquired by usage a certain meaning, which becomes lost in a word-for-word translation into another language ; so that in order to convey the meaning in that other language the form of expression must be changed.

108. Thus **tha an leabhar aig an duine** is a Gaelic Idiom, for its sense is lost in a word for word English translation like " the book is at the man," and, in order to convey the true meaning, the English expression must be changed to " the man has the book."

109. Idioms constitute one of the chief difficulties in learning any language, and the student is recommended to master the few Gaelic Idioms which will now be introduced into these exercises.

110. These Idioms enter much into the spoken and written language and well deserve particular attention, for there is not a page written in which they are not to be found, nor can there be a single conversation without their use.

To DENOTE POSSESSION.

111. VERB " HAVE " **bi** WITH THE PREPOSITION **aig**.

The verb " have " is in English generally an auxiliary verb, but it is not always such. When it is used in English to indicate " possession " it must be translated by the Gaelic verb **bi** along with the preposition **aig**, at. Thus " I have a book " becomes in this idiom " a book is at me," or " there is a book at me " or " to me," and similarly through all the pronouns. This is a somewhat similar idiom to the Latin form, "**est mihi liber**," " there is a book to me," etc.

112. Such a sentence one might expect to be translated into Gaelic **tha leabhar aig mi**, " a book is at me." Instead, however, we use a combination of pronoun and preposition called a prepositional pronoun. Hence we write **tha leabhar agam.** (Prep. Pro. par. 404).

113. Observe that in this construction the subject of the English sentence becomes the object in Gaelic idiom. In **tha leabhar agam**, " I have a book," **leabhar** is nominative to **tha** (and so comes after the verb), and not as in the corresponding English sentence " I have a book," in which " book " is in the objective case. This order of the words holds good no matter how many subjects to the verb are introduced. They are all in Gaelic nominatives to **tha**, and in English objectives after " have."

1.14.   PREPOSITIONAL PRONOUNS FORMED FROM
aig " AT."

aig mi	becomes	**agam** (*akŭm*)	at me	= I have.
aig thu	,,	**agad** (*akŭd*)	at thee	= thou hast.
aig e	,,	**aige** (*ākŭ*)	at him	= he has.
aig i	,,	**aice** (*āch-kŭ*)	at her	= she has.
aig sinn	,,	**againn** (*ak-ynn*)	at us	= we have.
aig sibh	,,	**agaibh** (*akyv*)	at you	= you have.
aig iad	,,	**aca** (*ach-kŭ*)	at them	= they have.

115. Examples of the use of these prepositional pronouns :—

Tha peann agad (agad-sa)	*thou hast a pen.*
Tha bo aige (aige-san)	*he has a cow.*
Tha ad aice (aice-se)	*she has a hat.*
Nach eil sgian aig a' ghille ?	*has the boy not a knife ?*
Cha'n eil da leabhar aig a' chaileig.	*the girl has not two books.*
Ged nach robh an t-airgiod aige an de, bithidh e aige am maireach,	*though he had not the money yesterday he will have it to-morrow (though the money was not at him yesterday it will be at him to-morrow).*

116. These pronouns, **agam**, etc., denote possession but do not necessarily signify ownership, take this example : **tha tigh aige**, "he has a house," which means that he possesses a house which may or may not be his own, i.e. he may be only a tenant. (par. 184).

117. And the idiom which thus expresses our relation to our material property is also used to express our relation to our immaterial properties, or bodily and mental activities, which are in some way subject to our control.

Tha fuath agam da (*foŭ*)	*I hate him* = *hate is at me to him.*
Tha truas agam ris (*trooŭs*)	*I pity him* = *I have pity for him.*
Tha gaol agam (*gŏll*)	*I love* = *I have love.*

But I cannot say **tha tinneas agam**, " sickness is at me," when I mean to tell you that " I am sick." Sickness is generally outside our control and is looked on as an infliction which comes " on us," as will be shown.

118.   *Vocabulary.*

an leabhar (*ŭn llyo-ŭr*) the book.
aig a' chaileig (*āk ŭ challyk*) nf. at the girl.
peann (*pyawnn*) nm. a pen.   **a' bho** nf. the cow

119. Read in Gaelic and translate into English :—

1. Am bi bo agam? 2. Bithidh bo agam agus cha bhi bo agad-sa.
3. Ged nach eil bo agad. 4. Ma bhitheas bo aice. 5. Tha peann aige.
6. Tha tigh agad. 7. Nach eil sgian agam ? 8. Cha'n eil sgian agam.
9. Tha an sgian aig a' ghille. 10. Tha am bàta aige. 11. Tha na h-eich so agad. 12. Tha an sgian agad. 13. Tha na coin aca ach tha bo againn. 14. Tha an t-each agam ach tha an cu agad. 15. Tha an leabhar agam agus tha leabhar aig a' chaileig. 16. Bha na h-eich sin againn an raoir.

120. Translate into Gaelic :—

1. I have a horse. 2. He has a house. 3. Has he not a house ?
4. We have a horse and a dog. 5. He had a dog but he has not it now. 6. We have a cow. 7. Have you a hat ? 8. She has a hat.
9. I have not a hat now. 10. I pity him. 11. Has he not the book ?
12. He had the book yesterday. 13. He has not a knife to-day.
14. You had the knife last night. 15. We had the dogs on the hill but the cow was in the pen there. 16. She is there now. 17. You will have a cow to-morrow. 18. Will the farmer have a cow to-day ?
19. Will the girl have that book now ? 20. I have the book to-day, the boy will have it to-morrow, and the girl will have it the day after.
21. The man had it last night.

LESSON XIII.

THE VERB " TO WANT " = " TO NEED."

121. In a similar idiomatic manner the English verb " to want," with a wish or desire " to have," is translated. The verb **bi** is used in all its tenses with the preposition **o** or **ua** " from," or the prepositional pronouns formed therefrom.

122. Prepositional pronouns formed from **o, bho,** " from."

uam   (*oo-ŭm*)   or **bhuam**   (*voo-ŭm*)   from me.
uait   (*oo-atch*)   or **bhuait**   (*voo-ahtt*)   from thee.
uaithe (*oo-ây-hŭ*)   or **bhuaithe** (*voo-ây-hŭ*)   from him.

uaipe	(*oo-ây-pü*)	or	**bhuaipe**	(*voo-ây-pü*)	from her.
uainn	(*oo-âynn*)	or	**bhuainn**	(*voo-âynn*)	from us.
uaibh	(*ooâ-yv*)	or	**bhuaibh**	(*vooâ-yv*)	from you.
uapa	(*oo-âh-pü*)	or	**bhuapa**	(*voo-âh-pü*)	from them.

123. Examples of their use :—

Tha leabhar uam,	*I want a book (a book is from me).*
Tha sgian uait,	*you want a knife (a knife is from you).*
Ciod tha uait ?	*what would you have ?—you want ?*
De tha uaithe ?	*what does he want ? what is he after ?*
Tha uam thu bhi sona,	*I want you to be happy.*
Tha uam e a bhi agad,	*I want you to have it (to be in possession of it).*
Uam no agam e	*whether it is mine or not (from me or to me).*
Tha an t-airgiod sin uainn a nis,	*we want that money now.*
Tha uam a bhi ann,	*I want to be there.*
Tha thu ri bhi ann,	*you are to be there.*
Tilg uait an sgian sin.	*throw from you that knife.*

Cha chomasach do dhuine an ni nach eil aige a thoirt uaithe.
It is impossible for a man to give away what he does not possess. (lit. *It is not possible for (with) a man the thing which would not be with (at) him to give from him).*

124.   *Vocabulary.*

cuan m. (*kooün*) an ocean.   **tilg** (*cheeleek*) throw.
aig an iasgair (*āk ün y askür*) at the fisherman.
an trath so adv. (*ün tra sho*) just now.
Seumas (*shāmus*) James.   **ad**, *nf.*, a hat.
an t-airgiod (*ün ttārygytt*) the money.
c'uine a? (*koon-ü*) when? (what the time that ?).

125. Read in Gaelic and translate into English :—

1. Tha leabhar uait. 2. Tha am bàta uapa. 3. Bha am bàta aca an raoir ach tha i uapa a nis. 4. Ciod tha uaipe ? 5. Tha uapa a bhi ann. 6. De tha uam ? 7. Tha an leabhar uam an nochd. 8. Am bheil leabhar uait ? 9. Cha'n eil an leabhar bho 'n chaileig. 10. Bha peann uaipe. 11. Tha an cuan o'n iasgair. 12. Bithidh am bàta aig an iasgair an trath so.

126. Translate into Gaelic :—

1. Throw from you that book. 2. James wants the hat to-day. 3. Do you want the money ? 4. I want that money now. 5. You want to be there to-morrow. 6. What does she want ? 7. She wants a hat. 8. What would he have ? 9. He wanted a book but he will not have it now. 10. Did he not have a book yesterday ? 11. He had a book yesterday but he wants it to-day. 12. Whether it is his or not I have it now. 13. He wants this book the day after to-morrow.

LESSON XIV.

The Verb " To Know."

127. The English verb " know," is translated by the Gaelic noun **fios** " knowledge," and is used in the idiomatic form illustrated in the preceding lesson.   **Tha fios aig** (*ha feess āk*) " to have knowledge " (knowledge is at).

128. We use **fios** when the verb " know " means " to recollect," " to be aware of," " to be sensible of," or when we ask or give information of intelligence, etc.   It is always used when " know " is followed by " who, what, where," or other dependent clause.

Tha fios agad na thubhairt e,	*you know what he said.*
Tha fios agad gu de thubhairt e. '	
Tha fios agam far an robh e.	*I know where he was.*
Tha fios agad c'aite an robh e.	*you know in what place he was.*
Tha fios aice co a tha aig an dorus,	*she knows who is at the door.*
Am bheil fios agad cuin a tha e tighinn ?	*do you know when he comes ?*
Am bheil fios agad ma tha bàta aige ?	*do you know if he has a boat ?*
Cha'n eil fios agam,	*I do not know (there is no knowing at me).*
Mur an robh fios aige far an robh am bàta, cia mar a bha fios aige gu'n robh i agaibh ?	*If he did not know where the boat was, how did he know that you had it ? (If knowledge was not at him where the boat was, etc.)*
Cuin' a fhuair thu fios ?	*when did you get the information ? (knowledge).*
Bheir mi fios,	*I will inform (give notice).*
Is beag fios dhomh-sa,	*Little do I know.*

129. In the same construction **aithne** is the " knowledge " by which we " recognise " or " acknowledge acquaintance," " to know by sight " a person, place or thing, etc.

An aithne dhuit an leabhar so ?	*do you know this book (by sight)? = have you heard of this book ?*
Cha'n eil aithne agam air,	*I have no knowledge of it.*
Tha aithne agam air,	*I know it (lit.. there is knowledge at me on it=of it).*
An aithne dhuit Domhnull ?	*do you know Donald ?*
Is aithne dhomh Domhnull,	*I know Donald (by sight).*

130. When " to know " means to be well versed in the subject or well acquainted with it—to know a fact ;   that a thing is :   to know by heart ;   we use **eolach** (*yolach*).

Am bheil thu eolach air an leabhar so ?	do you know (all) this book ?
Am bheil thu fada eolach air Domhnull ?	do you know Donald well ? (are you long acquainted with Donald ?)
Tha mi fada eolach air Domhnull,	I know Donald well (I am long acquainted with Donald).
An robh thu eolach air an tir bhur n-eòlais ?	did you know him in your own country (lit.), were you acquainted with him in your own country ?
Tha e 'na dhuine eolach	he is a man well acquainted. he is an intelligent man.

131. Vocabulary.

Co aig am bheil ? (ko āk um vāl) who at whom is = who has ?
co aig an robh ? (ko āk un ro) who had ?
toilichte (tolychtchü) adj., pleased.
coig (kō-yk) nu. adj. five.
tasdain (ttasttan) nf. shillings.
gu cinnteach (goo keenn-tchach) adv. certainly.
an uiridh (ün oor-y) adv. last year.
dhomh, dhuit (gov, gootch) to me, to you.

132. Read in Gaelic and translate into English :—

1. An aithne dhuit Seumas ? 2. Cha'n eil aithne agam air. 3. Tha an t-each aig an tuathanach. 4. Co aig am bheil an t-airgiod ? 5. Tha e aig an duine. 6. Co aig an robh am bàta ? 7. Bha e aig an iasgair. 8. Bha am bàta aig Seumas ach cha'n eil e aige a nis. 9. Ma bhitheas an t-airgiod aig a' chaileig bithidh an tigh aig a' ghille. 10. Tha cu aig a' chiobair. 11. Nach eil leabhar agaibh ? 12. Cha'n eil. 13. Bithidh sgian aig a' ghille. 14. Bha coig tasdain aig a' chaileig. 15. Bha sgian aig an iasgair an de ach cha'n eil i aige an diugh. 16. Na'n robh sgian aig an duine bhitheadh e gle thoilichte. 17. Cha robh fios agam gu'n robh sibh an sin. 18. Mur eil fios aig an tuathanach gu'n robh an gille an sin bithidh fios aige a nis. 19. Tha tigh aige anns a' bhaile. 20. Cha'n eil aithne agam air. 21. Cuin a fhuair thu fios ? 22. Bha fios agam far an robh an tigh aige.

133. Translate English into Gaelic :—

1. Do you know (**aithne**) this book ? 2. I do not know it. 3. I have not that book. 4. Have you not this book ? No. 5. Who had it ? 6. James had the book yesterday. 7. I want this book. 8. The fisherman has not a boat now, but he will have it to-morrow. 9. I hadn't five shillings. 10. The boy has not the knife. 11. Who has it ? 12. Do you know who had it ? 13. I know the girl had it last night. 14. Do you know if the farmer has the money now ? 15. I know that he will not have it. 16. Will he have it to-morrow ? 17. Yes, certainly. 18. Do you know if he wants a horse ? 19. Do you know if that man has a dog ? 20. I do not know if he has a dog now, but he had a dog last year. 21. Do you know the shepherd well ? 22. I am well acquainted with him. 23. He is an intelligent man. 24. He was at the house yesterday. 25. Was he there this morning ?

LESSON XV.

IDIOMS OF THE VERB **bi, bi** WITH **air**.

134. The use of the verb **bi** with the preposition **air** " on," and the prepositional pronouns formed from it is also the cause of several peculiar idiomatic forms of expression.

135. The things which are ours we keep as near us as we can ; they are the things " at us " ; but there are things that come " to us " not by any act of ours, but against our will ; they are visitations, they come " to us " from without and probably from the Unseen. In Gaelic idiom these involuntary visitations are said to be " on us." Hunger, thirst, sickness, sadness, fear, joy, death, in fact any state, quality, feelings or sufferings which affect the body, mind or soul, are expressed in Gaelic as being a burden laid upon the individual or sufferer.

136. Thus " I am thirsty " becomes in this idiom " thirst is on me " ; " are you angry ? " " is anger on you ? " etc.*

Ciod e a tha ort ?	*what ails thee ? (what is it that is on thee).*
Tha gradh agam ort-sa,	*I love thee (love is at me on you).*
Tha bron mor oirnn,	*we are very sorrowful (great sorrow is on us).*
Tha am fiabhras air,	*he has the fever (the fever is on him).*
Tha eagal oirre,	*she is afraid (fear is on her).*
Tha an t-acras air,	*he is hungry (hunger is on him).*
Bha iongantas air an duine,	*the man was astonished (astonishment was on the man).*
Na biodh eagal ort,	*be not afraid (let not fear be on thee).*

137. The same idiom applied to money betokens debt. The fact that " I owe John money " or that " I am under any obligation to pay money to John " is expressed by saying, " John has money on me," the preposition **air** being used before the name of the debtor, and the act of " having " being expressed by **tha** and **aig** as in the previous lesson. " I owe John a hundred pounds " is translated according to idiom, " John has a hundred pounds on me,"

---

* It is because Gaelic has no primary adjectives for a number of these terms that the noun is used in this idiom. Where primary adjectives are available they are used. **Tha mi tinn.** *I am sick.*

tha ceud punnd Sasunnach* aig Iain orm. (*lit.* there is a hundred pounds at (of) John on me).

Tha deich tasdain agam air an fhear sin,	*that man owes me ten shillings* (lit., *I have ten shillings on that man*).

138. The following are the prepositional pronouns formed from **air** :—

air mi	becomes	orm	(*or-üm*)	on me.
air thu	,,	ort	(*orst*)	on thou.
air e	,,	air	(*är*)	on him.
air i	,,	oirre	(*orrü*)	on her.
air sinn	,,	oirnn	(*orynn*)	on us.
air sibh	,,	oirbh	(*or-yv*)	on you.
air iad	,,	orra	(*orrüh*)	on them.

139. *Vocabulary.*

adhaircean (*ö arkün*) horns.
slat (*slläht*) a rod.
ciod ? (*kut*) **de ?** (*jä*) what ?
cluas (*klooüs*) ear.
gu trath (*kootra*) soon.
fhuair (*hooür*) got.
an d'fhuair . . . ? (*un dooür*) did . . . get ?
breac (*bprächk*) a trout.

sporan, a purse.
damh (*dav*) a stag.
air na h-eildean (*är nü häldjen*) on the hinds.
punnd (*poont*) pound.
arbhar (*arrar*) corn.
uaireadair (*oo-är-ütür*) watch.
lion (*leen*) a net.
ag iasgach (*ak y üsküch*) fishing.

140. Read in Gaelic and translate into English :—

1. Bha an t-acras air an duine. 2. Bha adhaircean air an damh. 3. Cha'n eil adhaircean air na h-eildean. 4. Tha punnd aig a' chaileig. 5. Tha cluas air a' chat. 6. Mur eil fios aig an tuathanach gu'm bheil na caoraich anns an arbhar, bithidh fios aige gu trath. 7. C'ait an robh sibh an de ? 8. Bithidh mi anns a' bhaile gu trath. 9. Bha bron mor ort. 10. Ciod e a tha air ? 11. Tha eagal orra. 12. An robh sibh ag iasgach air an loch an de ? Bha. 13. An d'fhuair thu breac ? 14. Bha bron mor air an duine. 15. Am bheil fios agaibh de'n uair a tha e ? 16. Cha'n eil uaireadair agam.

141. Translate into Gaelic :—

1. The horse is lame. 2. Did the man not know that his horse was lame ? 3. He did not know. 4. James has a purse. 5. We had a rod and a net when we were fishing. 6. I did not know that the sheep were in the corn. 7. Was it not very warm when you were in town ? 8. It was. 9. Are you going fishing to-day ? 10. Yes. 11. I do not know if he has the watch. 12. Have you a watch ? 13. James has a watch now. 14. Was the boy not hungry ? 15. He was not hungry but he was very tired. 16. The man was very astonished.

---

* **Punnd Sasunnach** (£1) pound sterling. **Sasunnach** (from Eng. **Saxon—Lowlander**) is generally placed after **punnd** when money is inferred.

17. He was afraid. 18. I was astonished. 19. There are no horns on the hinds but the stag has horns. 20. The man was hungry. 21. I got a pound from the girl. 22. She will be home soon. 23. What ails her ? 24. She has the fever. 25. He loves her. 26. They were hungry last night. 27. Did they get home last night.

LESSON XVI.

THE PARTICLE **ann.**

142. The verb **bi** with the particle **ann** is used to denote existence, the particle **ann** generally coming last in the phrase, or forming the chief portion of the predicate. In this position it is adverbial, and is equal to the English locative adverb " there." The verb **bi** denotes existence connected with locality ; **ann** serves to strengthen it in that meaning.

143. This combination of **bi** and **ann** is always used in this sense to express the phenomena of nature. Thus in the sentence—" The showers were heavy," something is stated about the showers, but their existence is not questioned, so in Gaelic this is simply **bha na frasan trom**, but if the sentence ran " there were heavy showers," it is simply a statement that they existed, and the sentence would be **bha frasan troma ann.**

Tha aran air a' bhord,	*there is bread on the table.*
Am bheil aran ann ?	*is there bread ?*
Cha'n eil im ann,	*there is no butter.*
Tha fuachd ann an diugh,	" *it is cold to-day* " (*there is cold-ness to-day*).
Tha e fuar an diugh,	" *it is cold to-day.*"
Nach bithinn ann na's mo,	" *That I should not be any more* " (*That I should not be* (*in existence*) *there any more*).
Ciod a tha ann ?	" *what is it ?* " (*what is that there* (*in existence*) *or what is that there that exists*).
Tha abhainn ann,	" *there is a river* " (*a river is there*).
Am bheil thu ann ? Iain,	" *are you there ? John.*"
Is e duine math a tha ann,	" *he is a good man* " (*it is* (*he*) *a good man that is there*).

144. In all these phrases **ann** agrees in meaning with the English adverb " there," in such phrases as " there are," " there was," " there exists," etc., in which the adverb originally signified location " in that place," but now also

expresses mere existence. It is not difficult to account for this transition.* To be able to say that a thing is in a certain place is to give an emphatic assurance that it exists ; and hence the localising statement has become the statement of existence. Instead of saying " a road is " or " exists," we say " there is a road." In English " there " in this sense always precedes the verb, but in Gaelic the verb always precedes the adverbial particle **ann.**

145. Ann as a preposition governs the dative case of nouns and means " rest in."

Ann an tigh,	" *in a house.*"
Anns a' bhaile,	" *in the town.*"

146. Ann after a verb of motion means " motion in " and " into," and governs the dative case.

Cuir uisge anns an t-soitheach,	*put water into the dish.*
Cuir an t-airgiod anns an sporan,	*put the money into the purse.*
Tha an t-iasg a' snamh anns an uisge,	*the fish is swimming in the water.*
Chaidh e ann an laigse,	*he went into a faint (he fainted)*

147. Ann as a prepositional pronoun, meaning " in it," " in him " (201).

Cha'n eil ann ach Sasunnach,	"*he is but an Englishman*" (lit., *there is not in him but an Englishman*).

148. *Vocabulary.*

abhainn (*avynn*) nf. a river.
fras -an nf. shower, -s,
iasg (*eeüsk*) nm. fish.
im (*eem*) nm. butter.
chaidh (*chà y*) irr. v. went.

muir (*moor*) nm. sea.
uisge (*ooshkü*) nm. water, rain.
bord (*bawrd*) nf. a table.
aran nm. bread.
cuir (*koor*) put.

149. Read in Gaelic and translate into English :—

1. Am bheil aran ann ? 2. Tha uisge ann a nis. 3. Am bheil thu ann ? 4. Tha uisge ann an diugh. 5. Tha am breac anns a' mhuir. 6. Tha abhainn ann. 7. Cuir an t-iasg anns an abhainn. 8. Tha an gille anns a' bhaile. 9. Chaidh e do'n bhaile. 10. Tha mi anns a' bhàta. 11. Nach e an t-uisge a bhios ann ? 12. Bithidh uisge. ann. 13. Tha la math ann. 14. Tha oidhche fhliuch ann. 15. Bha e ann.

150. Translate into Gaelic.

1. There is a boat on the river. 2. There is a man in the boat. 3. The man had bread and butter on the table. 4. There is bread on

---

* **Dr. Bain's Higher English Grammar.**

the table, but there is no butter. 5. There is fish in the river. 6. There was rain last night. 7. It was cold and wet yesterday. 8. The showers were heavy last night. 9. It rains now. 10. If we had bread we would not be hungry. 11. Are you there ? 12. Is that you ? (*lit*. Is it you that is there ?) 13. It will rain to-morrow. 14. It is wet to-night. 15. There is rain now.

LESSON XVII.

THE ASSERTIVE VERB **is**.

151. You have already been introduced to the verbs **tha** and **bheil**. We have a third verb which is also used to translate into Gaelic the English verb " am, art, is, are."

152. This verb is **is,** pronounced like " iss " in the English word " hiss." It serves to express a simple assertion, to connect an attribute with its subject, to predicate one thing of another, as :—**is mise an treoraiche,** " I am the guide." **An treoraiche** here is the attribute of **mise**, or is predicated of **mise** by the verb **is**. **Tha** denotes a qualified existence ; i.e., in relation to time, place, or some qualifying condition. **Is** denotes simple existence without reference to anything else whatsoever. Examples of both verbs are given in the following sentence, which the student would do well to analyse—**Is mise a tha ann,** " It is I who am there— in a certain place—here."

153. The verb **is** is generally used impersonally. In such cases a neuter pronoun subject is contained in the verb, so that the noun or pronoun that follows it is not a subject but a predicate ; when the latter is a definite or proper noun it will be a double predicate. Thus : **is mise,** " it is I " ; **is tusa,** " it is thou " ; **is e Seumas,** " it is (he) James." Being an emphatic and assertive verb, the emphatic pronouns are generally used.

154. This is a defective verb, having only a present tense **is,** and a past tense **bu**. But they enter into many combinations and idiomatic clauses along with a noun and preposition, verbs and adverbs, as :—**Is urrainn do,** can ; **is leir do,** see ; **is coir do,** ought ; **is tu bhios sona,** 'tis you who will be happy : **is gorm a dh' fhas e,** green did it grow.

155. There is no dependent form in either the present or past tense. In the present tense, after the particles, the

verb **is** is omitted and only the particles remain, but the idea is as distinctly conveyed as if the verb had been expressed ; as, **cha mhi,** " it is not I."

Present Tense.		*Past Tense.*	
is	it is.	**bu**	it was.
is mi	it is I *or* I am.	**bu mhi**	it was I *or* I was.
is tu	it is thou.	**bu tu**	it was thou.
is e	it is he, it.	**b'e**	it was he, it.
an ?	is it ?	**am bu** ?	was it ?
am mi ?	is it I ? am I ?	**am bu mhi** ?	was it I ?
an tu ?	is it thou ? are you ?	**am bu tu** ?	was it thou ?
cha	it is not.	**cha bu**	it was not.
cha mhi	it is not I.	**cha bu mhi**	it was not I.
cha tu	it is not thou.	**cha bu tu**	it was not thou.
cha'n e	it is not he.	**cha b'e**	it was not he.
nach ?	is it not ?	**nach bu** ?	was it not ?
ma's	if it is.	**na'm bu**	if. it was. were
mur	if it is not.	**mur bu**	if it was not.
ged a's	though it is.	**ged bu**	though it was.
ged nach	though it is not.	**ged nach bu**	though it was not.
gur	that it is.	**gu'm bu**	that it was.
nach	that it is not.	**nach bu**	that it was not.

156. In the past tense **bu** causes aspiration of words immediately following :—**bu mhi,** " it was I " ; **bu mhor am bonnach,** " the cake was large " ; but words beginning with a **d** or **t** are not aspirated—**bu tu,** " it was thou "; **bu dalma,** " 'twas impertinent." **Bu** loses its vowel when followed by a vowel—**b'e,** " it was he "; **b'iad,** " it was they "; **b'urrainn domh,** " I could."

WHERE THE VERB **is** MUST BE USED.

157. The verb **is** is used when both subject and predicate are definite ; when in the English sentence the verb " to be " is followed by a definite noun, i.e., (a) a proper noun ; (b) a common noun with the definite article ; (c) a common noun with a possessive pronoun ; (d) or by a pronoun predicate.

(a) is e Seumas	*it is (he) James.*
(b) is tusa an righ,	*you are the king.*
(c) is tusa mo mhathair	*you are my mother.*
(d) is mise e, is e so,	*I am he, it is this.*

158. The rule is :—The verb **tha** cannot predicate a definite noun or its equivalent. We can say (1) **Tha e 'na righ** for " He is a king " ; but we cannot say (2) **Tha e an**

righ for " He is the king " No. (2) expresses an absolute and definite identity, an assertion which can only be expressed by **is**.

159. Note another rule :—The verb **is** cannot be followed immediately by either a definite or a proper noun. Usage has determined that in addition to pronouns, only indefinite expressions such as adjectives and indefinite nouns should follow immediately after **is**.

160. In these last examples we have a personal pronoun as the subject. If we have a definite noun or its equivalent as subject, it will be a double subject, as it requires a corresponding personal pronoun to follow **is**. " Malcolm is the king " becomes **Is e Calum an righ**. Observe the introduction of the pronoun in accordance with rule noticed in preceding paragraph.

Is e Iain am fear (*fer*),	*John is the man.*
Is iad na fir (*fyr*) so iad,*	*these men are they.*
Is e Inbhirnis an t-aite,	*Inverness is the place.*
Is i so a' bhean (*ven*),	*this is the woman.*
Is e Dia mo bhuachaill,	*God is my shepherd.*

* Observe the phenomenon of the double pronoun here which is an exact application of the preceding rule ; also consider

Is e so e,	*this is he.*
Is (e) duine math e,	*he is a good man.*
Is e baile an righ mhoir e,	*it is the city of the great king.*

161. Notice that in these expressions the pronouns following **is** are not in the emphatic form. These pronouns are merely temporary subjects, and the emphasis caused by **is** is carried on to the words following **is e, is i,** or **is iad**. The verb **is** is always in a state of dependence or decay, and has a tendency to become contracted or to vanish altogether ; hence we find occasionally **So tigh Sheumais**, instead of **Is e so tigh Sheumais** (par. 464).

162. We must use **is** when both subject and predicate are indefinite nouns, either of which may have an adjective attached. These sentences generally signify species or class. Note that in these sentences the rule is to place an indefinite predicate immediately after the verb, so that we may term them " inverted sentences." A few examples will explain. In saying that " a hen is a bird," we mean that it is of the bird species or class.

C*

Is iasg breac,	*a trout is a fish.*
Cha'n iasg cearc,	*a hen is not a fish.*
Is eun cearc,	*a hen is a bird.*
An eun cearc ?	*is a hen a bird ?*
Is saor e,	*he is a joiner.*
An gille fear ?	*is a man a boy ?*
Is duine mise,	*I am a man.*
Is e la fuar an so	*this is a cold day.*

163. Generally we use **is** when an assertion is made which admits of no idea of doubt (or condition as to locality), or when in case of contrast one is selected before others. Hence **is** is used to point out the comparative and superlative of adjectives, because contrast is pointed out with certainty.

164. What has been said of **is** applies of course to its past tense **bu.**

165. *Vocabulary.*

Iain (*eeün*) John.
Calum (*callŭm*) Malcolm.
mathair (*ma-ŭr*) mother.
athair (*a-ŭr*) father.
saor (*sör*) nm. a joiner.
eun (*ān*) nm. a bird.

gual (*gooül*) nm. coal.
dubh (*dtooh*) adj. black.
cat (*kaht*), nm. a cat.
mo, m' (*mō*) my, (aspirates)
righ (*ree*) nm. a king.
cearc (*kyark*) nf. a hen.

166. Read in Gaelic and translate into English :—
1. An e so cu ? 2. Is e so cu. 3. Is e sin cat. 4. Is e sin gual. 5. Nach dubh gual ? 6. Is e gual. 7. C'aite am bheil an gual ? 8. Is tusa Calum. 9. An e so Iain ? 10. Is e. 11. Am bheil e 'na fhear ? Tha. 12. Am mi an gille ? 13. Bu mhise an gille. 14. Is e Calum an tuathanach. 15. Nach ciobair e ? 16. An e saor e ? 17. Is e. 18. Am fear gille ? 19. Is i mo mhathair agus is e m' athair. 20. Is i so a' chearc. 21. An eun cearc ? 22. Is e. 23. Is fuar an la so. 24. Cha bu tu an saor. 25. Nach bu chearc i ? 26 Ged nach cearc e is eun e. 27. Is e so an righ. 28. Is mise an righ.

167. Now translate into Gaelic :—
1. Though it is a' dog it is swift. 2. Is a trout a fish ? 3. A bird is not a fish. 4. A hen is a bird. 5. This is a hen. 6. That is a cat. 7. Yonder is a dog. 8. It was the boy who was here. 9. Is this the boy ? 10. That is John. 11. Is it not Malcolm ? 12. If that is the boy who was here last night he is not lame. 13. I am the man. 14. You are not the man. 15. He was the boy. 16. Was it not the hen that he had ? 17. It was not the boy who was here. 18. John is a man. 19. A trout is a fish. 20. That is the king. 21. This is the man. 22. These are the horses. 23. John is the king. 24. Is this coal ? 25. Is not coal black ?

LESSON XVIII.

APPLICATION OF **is** AND **bi.**

168. As there is a peculiar distinction in the application of these two verbs **is** and **tha,** a few more examples will be helpful.

169. As we have seen in previous exercises, we must examine carefully a sentence containing any part of the verb " to be " before we translate. We have given examples where the verb **is** MUST be used and the verb **tha** cannot be used. In some of the sentences we had in the earlier exercises, where we used **tha** we can also use **is,** but with a slightly different meaning, as we hope to illustrate by example.

170. An indefinite noun or adjective in predicate.

Tha e 'na fhear,	*he is a man (in his man).*
Tha an la fuar,	*the day is cold.*

Now we can also use the verb **is** here, and say **is fear e, is fuar an la.** Notice that up to this the order of the words in our Gaelic sentence has been (1) verb, (2) nominative case, and (3) predicate, which may be a noun, adjective, or a phrase which followed the English verb. When we use **is** this order is changed, and we always have the predicate when it is an indefinite noun or an adjective coming immediately after **is,** and uniting with it in making an assertion. We cannot say **is e fear,** because **fear** is an indefinite noun predicate, and according to rules comes immediately after **is.**

171. The position of the adjective modifies the sense and structure of the sentence, as in the following example :—

Is fuar an la so,	*this day is cold.*
Is e la fuar an so	*this is a cold day.*

This last example is somewhat analogous to what is sometimes heard in English, " 'Tis a cold day this."

172. We have shown that **tha** means " is now "; it also implies a state, quality, condition, or location, and **is** means " is always," implying kind, species, impression, and comparison. Thus if you say to me **is fear e,** your assertion

means to me that " he is a man " = " he is a real man," every inch a man, not a woman, an animal, or a coward. If we see a figure approaching, and you tell me **is fear e** as soon it is made out that it is a man, you will use **is fear e** correctly. But if you say **tha e 'na fhear** " he is a man " = " he is in his man," here I take you to mean a very different thing, that " he is now a man," no longer a boy, having grown up to be a man, and is now in his quality of " manhood." **Tha e 'na mhinistear,** " he is a minister," means that he is now a minister, after his studying he has become " a minister " and " is now " in his quality of minister.

173. All this is very important, because if there is any idea of a change of state in the mind, we cannot use **is**. If we wish to convey the idea that a person or thing has become what he (or it) is, and that he or it was not always so, we must use the verb **tha**. And the verb **tha** must in such construction be always followed by the preposition **ann** and a suitable possessive pronoun, as **tha e 'na fhear**, " he is in his man(hood) " (Lesson xxxv.)

On the other hand the preposition **ann** is not necessary when the predicate is an adjective, as, **tha e fuar**, " he is cold," for the simple reason that the adjective itself denotes posture and local condition equivalent to an adverbial phrase, " Cold = in cold."

Tha + Preposition + Noun.

174. Whenever in English the verb " to be " is followed by a preposition **tha** is the verb to use. This follows from the nature of the prepositions, for when we say a thing or someone is " at a place," " on a place," " from a place," etc., " is " always means " is now," or has reference to a state or condition. Again, when we talk about the weather or any thing that is changeable, " is cold," " hot," etc., we mean that it " is now " hot, cold, etc., and use **tha**.

175. *Vocabulary.*

bronach adj. sad.
ard (*ardt*) adj. tall, high.
laidir (*là tch ür*) adj. strong.

EXERCISE.

176. Use the verb **is** and **bu** in the following sentences in place of **tha,** and translate both sentences.

1. Tha e 'na fhear.   2. Tha an la fuar.   3. Tha mi 'nam shaor.   4. Tha thu bronach.   5. An robh an la fuar ?   6. Cha n'eil an la fuar. 7. Am bheil thu bronach ?   8. Tha am fear fliuch.   9. Tha mi sgith. 10. Tha an gille ard ach cha n' eil e laidir.   11. Bha na h-eich so sgith. 12. Nach 'eil mi crubach?   13. Ged nach robh thu leisg.   14. Mur an robh mi samhach.   15. Nach robh thu treun ?

LESSON XIX

is AND **tha** IN QUESTION AND ANSWER.

177. When asking a question thus :   we use **tha**

De tha so ?   *what is this ?*   Co tha sin ?   *who is that ?*

When a statement would be made in answer to these questions or in answer to the question, **an e so ?** " is it this," we use the verb **is.**

Is e so cu,   *this is a dog.*   Is e sin Calum, *that is Malcolm.*

When a question has been asked by using one of the dependent verbs **bheil** or **robh**, the answer must be made with the independent forms **tha** or **bha** or the negative **cha'n eil** or **cha robh.**

Am bheil thu a' dol ?	*are you going ?*	Tha,	*I am=yes.*
		Cha'n eil,	*I am not=no.*
An robh thu sgith ?	*were you tired ?*	Bha,	*I was=yes.*
		Cha robh,	*I was not=no.*

178. When answering " yes " or " no " to questions asked by the verb **is**, or by any of the particles which have the force of this verb but do not suffer it to be expressed, we use the verb **is** to reply, supported by the predicate of the questioning sentence repeated in the answer ;   the verb **is** cannot stand alone as **tha** does ;   it must always be supported by a pronoun.

An e so ?	*is it this ?*	Is e sin,	*it is that=yes.*
An e an duine ?	*is he the man ?*	Is e,	*he is=yes.*
		Cha'n e,	*he is not=no.*
Co e ?	*who is he ?*	Is e Calum,	*he is Malcolm.*
An e clachair a tha annad ?		Is e,	*I am=yes.*
	are you a mason ?	Cha'n e,	*I am not—no.*
Nach e Seumas a tha ann ?		Is e,	*It is=yes.*
	isn't that James ?	Cha'n e,	*it is not=no.*

179. **Seadh** (**is** + **eadh**) = " that's it " or " 'tis so."

We have already illustrated **tha** and **cha'n eil**, and **is e** and **cha'n e** as the common answers equivalent to " yes " and " no " in English. There is, however, another question form taking for answer **seadh** (*shögh*) " it is so " and **cha'n eadh** " it is not so." The question is usually made by the interrogative negative **nach** ? " is not ? " followed by an adjective. This pronoun **eadh** is a survival of an old neuter form.

Nach milis am bainne so ?	seadh	*it is so=yes.*
is this milk not sweet ?	cha'n eadh *it is not so=no.*	
Nach fliuch an la a tha ann ?	seadh	*it is so=yes.*
isn't it a wet day ?	cha'n eadh *it is not so=no.*	
Nach fearail e ? *isn't he manly ?*	seadh, cha'n eadh.	
Nach modhail sin ? *isn't that polite ?*	seadh, cha'n eadh.	
Is fearail an duine e.	seadh,	*he is.*
manly the man he is.	cha'n eadh *he is not.*	

THE VERB **is** WITH THE PARTICLE **ann**.

180. The combination of the verb **is** with the particle **ann** gives us a decisive emphatic form, an emphasis which is not conveyed by the English translation. The verb **is** emphasises the words immediately following it ; combined with **ann** it is rendered still more emphatic. **Is ann** is generally used to express indignation, surprise, or impression. **Is ann** may be literally translated " it is " " there is," " it has happened," " occurred."

Is ann air an duthaich a thainig an da la,	*what a change has come over the country.*
Is ann mar sin a bha e,	*it happened thus (like that).*
Is ann leis a thig iad,	*it is with him they will come.*
B' ann mar sin a thachair,	*it was in that way things happened*
Is ann aige tha fios,	*it is he who knows.*
B' ann as an aite sin a thainig e	*he came from that place.*
Is ann gu bronach a tha e,	*he is very sorrowful.*
Is ann daibh is aithne bualadh,	*they know how to thresh.*
Is ann an sin a bhitheas sinn,	*it is indeed there we shall be.*
An aite seasamh is ann a theich iad,	*instead of standing they fled.* (lit. *in place standing keeping their ground, it happened they fled.*)
B' ann air eiginn a thair e as,	*it was with difficulty he got òff* (lit. *there was* or *it occurred that by difficulty he came out of it* or *escaped*).
Is ann uaithe so a tha e tachairt,	*thus it happens* (lit. *it is from him thus that it is happening*)

It will be observed that **is ann** is most frequently used

before adverbs or adverbial phrases or clauses. The idioms are difficult in some of the examples shown, too difficult to be introduced at this stage.

181. *Vocabulary*.

trom adj. (*trowm*) heavy. **idir** adv. (*y tch ür*) at all.
loch nm. (*lawch*) a loch. **bainne** nm. (*bpan-nyü*) milk.
teine nm. (*tchănü*) a fire. **clachair** nm. (*klachür*) a mason

182. Read in Gaelic and translate into English :—

1. De tha sin ? 2. Is e sin gual. 3. C'aite am bheil an gual ? 4. Tha an gual anns an teine. 5. Am' bheil bàta air an loch ? Tha. 6. C'aite am bheil an gille ? 7. Bha an gille air a' mhonadh leis na coin 8. Is e so bàta. 9. De tha anns a' bhàta ? 10. Tha na caoraich anns a' bhàta. 11. Is bainne so, nach eadh ? 'seadh. 12. An eadh ? 13. Cha'n eadh idir. 14. Tha an t-uisge trom ann an diugh agus bha e trom an de. 15. Is ann 'na chlachair a tha Iain—nach ann ? 16. Is ann ach is ann 'na shaor a tha Seumas. 17. Is e so am fear. 18. An e an duine ? 19. Is mise an duine. 20. Am mise an gille ? 21. Am bu mhise an gille ? 22. Bu tusa an duine. 23. B'e an gille.

183. Translate into Gaelic :—

1. Is he the man ? 2. He is not the man at all. 3. I am the boy. 4. Was I not the boy ? 5. He was the man. 6. Thou art the man. 7. Is not that water ? 8. No, it is milk. 9. It was wet last night and it rains now. 10. The showers are not heavy. 11. It is wet to-day. 12. I am hungry and there is no bread in the house. 13. Had he the fever last night ? Yes. 14. Is John not going home ? Yes. 15. Are you going ? No. 16. Were you tired yesterday ? 17. I was not tired. 18. I would have been tired. 19. Were you the man ? No. 20. Is it this man ? 21. That's he. 22. John was the boy. 23. He wasn't. 24. Is this the bread ? 25. That's not it at all. 26. There is bread on the table. 27. This ! 28. That's it.

LESSON XX.

IDIOMS OF THE VERB **bi—is** WITH **le**.

184. We have already seen how " possession " is translated by the verb **tha**, with the prepositional pronouns formed from **aig**, " at." To describe " absolute possession or ownership " we use the verb **is**. " The book is John's " is translated " the book is with John." Here " is with " has the idea of being permanently connected with, as a thing is with the owner, so the verb used is **is** not **tha**. Note also the order of words in the Gaelic sentence when we use the verb **is**. First, the verb, which is followed by the adjective or noun which in English followed the verb, and last, the nominative case of the English sentence.

185. **Is le Iain e,** " it is John's " ; **is le Mairi an leabhar so,** " this book is Mary's " ; but in such a sentence as " the book is mine," we do not translate **is le mi an leabhar,** but use a prepositional pronoun formed from **le mi,** which becomes **leam.** The following are the prepositional pronouns formed from **le,** " with."

le mi becomes	**leam**	*(lem)*	with me, mine.
le thu ,,	**leat**	*(leh-t)*	with thou, thine.
le e ,,	**leis**	*(lāsh)*	with him, his.
le i ,,	**leatha**	*(lehüh)*	with her, hers.
le sinn ,,	**leinn**	*(lā-ynn)*	with us, ours.
le sibh ,,	**leibh**	*(lā-yv)*	with you, yours.
le iad ,,	**leotha**	*(lyo-hü)*	with them, theirs.

186. This prepositional pronoun can be used with more emphasis thus :—

is leamsa, " it is mine " (it is with me)
is leinne, " it is ours " (it is with us).

187. As illustrating the difference in meaning of **aig** and **le,** picture a banker handling his cash and saying—**tha airgiod agam ach cha leam fein e,** " I have money, but it is not my own." **Tha agam** shows that the money is in hand ; **cha leam,** " not with me," indicates the person's right to it. **An le Seumas an leabhar so ?** " Is it with James this book ? "=" Does this book belong to James ? " **Is leis e,** " It is with him "=" It does " ; **Bu leis e,** " It was with him "=" It did."

188. The interrogative possessive pronoun " whose " is translated into Gaelic in the form " whom with," **co leis,** as :—**co leis an leabhar so ?** " whose is this book " (idiomatic —whom with the book this) **leamsa,** " with myself = mine." **Co** with a pronoun asks a question without the verb **is** being expressed, **co e ?** " who is he ? "; **Co iad ?** " who are they ? " (par. 456).

189. *Vocabulary.*

reic *(rāchk)* sold.
cheannaich *(chyannych)* bought.
im saillte *(eem sāltchü)* salt butter.
clach *(klach)* nf. a stone.

abhag nf. *(ăvük)* a terrier.
im ur *(eem oor)* fresh butter.
dubh (duibhe), *adj.,* black.
mor *(mōr)* big, large, great.

190. Read in Gaelic and translate the following :—

1. Bu duine math e. 2. Am b'e an duine ? 3. Is e an duine. 4. Co tha so ? 5. Is e so Seumas. 6. De tha sin ? 7. Is e sin cu. 8. Is e so an t-each. 9. C'aite am bheil an cu ? 10. Tha an cu aig an dorus. 11. Am bheil an t-im ur ? 12. Cha'n eil. 13. De tha so ? 14. Is e so lion. 15. Co tha sin ? 16. Bha e 'na shaighdear. 17. An e an cu ? 18. Cha'n e. 19. Is i so an abhag. 20. Bu fhear og Seumas. 21. Tha fios agam. 22. Co leis an leabhar so ? 23. Is mise do mhac agus is tusa m'athair. 24. An iad so an righ agus m'athair? 25. An ·tusa fear an tighe ? 26. Is mise e. 27. Is mise a. tha tinn. 28. Tha an la fuar. 29. Is leisg am fear e. 30. Is trom a' chlach i. 31. Co leis an t-aite ? 32. Is fearr am fear thusa, a Sheumais. 33. C'aite an robh e ? 34. Bha e anns a' bhaile an raoir. 35. An robh fios agad air sin ? 36. Co thu ? 37. Cha'n eil acras orm. 38. Am bheil im saillte agad ?

191. Translate into Gaelic :—

1. Have you a book ? 2. Yes. 3. Is this it ? 4. No, this book is the girl's ;*that is mine. 5. Whose boat is that ? 6. Is it the fisherman's ? 7. No, it was his last year, but he sold it, and it is the shepherd's now. 8. Has the fisherman not a boat ? 9. He has not now, but he will have it to-morrow. 10. Is this book not John's ? 11. No, it is James'. 12. How do you know ? 13. I am not certain. 14. James, is this book yours ? 15. Yes. 16. Is this dog yours ? 17. No, I have a black terrier. 18. That is not mine. 19. Where is yours ?* 20. It is at home. 21. Is it a big dog ? No. 22. Where did you get it ? 23. I bought it last year. 24. Have you it now ? 25. Yes. 26. Is this fresh butter ? 27. No, it is salt butter. 28. Is there any bread ? 29. There is bread on the table. 30. Have you the money ? 31. Yes, it is here. 32. Thank you.

* *lit.* " that one " 'your one " inferred. See footnote to **fear** par. 47²

LESSON XXI.

THE VERB **bi** AND THE COMPOUND TENSES OF ALL VERBS.

192. With the exception of the verb* **bi**, no Gaelic verb has a present time tense.† The present tense of all Gaelic verbs is composed of the verb **bi** and a verbal noun which is translated by the English present participle. A com-

---

* Many of the future forms of both regular and irregular verbs might be used for present time, but particularly the verb **chi** " I see " or " will see "—**chi mi sin** I see that (par 513).

† In English, the regular verb has only two different forms to express time, thus **I love, I loved** ; all the other tenses are formed with the help of auxiliaries.

pound tense may be used to refer to an action whether present, past, or future, active or passive.

193. These compound tenses are formed thus—" She sings a song " becomes in Gaelic idiom " she is at the singing of a song," **Tha i a' seinn orain.**

194. When used in the present, to express an action progressing, as " singing," " going," " running," etc., the verbal noun is preceded by **ag,** " at," the **g** of which is dropped before all consonants, except in the case of **radh** and retained before all vowels, as :—**ag radh** (*üg ra*), "saying" **a' dol** (*ü dawl*), " going "; **ag iarraidh** (*üg keer-y*), " asking."

195. When used in the past to express a completed action, as—" sung," " spoken," etc., the verbal noun is preceded by the preposition **air,** " after," and thus the sentence, " she has sung a song " becomes in this Gaelic idiom " she is after the singing of a song," **tha i air seinn orain.**

196. When a noun follows these participles or verbal nouns it is put in the genitive case. **Orain** here is the genitive case of **oran,** and means " of a song." " Of " coming between two nouns is not translated, the inflection of the genitive noun is a sufficient indication.

197. Thus a whole series of compound tenses of an active signification may be formed by the use of the verbal noun, preceded by the prepositions **ag** and **air** and the verb **bi** in all its inflections, as :—

Tha e a' dol dachaidh,	*he is going home.*
Tha e air dol dachaidh,	*he has gone home (he is after going home).*
Bha e a' dol dachaidh,	*he was going home.*
Bha e air dol dachaidh,	*he had gone home (he was after going home).*
Bhitheadh e a' dol dachaidh,	*he would be going home.*
Bhitheadh e air dol dachaidh,	*he would have gone home.*
Bithidh e a' dol dachaidh,	*he will be going home.*
Bithidh e air dol dachaidh,	*he will have gone home.*
Bitheam a' dol dachaidh,	*let me go home.*
Am bheil e a' dol dachaidh ?	*is he going home ?*
Cha'n eil e a' dol dachaidh,	*he is not going home.*

198. When the personal pronoun is the object of a progressive participle in English, as " he is striking me ";

it is translated by a combination of the corresponding possessive pronoun and the preposition. Such combinations may be called prepositional possessives.

199. Thus, the possessive pronouns **mo, do, a, ar, ur, an,** or **am,** along with the preposition **aig** " at " give us

'gam,	'gad,	'ga,	'gar,	'gur,	'gan,
at my.	at thy.	at his,	at our.	at your.	at their.

200. Thus we have " he is striking," **tha e a' bualadh** ; but " he is striking me " i.e., " he is at the striking of me " **tha e 'gam bhualadh*** (he is at my striking). " He is breaking stones," " he is at the breaking of stones " **tha e a' briseadh chlach** ; but " he is breaking them," **tha e 'gam briseadh** (he is at their breaking)

201. These possessives along with the preposition **ann** " in," give :—

am,	ad,	'na,	'nar,	'nur,	'nan,
in my.	in thy.	in his.	in our.	in your.	in their.

Ann is used to denote a state or condition :—

Bha mi am* shuidhe,	*I was sitting (I was in my sitting).*
Tha e 'na laighe,	*he is lying down (in his lying down).*
Bha na fir 'nan suidhe,	*the men were sitting.*
Tha e 'na *dhuine,	*he is a man* (lit. *in his man*).

202. In the same relation and in the same order of construction, the preposition **air** is used to express a completed action ; and **gu** (contracted **g'**) to express a purpose.

Tha e air mo bhualadh,	*he has struck me (he is after my striking).*
Bha an tuathanach air a bhualadh,	*the farmer had struck it.*
Chaidh e gu m' *bhualadh,	*he went to strike me.*
Thog e lamh g'am bualadh,	*he raised a hand to strike them.*

203. When the possessive pronoun or prepositional pronoun preceding a verbal noun agrees with its nominative noun or pronoun in person and number, the sentence assumes a passive signification.

---

* The possessive pronouns which aspirate their nouns when used in their simple form aspirate in these combinations also. (par. 409).

Bha e a' togail na cloiche,	*he was lifting the stone.*
Bha a' chlach 'ga togail,	*(the stone was at its lifting),the stone was being lifted.*
Bha e 'gam bhualadh.	*(he was at my striking), he was striking me.*
Bha mi 'gam bhualadh,	*(I was at my striking), I was being struck.*

204. EXERCISES.

Vocabulary.

briseadh (*bprees ügh*), breaking.
breabadh (*bprāpügh*)† kicking.
bualadh (*booalügh*) striking.
reic (*rāchk*) selling.
togail (*tokül*) lifting.
air falbh nm. gone away
a' charbad-iaruinn (*ü charapüt eeürynn*) the train.

ceannach (*kyannŭch*) buying.
an eich (*un āch*) of the horse.
a' choin (*ü choyn*) of the dog.
leis a' ghille (*lāsh ü yillü*) by the boy.
cuideachd, *adv.*, also
do, to, into.

205. Read in Gaelic and translate into English :—

1. Tha e air dol dachaidh. 2. Bha an uinneag air a briseadh leis a' ghille. 3. Am bheil e a' dol an sin? 4. Cha'n eil. 5. Tha e a' tighinn an so. 6. Am bheil thu a' dol a nis? 7. Tha an gille a' breabadh an eich. 8. Bha am fear a' bualadh a' choin. 9. Am bheil a' charbad-iaruinn a' dol a *dh'fhalbh? (*to go*). 10. Cha'n eil fios agam. 11. Nach robh e air falbh an raoir? 12. Tha mi a' ceannach na caorach sin. 13. Am bheil thu air reic a' choin? 14. Tha mi air seinn orain. 15. Bithidh e a' seinn orain am fheasgar so. 16. Tha e 'na laighe[1] a nis. 17. Thog mi mo lamh[2] g'a bhualadh. 18. Bha e 'gam bhualadh. 19. Bha an tuathanach air a bhualadh.

206. Translate English into Gaelic :—

1. I have bought these sheep this afternoon. 2. Have you bought the dog to-day also? 3. No. I had bought it last night. 4. Are you going home now? 5. I am going to the train immediately. 6. When are you going home? 7. I am selling these sheep to-day and I will be home to-night. 8. Has the train not gone away now? 9. No, but it is going to-morrow. 10. Has the boy broken that window? 11. I do not know. 12. The window was broken last night. 13. The boy had struck the horse this morning. 14. It had kicked the dog yesterday. 15. I was lifting the stone. 16. The stone was being lifted by the boy.

---

* Pron : *ü ghall-üv.* [1] *lla yü.* [2] *llâv.*

† *a + dh* or *gh*. In the case of *adh* or *agh*, after the sound of *a* = modified *ŏ* the *dh* or *gh* comes in very much like the momentary sound of a teaspoonful of gargle in the throat—a gargle sound.

LESSON XXII.

THE ARTICLE.

207. There is no indefinite article in Gaelic :—

duine, " a man." **daoine**, " men."

Notice that the indefinite article is also omitted in the English plural, where the absence of the " a " or any form of it serves exactly the same purpose as the presence of it in the singular.*

208.   THE DEFINITE ARTICLE.

In English we say :—" the man "; plural, " the men."
In Gaelic we say :—**an duine** ; plural, **na daoine**.
an and **na** we may call the primary forms of the article.
It is declined for gender, number and case as follows :—

	masc. sing	*fem. sing.*	*plural.*	
Nom.	**an, am, an t-,**	**an, a', an t-,**	**na**	" the "
Gen.	**an, a', an t-,**	**na, na h-,**	**nan, nam**	" of the "
Dat.	**an, a', an t-,**	**an, a', an t-,**	**na**	"(to) the "

209. The **n** of the article becomes **m** before nouns with initial **b f m** and **p** as—**am fear**, " the man " ; **am bàta**, " the boat " ; **am maireach**, " to-morrow."

210. The article causes aspiration in certain cases. The **n** then drops out and its elison is marked by an apostrophe ('), as :—**a' bhean**, " the wife " ; **a' ghille**, " of the boy."

211. When the article follows a preposition ending in a vowel it is the **a** that is dropped and its place taken by an apostrophe ('n) as—**do 'n righ**, " to the king " ; **o'n tigh**, " from the house." In cases where the **n** would be dropped before an aspiration, and the **a** after a preceding vowel, the **n** is retained and the **a** is dropped, as—**do'n mhac**, " to the son."

---

* The absence of the indefinite article in Gaelic is not unique ; in other languages, notably Greek, there is no indefinite article ; French plurals all require an article ; but Latin again has no articles at all. The Latin **filius viri** may mean " a son of a man," " a son of the man," " the son of a man," or " the son of the man."

212. In translating the English possessive case noun we use in Gaelic the noun in the genitive. This genitive noun, in which "of" is an understood component part, comes after the noun it qualifies and defines. The qualifying genitive noun only can take the article before it, even though both nouns may have a definite signification. When a possessive pronoun is used before the qualifying noun, the definite article is excluded altogether. The absence of an article from either noun in Gaelic does not signify that both nouns are indefinite (see example 3).*
A definite compound noun takes the article before the first element of the compound (par. 298, 9).

lamh a' ghille,	*the hand of the boy*	*the boy's hand.*
lamh mo ghille,	*the hand of my boy,*	*my boy's hand.*
lamh gille,	*the hand of a boy,*	*a boy's hand.*
solus-greine,	*sunlight,*	*sunlight.*
solus na greine,	*the light of the sun,*	*the sun's light.*
an solus greine,	*the light of the sun,*	*the sunlight.*

213. If an adjective simple or qualified precedes the noun, the article is placed before the adjective. The article so placed is subject to all the modifications, and aspirates the adjective as it would a noun beginning with the same letters.

An droch dhuine, *the bad man.*
am fior dhroch dhuine, *the truly bad man.*

214. The article is used before a noun when followed by the demonstrative pronouns **so, sin, ud** : **an tigh so,** " this house " ; **an cnoc ud,** " yonder hill " ; when the noun is preceded by **is** and **bu,** and an adjective : **is math an t-each e** " he is a (the) good horse " ; and between the interrogatives, **co, cia, ciod,** and the noun : **co am fear** ? " what man ? " (*lit.* : who (is) the man).

215. The article is frequently used before abstract nouns, and nouns which represent their class or kind ; as **an leisg,**

---

* I have stated it in this way, as it is more correct than to say, like Gillies and others, " that one noun governs another in the genitive." Whose " hand " ? the " boy's " hand ; it might be anyone's hand, and so we qualify and govern the noun " hand " by " boy's " instead of the reverse being the case. A compound illustrates this point even more so (par. 295). It is incorrect to say as Gillies does that both nouns are indefinite in the absence of any article (Gillies 179).

" laziness " ; **an duine**, " man " (signifying mankind) ;
before names of certain countries ; as **an Eadailt**, " Italy " ;
an Roinn-Eórpa, " Europe " ; **an Fhraing**, " France " ;
Eachdraidh na h-Alba, " History of Scotland."

216. As the vagaries of the article are many, we will,
in order to fully describe and illustrate all its combinations,
decline it with the noun. As already shown, the article
changes according to case, number, gender, and the initial
letter of the noun which it qualifies. We will divide the
nouns into four groups in order to illustrate all these changes.

Group 1.—All nouns beginning with **d, t** ; **l, n, r** ; **sg,
sm, st, sp.**

Group 2.—All nouns beginning with **b, c, g, f, m,** or **p.**

Group 3.—All nouns beginning with **s** followed by **l, n,
r,** or **s** followed by a vowel.

Group 4.—All nouns beginning with a vowel.

217.   THE ARTICLE FOR NOUNS IN GROUP 1.

All nouns beginning with **d, t, l, n, r** ; **sg, sm, st,** or **sp.**

In this group no alteration or addition is made, and the
article remains in its primary form. The final lingual **n**
of the article prevents aspiration of initial **d** or **t** of a noun
or adjective immediately following it ; the lingual termination and dental initial letters blending into each other
naturally. Initial **l n r** never show aspiration in any position (pars. 21, 38).

ramh (m) an oar.		**spog** (f) a claw.	
N.	**an ramh,**	the oar.	**an spog,**	the claw.
G.	**an raimh,**	of the oar.	**na spoige,**	of the claw.
D.	**an ramh,**	the oar.	**an spoig,**	the claw.
N.	**na raimh,**	the oars.	**na spogan,**	the claws.
G.	**nan ramh,**	of the oars.	**nan spog,**	of the claws.
D.	**na raimh,**	the oars.	**na spogan,**	the claws.

218.   THE ARTICLE FOR NOUNS IN GROUP 2.

Nouns beginning with **b f m p** and **c** and **g.** Masculine
nouns in this group aspirate in the genitive and dative
singular ; feminine nouns aspirate in the nominative and
dative singular. The **n** of the article drops out before the
aspirated consonant in these cases and an apostrophe takes
its place ('). Before **c** and **g** in the nominative singular

masculine and the genitive plural the article **an** and **nan** is pronounced with a **g** sound attached to it, as—**an cu** (*ung-koo*) the dog ; **nan gleann** (*nung-glaunn*) of the glens.

gille (m) a boy. **clach** (f) a stone. **bard** (m) a poet. **poit** (f) a pot.

N.	**an gille.**	a' **chlach.**	am **bard.**	a' **phoit.**
G.	a' **ghille.**	na **cloiche.**	a' **bhaird.**	na **poite.**
D.	a' **ghille.**	a' **chloich.**	a' **bhard.**	a' **phoit.**
N.	**na gillean.**	na **clachan.**	na **baird.**	na **poitean.**
G.	**nan gillean.**	**nan clach.**	**nam bard.**	**nam poit.**
D.	**na gillean.**	na **clachan.**	na **baird.** na **poitean** *or* **poitibh.**

Observe that in the nominative singular masculine and in the genitive plural, both masculine and feminine, the **n** of the article changes to **m** before **b f m** and **p**.

219. In nouns beginning with **f**, both mas. and fem., the article **an** is retained in full before aspiration ‚as the **fh** which follows is silent and thus there is no harsh sound to break down, **an fhras**, pronounced *un rass*.

fear (m) a man. **fras** (f) a shower.

N.	**am fear,**	the man.	**an fhras,**	the shower.
G.	**an fhir,**	of the man.	**na froise,**	of the shower.
D.	**an fhear,**	the man.	**an fhrois,**	the shower.
N.	**na fir,**	the men.	**na frasan,**	the showers.
G.	**nam fear,**	of the men.	**nam fras,**	of the showers.
D.	**na fir,**	the men.	**na frasan,**	the showers.

220.   THE ARTICLE FOR NOUNS IN GROUP 3.

Nouns beginning with **sl, sn, sr,** or **s,** when followed by a vowel. Nouns in this group add a **t-** in the genitive and dative singular masculine, and in the nominative and dative singular feminine. No change in the article takes place in the plural. The **s** is always silent after **an t-**.

sruth (m) a stream. **slat** (f) a rod.

N.	**an sruth,**	the stream.	**an t-slat,**	the rod.
G.	**an t-srutha,**	of the stream.	**na slaite,**	of the rod.
D.	**an t-sruth,**	the stream.	**an t-slait,**	the rod.
N.	**na sruthan,**	the streams.	**na slatan,**	the rods.
G.	**nan sruth,**	of the streams.	**nan slat,**	of the rods.
D.	**na sruthan,**	the streams.	**na slatan,**	the rods.

221.   THE ARTICLE FOR NOUNS IN GROUP 4.

All nouns beginning with a vowel. Masculine nouns in this group add a **t-** in the nominative singular ; feminine nouns take an **h-** in the genitive singular ; and nouns of both genders take an **h-** in the nominative and dative plural.

	athair (m), a father.		**abhainn** (f), a river.	
N.	**an t-athair,**	the father.	**an abhainn,**	the river.
G.	**an athar,**	of the father.	**na h-aibhne,**	of the river.
D.	**an athair,**	the father.	**an abhainn.**	the river.
N.	**na h-aithrichean,**	the fathers,	**na h-aibhnichean,**	the rivers.
G.	**nan athair,**	of the fathers.	**nan abhainn,**	of the rivers.
D.	**na h-aithrichean,**	the fathers.	**na h-aibhnichean,**	the rivers.

222. In declining the dative case, always say **air a' ghille** or **do 'n ghille,** " on the boy " or " to the boy," **do na gillean,** " to the boys," and so on for the other nouns. The dative case always requires a preposition before it, as it expresses no terminational variety of meaning in either number without it ; any other simple preposition may be used, as : **aig, as, de, fo, mu, o,** etc. (par. 594).

223.   QUESTIONS ON THE ARTICLE.

If you can answer the following questions correctly it will be a guide as to whether you have understood the different forms of the article. The answers are to be found in the preceding two pages, but we will give a further definitive answer in the key.

1. Why is **abhainn** with the article not written **an t-abhainn** ?
2. Why is **bard** with the article not written **an bard** ?
3. Why is **an duine** written and not **a' dhuine** ?
4. Why **a' chlach** and not **an clach** ?
5. Why **an saoghal** and not **an t-saoghal** ?
6. Why **an spog** and not **an t-spog** ?
7. How do we translate into Gaelic the indefinite article " a " or " an " before an English noun ?
8. How do we translate "of a father," " to a father," " on a father."

224.   EXERCISE ON THE ARTICLE.

Apply the Article to the following nouns :—

ann am bàta, in a boat.
bàta, m. (*bpátü*), a boat.
bean, f. (*pen*), a wife.
bord, m. (*bawrd*), a table.
buird (*boord*), of a table.
long, f. (*lonk*), a ship.
luinge (*looyngü*), of a ship.

saoir m. (*söyr*), of a joiner.
leabhar, m. (*llyo-ür*), a book.
bruachan (*bprooückün*), banks.
each, m. (*ăch*), a horse.
fiadh, m. (*feeügh*), a deer.
eich (*ăeech*), horses.
feidh (*fā-y*), of a deer.

ord, m. (*awrd*), a hammer.
uird (*oortch*), of a hammer.
lorg, f. (*lorŭk*), a track.
luirge (*loorkŭ*), of a track.
mac, m. (*machk*), a son.
mic (*meechk*), of a son.
fear, m. (*fer*), a man.
fir (*fyr*), of a man.
air creig (*ār krāg*), on a rock.
slat, f. (*sllaht*), a rod.
slaite (*slātchŭ*), of a rod.
slatan (*slātŭn*), rods.
le slait (*le slātch*), with a rod.
cu, m. (*koo*), a dog.
air cat (*ār cāht*). on a cat.
facal, m. (*fǎchkŭl*), a word.
taobh, m. (*tŏv*), a side.

cas, f. (*kǎss*), a foot.
air cois (*ār koysh*), on a foot.
do righ (*dtŏ ree*), to a king.
air luing (*ār looynk*), on a ship.
air craobhan (*ār krŏvŭn*), on trees.
muice, f. (*mooychkŭ*), of a pig.
iasg, m. (*eeusk*), a fish.
eisg (*āshk*), fishes.
lamh, f. (*llǎv*), a hand.
laimhe (*llǎyvŭ*), of a hand.
sgian, f. (*skeeŭn*). a knife.
sruth, m. (*sroo*), a stream.
srutha (*srooŭ*), of a stream.
air sruth, on a stream.
le laimh (*le llayv*), with a hand.
eun, m. (*ān*), a bird.
eoin (*yoin*), birds.

lamh caileige (*lǎv kallǎkŭ*), a girl's hand (the hand of a girl).
ceann eich (*keeǎwn āeech*),, the head of a horse (a horse's head).
ceann circe (*keeǎwn keer-kŭ*), a hen's head (the head of a hen).
casan gille (*kassŭn keel-ŭ*), a boy's feet (the feet of a boy).
casan fhiadh (*kassŭn eeŭgh*), the feet of deer.
bun craoibhe (*poon krŏyvŭ*), a root of a tree.

225.   *Vocabulary.*

geur (*kāŭr*), sharp.
tapaidh (*tahpy*), clever.

a' seinn (*ŭ shāynn*), singing
raimh (*ra-yv*), oars.

226. Correct the article, etc., in the following sentences, read and translate :—

1. Bha an lamh a' chaileige dubh. 2. Cha robh am gille laidir.
3. Bha na gille fliuch. 4. Cha 'n eil an bàta air an cuan, tha e air an sruth. 5. Cha 'n eil a' ghille an so fathast, ach tha an caileag.
6. Tha an ceann an t-eich dubh. 7. Tha an ord an fir sin trom.
8. Tha an ceann a' ord trom. 9. Cha 'n eil na gillean anns am baile.

227. Translate the following into Gaelic :—

1. The son of the joiner is very clever. 2. Have you the rods? 3. No, the shepherd has them. 4. The book of the boy is on the table.
5. The father of the girl is at the town. 6. He was at the house of the fisherman. 7. Have you been at the house of the shepherd ? 8. Do you know where the boy's knife is ? (the knife of the boy). 9. If it is not at home it is lost. 10. The men have the oars in the boat. 11. Do you know where they are ? 12. The men had them last night.
13. Were they singing on the river last night ? 14. The birds were singing in the trees on the banks of the river. 15. Who was King of Scotland ? 16. The boy's knife is sharp. 17. The man had a boat at the side of the river to-day. 18. I was at the side of a stream last night.

LESSON XXIII.

THE NOUN.

228. There are only two genders in the Gaelic language, the masculine and feminine ; all Gaelic nouns therefore are either masculine or feminine gender. To know and remember the gender of ordinary Gaelic nouns is one of the great difficulties in learning the language, as it is in learning French and many languages. Without this knowledge, which can only be mastered by practice, no one can speak or write Gaelic correctly.

229. There are a few general rules which will very much help the learner to distinguish the gender of nouns ; they are only **general** rules, however, subject to many exceptions ; and where they do not apply, the student must depend on practice and memory.

230. The following nouns are usually masculine :—

(1) The names of males—**fear**, a man ; **torc**, a boar ; **righ**, a king.

(2) The young of all animals regardless of sex—**uan, a** lamb ; **searrach**, a foal.

(3) Diminutives in **an**—**bordan**, a little table ; **lochan**, a little loch.

(4) The names of trees, vegetables, grains, liquors, colours, metals, elements, the seasons, and the days of the week—**calltuinn**, hazel ; **cal**, kail ; **leann**, ale ; **iarunn**, iron ; **uisge**, water ; **samhradh**, summer.

(5) Derivatives in **as, ear, air, iche**, etc. **cairdeas**, friendship ; **taillear**, a tailor ; **piobair**, a piper ; **maraiche**, a seaman ; **marcaich**, a ride ; **oibriche**, a worker ; **aoradh**, worship ; **bualadh**, striking.

231. The following nouns are usually feminine :—

(1) Names of females—**caileag**, a girl ; **caora**, a sheep ; **muc**, a pig.

(2) Names of countries—**Alba**, Scotland ; **Eire** or **Eirinn**, Ireland.

(3) Names of musical instruments, heavenly bodies, diseases—**piob-mhor**, the bag-pipes ; **clarsach**, a harp ; **reul**, a star ; **grian**, a sun ; **siataig**, rheumatism ; **teasach**, fever.

(4) Diminutives, etc. in **ag** and **achd**—**duanag**, a little song ; **murlag**, a small creel ; **morachd**, greatness ; **bardachd**, poetry.

(5) Derivatives in " **e**," denoting attributes—**doille**, blindness ; **buidhre**, deafness.

232. The Gaelic noun has two numbers—singular and plural. Note that after certain numerals the singular is used, as after **aon**, one ; **fichead**, twenty ; **ciad** or **ceud**, a hundred ; **mile**, a thousand ; and any multiple of these. The plural is used after all other numbers.

233. The Gaelic noun has five cases, nominative and accusative, genitive, dative, and vocative. Practically speaking the Gaelic noun has only two forms, some feminines have three.

234. The nominative and accusative (or objective) case are alike in Gaelic. The nominative case is used when any person or thing is mentioned as the subject word of the sentence, or when it is the object word, and is directly governed by the action of the verb. There is no accusative case in Gaelic different from the nominative.

235. The genitive case in Gaelic corresponds to the English possessive case, or to the English noun preceded by the preposition " of " Thus " a man's hand " becomes " the hand of a man " ; " of a man " being translated by the genitive of " man." The genitive is generally used as a qualifying and limiting term to and after another noun.

236. The dative case is the case where the noun is governed by a preposition and corresponds to the indirect objective case in English.

237. When the noun represents the person or thing spoken to, we call its case the vocative or the nominative of address. It is usually preceded by the vocative particle **a**, which causes aspiration of all aspirable consonants. (par. 254).

238. The Gaelic noun has been variously divided into declensions. Sometimes in two—a noun whose last vowel is broad is said to be of the first declension as—**bard, oran,** etc. A noun whose last vowel is narrow is classed as of the second declension, as—**mir, coist,** etc.

239. The most general manner of forming the genitive singular of nouns of both these declensions is to insert an **i** after the last broad vowel of the nominative singular, and when this is not done we may say the noun is partly irregular and falls under some of the rules to be given hereafter for the formation of the genitive. The division of the noun into declensions seems unnecessary, as there is scarcely any variation in the manner of declining nouns either in broad or narrow vowels.

240. It will be observed that the various inflections in the genitive singular constitute the principal guide in classification. If different forms of the genitive singular are a sufficient reason for a separate declension, a survey of the various formations of that case as classified in this work will enable the reader to discover at once that no fewer than fifteen declensions should be adopted—a division that would confer no benefit whatever ; it will be found that ninety per cent. of the Gaelic nouns follow in some manner the general rule, and that, after forming the genitive singular a close uniformity of flectional formations pervades all the other cases.

241. The general rule for forming the genitive singular of both masculine and feminine nouns is to introduce an **i** after the last broad vowel of the nominative singular, or by leaving out the broad vowel or dipthongal part and substituting **i.** If the last vowel is **i** no change takes place ; feminine nouns also add a terminal **e.** Many classes of nouns have special variations in the genitive, on account of their vowel combinations ; examples of most of these are declined on the following pages.

242. A noun declined with the definite article we call a definite noun, a noun without the article we call an indefinite noun.

DECLINING THE INDEFINITE NOUN.

243. After forming the genitive a close uniformity of all flectional formations pervades all the other cases of Gaelic nouns. It will be found that in an indefinite masculine noun the nominative, accusative and dative singular are alike ; the genitive plural is usually formed by aspirating the nominative singular ; while the nominative, accusative and dative plural are the same as the genitive singular ; the vocative is like the genitive singular, but aspirated ; vocative plural is like the nominative singular, aspirated and a final **a** added, or like the nominative plural, aspirated.

244. In the case of indefinite feminine nouns, the nominative and accusative are alike ; the dative with the omission of the final **e** is the same as the genitive ; the nominative accusative and dative plural add **an** (**ean** to correspond to preceding small vowel) to the nominative singular ; the genitive plural and the vocative singular are like the nominative singular aspirated ; and the vocative plural is like the nominative plural, aspirated.

DECLINING THE DEFINITE NOUN.

245. The declension of a noun with the definite article is similar to that without the article. The initial letters of some nouns are aspirated in certain cases, others eclipsed, etc. (Lesson xxii.).

246. A definite noun has no vocative case.

247. A definite noun masculine beginning with an aspirable consonant is aspirated in the genitive and dative singular. A definite noun feminine aspirates the nominative, dative singular.

248. A definite noun, whether masculine or feminine, beginning with **d, l, n, r, s, t,** aspirates no case.

249. A definite noun, whether masculine or feminine, beginning with a consonant is never aspirated in the plural.

250. As we have already dealt fully with the definite article with the noun, a further two examples will suffice to compare the changes effected by their combination.

251. Any unaspirated case is subject to aspiration after words which cause aspiration, as :—**mo bhord,** " my table " ; **mo bhuird,** " of my table."

252. EXAMPLES TO ILLUSTRATE THE GENERAL RULE.

AN INDEFINITE MASCULINE NOUN.

	Singular.			*Plural.*	
Nom.	**bard,**	a poet.	**baird,**	poets.
Gen.	**baird,**	of a poet.	**bhard,**	of poets.
Dat.	**(air) bard**	on a poet.	**(air) baird,**	(on) poets.
Acc.	**bard,**	a poet.	**baird,**	poets.
Voc.	**a bhaird,**	oh ! poet !	**a bharda,**	oh ! poets !

WITH THE DEFINITE ARTICLE.

Nom.	**am bard,**	the poet.	**na baird,**	the poets.
Gen.	**a' bhaird,**	of the poet.	**nam bard,**	of the poets.
Dat.	**a' bhard,**	the poet.	**na baird,**	the poets.
Acc.	**am bard,**	the poet.	**na baird,**	the poets.

253. AN INDEFINITE FEMININE NOUN.

Nom.	**brog,**	a shoe.	**brogan,**	shoes
Gen.	**broige,**	of a shoe.	**bhrog,**	of shoes.
Dat.	**(air) broig,**	(on) a shoe.	**(air) brogan,**	(on) shoes.
Acc.	**brog,**	a shoe.	**brogan,**	shoes.
Voc.	**a bhrog,**	oh ! shoe !	**a bhrogan,**	oh ! shoes !

WITH THE DEFINITE ARTICLE.

Nom.	**a' bhrog,**	the shoe.	**na brogan,**	the shoes.
Gen.	**na broige,**	of the shoe.	**nam brog,**	of the shoes.
Dat.	**a' bhroig,**	the shoe.	**na brogan,**	the shoes.
Acc.	**a' bhrog,**	the shoe.	**na brogan,**	the shoes.

254. The vocative case is the same in the singular of masculine nouns as the genitive aspirated ; and in the feminine nouns as the nominative aspirated ; and in the plural generally as the nominative plural aspirated, often minus the final **n** where the noun has had a syllable added to it to make the plural. nouns of one syllable add **a** to the nominative singular aspirated. The vocative case is generally preceded by the sign **a,**

255. The old dative plural for a number of nouns, both masculine and feminine, added **ibh or aibh** to the nominative singular, and this termination is still used more or less in poetry, or to give touch of dignity to serious writing.

Air bharraibh nam biodag,	*on the points of the dirks.*
Fo chasaibh nan namh,	*under the feet of the enemies.*

256. There are a few exceptions to all these rules, as in the case of **duine,** " a man," nominative, dative, and genitive are alike ; **daoine,** " men," nominative and genitive

plural are also alike ; also **bean**, " a woman," an altogether irregular noun, is **mna** in the genitive singular and **bhan** in the genitive plural (par. 282).*

NOUNS DECLINED ACCORDING TO THE GENERAL RULES.

257. Monosyllabic and many other nouns whose vowels are broad (**a,o,u, ao** or **ua**)   form their genitive after the manner of the preceding general rules.

Laogh m. (*llōgh*), a calf.

Nom.	**laogh**	**laoigh**
Gen.	**laoigh**	**laogh**
Dat.	**laogh**	**laoigh**

Bruach f., a bank.

	bruach	**bruachan**
	bruaiche	**bhruach**
	bruaich	**bruachan**

Nouns similarly declined.

adag† f. (*adtak*) a stook.
al m. (*ál*) a brood.
Albannach m (*allupanŭch*) a Scotsman.
bàd m. (*pádt*) a tuft.
balach m. (*bpallŭch*) a boy.
bàs m. (*bás*) death.
biodag† f. *bpydtak*) a dirk.
bodach m. (*bpodtŭch*) an old man.
bonnach m. (*bponŭch*) a bannock.
cal m. (*kál*) a cabbage.
caol m. (*kŏll*) a strait. narrow.
cat m. (*kaht*) a cat.
clar m. (*klar*) a tablet, board.
cluas f. (*klooŭs*) an ear.
craobh f. (*krŏv*) a tree.
cuan m. (*kooŭn*) a sea.
cul m. (*kooll*) a back.
dan m. (*dtán*) a song.
dorus‡ m. (*dorŭs*) a door.
dos m. (*tos*) a tassel.

duan m. (*dooŭn*) a poem.
fraoch m. (*frŏch*) heath.
glas f. (*gklass*) a lock.
gradh m. (*grágh*) love.
lamh f. (*llắv*) a hand.
laoch m. (*llŏch*) a hero.
lòn m. (*lawn*) a meadow.
maor m. (*mŏr*) an officer.
oglach m. (*oklŭch*) a servant.
ospag† f. (*ospak*) a sob.
ramh m. (*rhắv*) an oar.
run m. (*roon*) darling.
saor m. (*sŏr*) a joiner.
sguab f. (*skooŭb*) a sheaf.
slat f. (*sllaht*) a rod.
sluagh m. (*slooŭ*) people.
srad f. (*strắtt*) a spark.
sron f. (*stron*) a nose.
tarbh m. (*tarŭv*) a bull.
tuadh f. (*tooŭ*) an axe.
tur m. (*dtoor*) a tower.

---

* The student who only knows the English language thinks the formation of the plurals in that language very simple, yet the varied inflections which characterise the plurals of many common nouns is surprising.   Here is a selection only :—man men, foot feet, cow kine, child children, brother brethren, box boxes, ox oxen, arch arches, loch lochs, wife wives, shelf shelves, staff staves, ruff ruffs, fly flies, penny pence, money monies, echo echoes, piano pianos, mouse mice, deer deer, alms alms, news news.   In comparison, Gaelic seems much more regular.

† These do not add an **e** in the genitive.

‡ **Dorus** also makes a plural in **dorsan**.

258. Exercises on the foregoing nouns :—
Decline the following with the definite article—
    cluas, al, dan, lon, laogh, bruach, maor, tuadh, slat, ospag.

Decline the following without the article—
    cat, cuan, gradh, dos, sguab, clar, salm.

259. Read in Gaelic and translate into English :—
1. Tha Albannach air a' mhonadh.   2. Tha tuadh an t-saoir briste
3. Tha dos air piob a' mhaoir.   4. Tha craobhan anns an lon.   5·
Bha an sluagh air seinn an orain.   6. Tha am bàta air cuan.   7·
Cha 'n eil a' ghlas air an dorus.   8. Bha glas an doruis briste an
raoir   9. Tha brogan a' bhalaich salach,   10. Bha coig tairbh air an
fhraoch.   11. Tha an t-acras air a' bhalach.   12. Tha an gille a'
seinn dain mu na bruachan.

260. Translate into Gaelic :—
1. A tree is on the hill.   2. The Scotsman is a hero.   3. The oars of
the boat are here.   4. A bull is in the field.   5. A dirk is in the
officer's hand.   6. The ears of a cat.   7. A lock is on the door.
8. The lock of the door is broken.   9. The darling of the people is here.
10. I was at the tower on the hill.   11. The boy sang an old man's
song.   12. The door of the tower is open.   13. The joiner's axe is
sharp.   14. The servant's ear was at the door.   15. The old man's
back is dirty.

LESSON XXIV.

The Noun. II.

Particular Rules for Forming the Genitive.

261. A number of nouns in **a** and **o** change these vowels
into **ui** in the genitive, and are then declined through the
other cases according to the general rules.

	carn m. a cairn, heap of stones.			**lorg**, f. a track.	
	Singular.	*Plural.*		*Singular.*	*Plural.*
Nom.	**carn**	**cuirn**		**lorg**	**lorgan**
Gen.	**cuirn**	**charn**		**luirge**	**lorg**
Dat.	**carn**	**cuirn**		**luirg**	**lorgan**

Nouns similarly declined :—

allt, m. (*ault*), a brook.
balg, m. (*bpaluk*) a wallet.
ball, m. (*paul*) a member.
boc, m. (*bpochk*), a buck.
bord, m. (*bawrd*), a table.
broc, m. (*bprochk*), a badger.

calg, m. (*kaluk*), a prickle.
car, m. (*kar*) a turn.
clag, m. (*klak*) a bell.
cnoc, m. (*krochk*), a hill.
cord, m. a string.
crodh, m. (*kro*) cattle.

D

falt, m. (*fallt*) hair.
fonn m. (*fownn*) a tune.
gob m. (*gop*), a bill, a beak
long, f. a ship.
olc, m. (*awlk*), evil.
ord, m. (*awrdt*), a hammer.
port, m. (*porst*), a harbour.

sloc, m. (*slochk*), a pit.
sop, m. a wisp.
spong, m. (*sponk*) a sponge.
toll, m. (*towll*) a hole.
tom, m. (*towm*) a knoll.
tonn, f. (*townn*) a wave.
tromp, f. a trumpet.

262. A number of nouns in **ea** or **io** contract these into **i** in the genitive, and are declined through the other cases according to the general rules.

ceann, m. (*kyaun*) a head.

	Singular.	Plural.
Nom.	ceann	cinn
Gen.	cinn	cheann
Dat.	ceann	cinn

cearc f. (*kyark*) a hen.

	Singular.	Plural.
	cearc	cearcan
	circe	chearc
	circ	cearcan

Nouns similarly declined :—

biadh, m. (*bpeeügh*) food.
breac, m. (*prechk*) a trout.
cinneadh, m. (*keennügh*) a clan.
coileach, m. (*koylüch*) a cock.
crioch, f. (*kreeüch*) an end.
fear, m. (*fer*) a man.

gleann, m. (*glaunn*) a glen.
leac, f. (*llechk*) a flagstone.
lion, m. (*lyeen*) a net.
preas, m. (*prās*) a bush.
mac, m. (*machk*) a son.
siol, m. (*sheell*) seed.

263. A number of nouns in **ea**, **eu**, and **ia** change these vowels into **ei** in the genitive, and are then declined through the other cases according to the general rules.

cliabh, m. a basket.

	Singular.	Plural.
Nom.	cliabh	cleibh
Gen.	cleibh	chliabh
Dat.	cliabh	cleibh

grian, f. sun.

	Singular.	Plural.
	grian	grianan
	greine	ghrian
	grein	grianan

Nouns similarly declined :—

breug, f. (*bprāk*) a lie.
caileag, f. (*kallük*) a girl.
cairdeas, m. (*karjess*) friendship.
coibhneas, m. (*koyvness*) kindness.
cealg, f. (*kyaluk*) deceit.
ceard, m. (*kyârd*) a tinker.
ceart, m. (*kyārst*) a right.
ceum, m. (*kām*) a step.
ciall, m. (*keeüll*) sense.
cleireach, m. (*klāruch*) a clerk.
coigreach, m. (*koykrüch*) a stranger.

creach, f. (*krech*) plunder.
creag, f. (*krāk*) a rock.
dealg, m. (*tchallük*) pin.
each (*āch*) horse.
fearg, f. (*feruk*) anger.
fiadh, m. (*fee-ügh*) a deer.
geug, f. (*gāk*) a branch.
iall, f. (*eeüll*) a thong.
iasg, m. (*eeusk*) a fish.
iteag, f. (*eetchak*) a feather.
neamh, m. (*nyāv*) heaven.
sealg, f. (*shaluk*) hunting.
sliabh, m. (*slleeuv*) a moor.

264. A number of nouns in **a** change the **a** into **oi** in the genitive, and are then declined through the other cases according to the general rules.

cas, f. (*kass*) a foot.

	Singular.	Plural.
Nom.	**cas**	**casan**
Gen.	**coise**	**chas**
Dat.	**cois**	**casan**

Nouns similarly declined :—

bas, f. (*bass*) the palm.
clach, f. (*klach*) a stone.
clann, f. (*klaunn*) children.
crann, f. (*kraunn*) a trunk, tree.

dall, m. (*tdooll*) a blind man.
fras, f. a shower.
gad (*gadt*), m. a thong.
Gall (*gâool*), m. a Lowlander.

265. A number of nouns of one syllable, both masculine and feminine, add **a** to form the genitive, and add **an** or **annan** to form the plural, and are declined as follows :—

loch, m. (*llawch*) a loch.

	Singular	Plural.
Nom.	**loch**	**lochan**
Gen.	**locha**	**loch**
Dat.	**loch**	**lochan**

Nouns similarly declined :—

anam, m. (*anüm*) a soul.
ath, f. (*âh*) a kiln.
barr, m. a point.
beus, f. (*bās*) virtue.
buth m. (*boo*) a shop.
cath, m. (*kah*) a battle.
cladh, m. (*klôgh*) a churchyard
cleoc, m. (*klyochk*) a mantel.
cnaimh, m. (*krāyv*) a bone.
dram (*dtrâm*), m. a dram.

earb, f. (*ārüp*) a roe.
feum, m. (*fām*) need.
fion, m. (*feen*) wine.
fios, m. (*feess*) knowledge.
guth, m. (*goo*) a voice.
lagh, f. (*llôgh*) law.
luch f. (*llooch*) a mouse.
modh, f. (*mogh*) a manner
piob, f. (*peep*) a pipe.
sruth m. (*strooh*), a stream

266. A number of nouns in **eu** change these vowels into **eoi** in the genitive, and are declined as follows :—

beul, m. (*bpāll*) a month.

	Singular.	Plural.
Nom.	**beul**	**beoil**
Gen.	**beoil**	**bheul**
Dat.	**beul**	**beoil**

Nouns similarly declined :—

deur, m. (*tchār*) a tear,
gleus, m. (*glās*) order
leus, m. (*llyās*) light.
eun, m. (*ān*) a bird.

neul, m. (*nyāll*) a cloud.
sgeul, m. (*skāll*) a story.
feur, m (*fār*) grass.
meur, m. (*mār*) a finger,

267. A number of nouns ending in **-chd** and **-dh** are indeclinable in the singular, that is all cases are alike, and form their plural in **an.**

> **beachd**, m. (*bechk*) an observation, an opinion.

Sing, N.G.D.   *Nom. and Dat. Pl.*   *Gen. Pl.*
    beachd   **beachdan**   **bheachd**

Nouns similarly declined :—

faidh, m. (*fāee*) a prophet.   **reachd**, m. (*râchk*) a law, statute.
cleachd, m. (*klechk*) a habit.   **fuachd**, m. (*foouchk*) a cold.
ucbd, m. (*oochk*) a breast.   **feachd**, m. (*fāchk*) a host.
beannachd, m. a blessing.   **rioghachd** f. (*ree-achk*) a kingdom.

268. A number of nouns whose final vowel is narrow (generally called the second declension), have both masculine and feminine nouns forming their genitive by adding an **e** ; and **ean** to form their plural.

> **mir** m. (*meer*) a piece.   **sraid** f. (*srādt*) a street.

	Singular.	*Plural.*	*Singular.*	*Plural.*
Nom.	**mir**	**mirean**	**sraid**	**sraidean**
Gen.	**mire**	**mhir**	**sraide**	**shraid**
Dat.	**mir**	**mirean**	**sraid**	**sraidean**

Nouns similarly declined :—

tir f. (*cheer*) land.   **mionaid**, f. (*my natch*) a minute.
aite, m. (*âh-tchü*) a place.   **tigh, taigh** m. (*ttâh y*) a house.
ceist, f. (*keest*) a question.   **uair** f. (*ooŭr*) an hour.
im, m. (*ym*) butter.   **cir**, f. (*keer*) a comb.
bid m. (*bpidt*) a chirp.   **ainm**, m. (*anām*) a name

269. Nouns of one syllable ending in a vowel are indeclinable in the singular, and to prevent a hiatus, insert a silent **th** before the plural terminations **an** or **ean.**

Singular N. G. and D. **cno** t. (*kro*) a nut.
Plural, Nom. **cnothan** nuts ; *Gen.* **chno** of nuts.

Nouns similarly declined :—

ceo, m. (*kvo*) mist.   **cliu**, m. (*klyoo*) praise.
clo, m. (*kllō*) cloth ; **cloithean** **gleo**, f. (*glyo*) a fight.
la, m. (*lla*) a day.   **ni**, m. (*nny*) a thing.

270. Decline as definite nouns, giving gender and translation, the following :—

calg, tromp, balg, tom, ceann, lion, mac, gleann, mir, bord.

271. Decline the following similarly, but as indefinite nouns :—

calg, clann, ord, crodh, long, cnoc, caileag, im, cir, sraid.

272. Read in Gaelic and translate into English :—

1. Bha am fear anns an t-sraid. 2. Bha coig bric ann an lion an fhir ud.
3. Tha an t-ord air a' bhord. 4. Bha am broc anns an toll air a'
chnoc. 5. Tha long mhor anns a' phort. 6. Tha an coigreach a'
sealg fhiadh air an t-sliabh. 7. Tha an t-each crubach. 8. Nach
eil iasg anns a' chliabh ? 9. Tha clachan anns a' chliabh a nis.
10. Tha eolas agam air dall. 11. Cha 'n eil fion anns an tigh. 12.
Bha mi aig ceann an locha an de. 13. Tha an sruth aig ceann an
locha. 14. Is i ceist na tire ceist nan ceistean. 15. Cha 'n eil eolas
agam air an lagh. 16. A' chaileag bheag le guth mor. 17. Tha an
gille aig ceann na sraide.

273. Translate into Gaelic :—

1. A big ship is in the harbour. 2. The badger is in a hole on the moor.
3. The hammer is on the table. 4. The man has five trout in the net.
5. The end of the string is at the flagstone. 6. A basket of seed is
on the table. 7. Is there fish in the basket ? 8. The stranger was
hunting deer on the hill. 9. The foot of the horse is lame. 10.
There are tracks of the feet of horses on the moor. 11. The girl
with the voice. 12. I had no knowledge of the law. 13. That
stranger's house is in this street. 14. There is bread and butter in
the house. 15. The land question is the question of questions.
16. A prophet gave a blessing on the house 17. The man is at the
top of the street. 18. Five trout are in the man's net.

LESSON XXV.
THE NOUN. III.

PARTICULAR RULES (CONTINUED)—POLYSYLLABLES.

274. In declining nouns of more than one syllable the
method of forming the genitive and plural depends on the
form of the last syllable.

Feminine nouns may not always add the terminal **e** in
the genitive singular.

275. Nouns ending in **air** may be of three kinds.

276 (a) A class indicating an agent or doer except (b).
These nouns are indeclinable in the singular and add **ean**
to form the plural.

sealgair (*shalügür*)	nm.	a hunter.
piobair (*peepür*)	nm.	a piper.
ciobair (*keepür*)	nm.	a shepherd.
morair (*mōrür*)	nm.	a nobleman.
murtair (*moorstür*)	nm.	a murderer.
lanntair (*llanntür*)	nm.	a lantern.
tosgair (*ttoskür*)	nm.	a herald.
iasgair (*y askür*)	nm.	a fisherman.

277. (b) A class indicating kinship. These drop the **i** from the air to form the genitive and contract and generally add **ichean** or **ean** to form the plural.

Nom. and Dat.	Gen.	* Plural, N.G.D.
athair (â-ür) a father.	**athar**	**athraichean**
mathair (ma-ür) a mother.	**mathar**	**mathraichean**
brathair (brahür) a brother.	**brathar**	**braithrean**
seanair (shānür) a grandfather.	**seanar**	**seanairean**
seanamhair, a grandmother.	**seanamhar**	**seanamhairean**
piuthair (pyoo-ür) a sister.	**peathar**	**peathraichean**

278 (c) A class indicating neither of these, but where **air** forms part of the word. These and nouns ending in **ar**, **al**, and **ail**, contract in the genitive and add **ach**, and form their plural by contracting and adding **ichean**. The following are all feminine :—

Nom. and Dat.	Gen.	Pl. N.G.†D.
acair (achkür) an anchor.	**acrach**	**acraichean**
		acairean
anail (anül) breath.	**analach**	**anailean**
barail (baral) opinion.	**baralach**	**barailean**
cathair (ka-ür) a chair.	**cathrach**	**cathraichean**
coir (kor) a right.	**corach**	**coraichean**
		coirean
dail (dahl) delay, a meeting.	**dalach**	**dalaichean**
faidhir (fâ-yr) a fair.	**faidhreach**	**faidhrichean**
		faidhrean
iuchair (yoochür) a key.	**iuchrach**	**iuchraichean**
litir (leetchür) a letter. m	**litreach**	**litrichean**
luachair (looüchür) rushes.	**luachrach**	
machair (machür) a field, plain.	**machrach**	**machraichean**
nathair (nahür) a serpent.	**nathrach**	**nathraichean**
peasair (pāssür) pease.	**peasrach**	
ponair (ponür) beans.	**ponarach**	
togail (tokül) a building.	**togalach**	**togalaichean**
		togailean

279. Some Nouns contract and add an **a** or an **e** to form the genitive and form the plural by adding **an**, **achan**, or **ichean** :—

Nominative.	Genitive.	Plural.
abhainn, f. (âvynn) a river.	**aibhne**	**aibhnichean**
buaidh, f. (boo-y) a victory.	**buadha**	**buadhan**
buidheann f. (booyün) a company.	**buidhne**	**buidhnean**

* The genitive plural when indefinite aspirates the nominative plural or genitive singular,) but a definite noun does not aspirate :— **bhraithrean** " of brothers " ; **nam braithrean** " of the brothers."

† The genitive plural if indefinite is aspirated according to rule.

Nominative.	Genitive.	Plural.
banais, f. (*ban ysh*) a wedding.	bainnse	bainnsean
coluinn f. (*koll ynn*) the body.	cola	coluinnean
duthaich f. (*dtoo-ych*) a country.	duthcha	duthchannan
fiacail f. (*fyach-kyl*) a tooth.	fiacla	fiaclan

280. Nouns of more than one syllable ending in a vowel are indeclinable in the singular, and add **achan** or **ichean** to form the plural :—

Sing. N.G.D.	Plur. N.G.D.*
balla m. (*pallü*) a wall.	**ballachan**
bàta m. (*bpatü*) a boat.	**bàtalchean**
cota m. (*koh ttü*) a coat.	**cotaichean**
cridhe m. (*hroo ü*) a heart.	**cridheachean**
canna m. (*kannü*) a jug.	**cannachan**
fairge f. (*farākü*) the sea.	**fairgeachan**
gloine f. (*kloynü*) a glass.	**gloinneachan**
linne f. (*llynnü*) a pool.	**linneachan**
leaba f. (*lyāpu*) a bed.	**leapaichean**
uisge m. (*ooshku*) water.	**uisgeachan**

281. Nouns ending in **l, n, le,** or **ne,** generally drop the vowel and add **tean** to form the plural :—

Sing. N.G.D.	Plur. N.G.D.*
baile m. a town.	**bailtean**
coille f. (*kolyü*) a wood.	**coilltean**
feill f. (*fāyll*) a festival.	**feilltean**
mile f. (*my-lü*) a thousand.	**miltean**
smuain f. (*smoo-ün*) a thought.	**smuaintean**
teine f. (*tchā-nü*) fire.	**teintean**
tuil f. (*ttoo yl*) a flood.	**tuiltean**

282. The following Nouns are altogether irregular :—

	Singular.			Plural.		
Nom.	Gen.	Dat.	Nom.	Gen.	Dat.
bean f. a woman	mna	mnaoi	mnathan	bhan	mnathan
bò f. a cow	ba	boin	ba	bhò	ba
braich f. malt	bracha	braich			
cu m. a dog	coin	cu	coin	chon	coin
cuid f. a share	codach	cuid	codaichean		
coir f. a right	corach	coir	coraichean		
caora f. a sheep	caorach	caora	caoraich	chaorach	caoraich
druim m. a back	droma	druim	dromannan		
dia m. a god	de	dia	diathan		
deoch f. a drink	dibhe	deoch	deochannan		
fuil f. (*foo yl*) blood	fola	fuil			
gobha m. a smith	gobhainn	gobha	goibhnean		
gobhar m. a goat	goibhre	gobhar	goibhrean or gobhair		
gniomh m. a deed	gniomha	gniomh	gniomharan		
muir f. (*moo yr*) the sea	mara	muir	marannan		
sail (*sal*) f. a heel	salach	sail	sailtean		
talamh m. the earth	talmhuinn	talamh	talamhanan		
suil f. (*sool*) an eye	sula	suil	suilean		
mil f. (*myl*) honey	meala	mil			
leaba f. (*lyāpu*) a bed	leapa	leabaidh	leapaichean		

---

* An indefinite genitive plural will be aspirated according to rule.

283. Read in Gaelic and translate into English :—

1. Co leis na leabhraichean so ? 2. Nach leat-sa fein iad ? 3. Tha geugan nan craobh ard. 4. Ceann circe. 5. Cinn chearc. 6. Bha iad aig taobh an uillt. 7. Am bheil fios agaibh far am bheil mac a' ghobhainn ? 8. Bha coin a' chiobair a' sealg nam fiadh air a' mhonadh sin. 9. Am fiadh sin ? 10. Is e. 11. Am bheil eoin air na geugan. 12. Ord an t-saoir. 13. Glas an doruis. 14. Cinn each. 15. Cinn nan each. 16. Casan nam bord. 17. Tha na h-uain air mullach a' chnuic. 18. Bha an lair aig dorus an stabuill. 19. Tha cas a' choin briste. 20. Tha casan nan con briste. 21. Bha cu a' ghille air an dun. 22. Tha e a nis aig an tigh. 23. Tha tigh an t-saoir aig taobh an locha. 24. Tha suil a' chait air an toll. 25. Tha barr nam fiacla briste. 26. Dh' fhalbh an gille anns a' mhaduinn le callach air a dhruim. 27. Dh' fhosgail mi leabhar an lagha. 28. Tha na laghan math.

284. Translate into Gaelic :—

1. A shepherd was on the moor this morning. 2. I was at the house of the piper last night. 3. The boat of the fisherman is in the harbour. 4. I will see the brother of the nobleman at the river. 5. The key of the door is here. 6. There is a chair on the right of the door. 7. The little girl has a jug of water. 8. That man had a glass of wine. 9. I had a bed of feathers last night. 10. There was a fire in the town this evening. 11. There was a wedding festival here yesterday. 12. There are woods in that country. 13. He has broken a glass. 14. There were fish in the nets this morning. 15. I found the boy's shoe this evening. 16. The joiner's hammer is broken. 17. The girls sang a song. 18. We found the boy's books on the banks of the river. 19. The books of that boy were wet. 20. Your grandfather's house is at the top of the road. 21. There are men at work at the end of the house. 22. A bull is on the plain.

285. Examination on the Noun :—

1. How is the genitive sing. of masculine nouns generally formed ? 2. What is the distinction of the genitive sing. feminine ? 3. Do both masculine and feminine nouns aspirate in the genitive sing. ? 4. What definite nouns resist aspiration ? 5. Do any definite nouns totally resist aspiration everywhere ? 6. How is the plural of masculine nouns generally formed ? 7. State what difference there is in the genitive plural of masculine and feminine nouns. 8. What is the old dative plural ? 9. How do we translate " at a poem," " of a poem," " to a poem," " of a voice," " to a voice," " of voices " ? 10. What effect has the definite article on the genitive sing. masculine ? 11. Why does an indefinite genitive singular feminine noun not aspirate ?

LESSON XXVI.

The Government of Nouns.

286. Nouns are influenced by other nouns and adjectives ; by verbs ; by prepositions ; causing in the noun a change of case. These cases are called Nominative, Genitive, Accusative, and Dative.

287. The term genitive covers the English possessive case, but as our Gaelic genitive noun does more than the term possessive implics, it is better termed genitive.

The Indefinite Possessive Case.

288. In English we can say (a) " a boy's book " or (b) " the book of a boy." The first (a) is the inflected form and (b) the uninflected form. Notice that the " the " disappears when written in the inflected form. Gaelic idiom may be said to be a combination of both forms. In Gaelic the " the " is not translated, and " of a boy " is translated by the genitive case of " boy " ; " of " coming between two nouns in this manner is not translated (par. 212). In Gaelic the qualifying noun comes after the noun it qualifies, thus we have. **leabhar balaich** " the book of a boy." A definite noun qualified by an indefinite noun.

The Definite Possessive Case.

289. Let us take the same phrase with the definite article attached to both nouns, " the book of the boy." The beginner invariably translates this wrongly **an leabhar a' bhalaich.** Write the English in the inflected form thus : " the boy's book." Notice that one " the " has disappeared ; note also that the " the " left belongs to " boy's " and not to " book." Now bearing this in mind we translate thus : **leabhar a' bhalaich.** " the book of the boy."

290. The rule here is, " A definite noun only, can be qualified by a noun which is definite and is in the genitive ; the definite noun so qualified never takes the article " (pars. 212, 303). A possessive pronoun excludes the article from both nouns, as similarly happens in the English inflected form.

Leabhar a' bhalaich,	*the boy's book,*	*the book of the boy.*
Leabhar a bhalaich,	*his boy's book,*	*the book of his boy.*
Leabhar a balaich,	*her boy's book,*	*the book of her boy.*

D*

291. To sum up. This specially defining use and non-use of the article in Gaelic is similar to the inflected English possessive in idiom, except that the position of the nouns in the one language is the reverse of their position in the other.

292. When two or more nouns are in a possessive phrase one noun only is translated in the genitive. The Gaelic usage is again like the English inflected possessive in its treatment of the article. Note again the complete reversal in the idiom of the two languages.*

                  1   2   3

Uninflected (**a**)   The beauty of the daughter of the king.

                            3   2   1

Inflected   (**b**)   The king's daughter's beauty.†

                            1   2   3

           (**c**)   **Boidhchead nighean an righ** (*not* nighinn).

In (b) it is the term " king " which has the article and in (c) its Gaelic equivalent **righ** also has the article.

293. A noun following a verbal noun is put in the genitive.

Ag itheadh arain,   *eating bread* (lit.) *at eating of bread.*

294. An indefinite noun of a partitive nature can only be qualified by another indefinite noun in the genitive. These generally denote quantity, plenty or scarcity. Some of these terms are : **moran** many, much ; **lan** full ; **sac** bag ; **beagan** a little ; similarly with an ounce, a lb., a stone, etc., any term indicative of a part or portion of anything (par. 302).

Moran sluaigh,	*many (of) people.*	Badan fraoich,	*a sprig of heather*
Lan oir,	*full of gold.*	Sac mine,	*a sack of meal.*
Pios arain,	*a piece of bread.*	Beagan uisge,	*a little water.*

295. But when we have an indefinite noun governing, qualifying, or descriptive of another indefinite noun we have generally a compound noun. The qualified noun we place first and it is declined regularly through all the cases. The qualifying noun comes second, but is not·

---

* A common feature is that the possessive and qualifying nouns (pars. 212, 295) which we translate by the genitive have really the limiting force of an adjective in both languages.

† We can also say in English " the beauty of the king's daughter." In Gaelic we have only one way we can properly translate all these English forms.

declined, keeping the genitive form throughout all cases ;
if the singular*aspirating like an adjective in agreement
with the gender of the first element;(par.327) if the plural
aspirating all the cases. A final **e** in the genitive of a first
element is deleted. Compound nouns take the gender
of their principal component except those compounded
with **ban** which are always feminine. A final lingual
prevents aspiration of an initial dental (par. 38).

Ban-tighearna (f)	*a lady.*
(Mullach) tigh-chearc (not tighe)	*(top) of a henhouse.*
Fear-ciuil	*a man of music = a musician.*
(Ceann) fir-chiuil (m)	*(head) of a musician.*

The following show a similar qualifying use of genitive :—

Cir mheala (f)	*a honeycomb.*
Peann oir (m)	*a gold pen = a pen of gold.*
Tom ghroiseid (f)	*a gooseberry bush.*
Tom fraoich(m)	*a heather bush.*
(Meud) tom fraoich (*not* tuim *par*. 292)	*(size) of a heather bush*
* (Ceann) toman fraoich (m)	*(top) of heather bushes.*

cf. French : une plume d'or ; une robe de soie.

296. A noun and adjective forming a compound are
declined as if each stood apart (see government of adjectives (pars 327-8).

Coileach-dubh, *a black-cock.* Coilich-dhuibh, *of a black-cock.*

297. When the adjective precedes the noun with which
it is compounded, the adjective retains the nominative
form, while the noun is regularly declined through all cases.

Dubh-fhacal, *a dark saying.* Dubh-fhacail, *of a dark saying.*

298. When a compound noun is definite the article is
placed before its first word whether noun or adjective,
and both the article and the first word are subject to all
the modifications already illustrated in Lesson xxii.
according to the initial letter of the first word.

An t-oig-fhear,	*the young man.*
An og bhean,	*the young woman.*
An seann duine,	*the old man.*
An t-seann-bhean,	*the old woman.*
A' choisir chiuil,	*the musical choir.*
A' chearc-fhraoich,	*the moor-hen.*

299. The application of the definite article to a compound
noun and the change arising in meaning from its use and
non-use before the first as well as before the second noun
can best be shown by example.

Long-chogaidh (f)	*a ship of war.*	*a warship.*
An long-chogaidh	*the ship of war.*	*the warship.*
Long (f) a' chogaidh (m)	*the ship of the war.*	*the war's ship.*

Observe the effect of the definite article when placed before **cogaidh** changing its meaning to some special and definite " war " and not " war " in general.

Take another example : **meadhon oidhche** " midnight " ; **am meadhon oidhche** " the midnight " ; now insert **an** before **oidhche** and its meaning is at once defined, **meadhon na h-oidhche** " the middle of the night " ; *i.e.* some special night named or known.

300. A study of these compound forms of the noun will show that here again is a similarity with continental languages. It will be observed there is an essential difference of construction from English. Gaelic is like French and other languages in that it goes from the general to the particular, while the English go from the particular to the general. The arrangement of the compound noun in English is exactly inverted in Gaelic.

Eng.	Cod	Liver	Oil.		Annual	General	Meeting
	3	2	1		3	2	1
French	*Huile*	*de foie*	*de morue.*		*Assemblée*	*générale*	*annuelle.*
	1	2	3		1	2	3
Gaelic,	**Uilleadh**	**gruthan**	**throsg.**		**Coinneamh**	**choitcheann**	**bhliadhnail**
	1	2	3		1	2	3

GOVERNMENT OF THE NOUN BY PREPOSITIONS.

301. Prepositions govern the dative case, in fact, simple prepositions govern no other case (par. 595). Compound prepositions govern the genitive case (par. 614).

A DEFINITE NOUN QUALIFYING AN INDEFINITE NOUN.

302. A definite noun qualifying an indefinite noun cannot be placed in the genitive case, though in English it is governed by " of." We cannot have a definite genitive noun qualifying an indefinite noun (par. 290). In Gaelic we place it in the dative case following the preposition **de**. If an indefinite noun which would otherwise be placed in the genitive (par. 294) is qualified by an adjective, it must be placed in the dative instead (pars. 342, 604b).

Sac de'n mhin sin,	a sack of that meal.
Air pios de'n aran,	on a piece of the bread.
(Air) pios de aran math,	(on) a piece of good bread.
(Air) pios de dh' aran math,	(on) a piece of good bread.
Gann de storas (par. 604b)	scarce of wealth.

303. When there is a demonstrative adjective attached to the first noun the article must be used with it as well as with the second noun, an exception to pars. 212, 602.

Air a' phios so de aran,	on this piece of bread.
Am pios so de aran math,	this piece of good bread.
Am pios so de'n aran sin,	this piece of that bread.
Am pios math so de'n aran sin,	this good piece of that bread.

304. When one noun is predicated of another by the verb **is** and an adjective of praise or dispraise is connected with the predicate, the noun is never put in the genitive. In English the noun is governed by the preposition "of," but in Gaelic it is actually in the nominative case after the verb **is**, which is here used as a relative, standing for "who is."

| Is e fear is mor rath, | he is a man of great prosperity. |
| Is e am fear is mo ciall, | he is the man of greatest sense. |

PROPER NAMES AND NOUNS IN APPOSITION.

305. When we have two or more nouns together denoting the same person, such as a proper name, they agree in the same case. The surname or second element is aspirated as a qualifying adjective (pars. 295, 327).

Bha Righ Tearlach an sin,	King Charles was there.
Tha Seumas Camshron aig an dorus,	James Cameron is at the door.
Tha Mairi Chamshron air dol dachaidh,	Mary Cameron has gone home.

306. If these are limiting or qualifying another noun, both name and surname are in the genitive.

Ceann Thearlaich Chaimbeil,	Charles Campbell's head.
Tigh Sheumais Chamshroin,	James Cameron's house.
cf. Ceann Righ Tearlach (not Thearlaich),	King Charles' head.

307. In the vocative : **A Mhairi, mo ghaol**, Mary, my love.

308. **Mac** "son" is prefixed for a masculine surname and **Nic** for a feminine. It means "one of the Clan." **Nic** for **ni mhic (nighean mhic)** is a distinction not made in English, in which it has no equivalent, it is always "Mac"

even for females. In usage **Mac** and **Nic** are followed by
the genitive which is generally aspirated (par. 295).

Domhnull Mac Dhughaill,	*Donald Mac Dougall.*
Iain Mac Thomais,	*John Thomson.*
Anna Nic Uilleim,	*Ann Williamson.*
Mairi Nic Dhomhnuill,	*Mary Mac Donald.*

309. A simple appellative may be used and be in apposition, descriptive of a person's position, trade, or calling.
These generally omit the article, though a feminine is aspirated as though an article were present.

Calum Ciobair,	*Malcolm the shepherd.*
Cu Chaluim Chiobair,	*Malcolm the shepherd's dog.*
Bha Calum ur n-athair an so,	*Malcolm your father was here.*
Ceit Bhanarach,	*Kate the milkmaid.*

310. **Calum an Ciobair** is not wrong, although it is not
as *native* as the form given, but if the second part is a
compound, the article is necessary—

Alasdair an Ceardumha,	*Alastair the coppersmith.*

Calum a' Chiobair is quite a different matter.   It means
" Malcolm of the shepherd—his son or his servant."

311. After a person's full proper name a term descriptive
of the trade, office, etc., requires the article.

Domhnull Camshron am maighstir-sgoil,	*Donald Cameron, the schoolmaster.*
Seumas Grannd an taillear,	*James Grant, the tailor.*

312. A noun in apposition to, and explanatory of another
noun in the genitive case, is not itself in the genitive case,
but in the nominative case.

Leabhar Dhonnachaidh Bhain am Bard.	*The book of Duncan Ban the poet.*
Mac Ioseiph an saor,	*The son of Joseph the carpenter.*

Notice that we have **am bard** and **an saor**, and not **a'
bhaird** or **an t-saoir** (the genitive case of them) though they
are explanatory of nouns which are in the genitive.

313. Compare the effect of the genitive if applied to this
example : **Mac Ioseiph an t-saoir.**   In this form the sense is
completely changed ;   the meaning being now "the son
of the carpenter's Joseph " (i.e. " the grandson of the
carpenter," or this Joseph may be an employee of the
carpenter).

314. A noun in apposition to a noun in the dative case is put in the nominative.

Thubhairt e ri Sarai a bhean *he said to Sarah his wife.*
(*not* a mhnaoi).

LESSON XXVII.

The Adjective.

315. The natural position of the Gaelic adjective is immediately after the noun which it qualifies, as :—

long mhor (*lonk vor*)   a big ship.
cu donn (*koo dtownn*)   a brown dog.
craobh ard (*krōv ardt*)   a high tree.

The exceptions to this rule are the following :—

316. When the adjective is specially emphatic and is ascribed to its noun by the verb **is** or its negative **cha**, etc., it is placed before the noun and immediately follows the verb.

Is fuar an la e,   *it is a* COLD *day.*
Is math a' bhean i,   *she is a* GOOD *woman.*

317. Numeral adjectives both cardinal and ordinal are always placed before their nouns.

Tri bliadhna,   *three years.*   An treas bhliadhna,   *the third year.*

318. Some adjectives of one syllable are placed immediately before the noun which they qualify and generally form a compound word. They suffer no change in termination, the initial letter of the noun may be aspirated. See government of compound nouns (pars. 295-8).

Seann duine,   *an old man.*   Droch dhuine,   *a bad man.*
Og bhean,   *a young wife.*   Gorm shuil.   *a blue eye.*
Deagh obair,   *a good work.*   Sar obair,   *choice work.*

319. The agreement of an adjective and noun is regulated by its position in the sentence.

When the adjective immediately follows the noun, it agrees with it in gender, number, and case. Suffering a change sometimes in the aspiration of its initial letter, sometimes a vowel change, according to the gender and case of the noun to which it is a qualification, and thus they have two forms of declension :—the one with masculine nouns and the other with feminine nouns.

Fear mor, *a big man.* Bean mhor, *a big woman.*

320. When the adjective is . one which qualifies and precedes its noun, the form of the adjective does not change in any respect dependent on its noun, but it is influenced by prefixed particles as if it were part of the substantive itself, and it aspirates the initial of its noun if aspirable, as if it formed a compound term (par. 298, 318).

321. When the adjective is in the predicate of the proposition and ascribes a quality to the noun which is the subject, the form of the adjective is not modified by its noun but is used in its simple form whatever be the gender or number of the noun.

Tha a' chlach (*f*) bheag ban,	*the small stone is white.*
Tha a' chlach bhan beag,	*the white stone is small.*
Tha a' chlach beag, ban,	*the stone is small and white.*
Tha a' chlach bheag, bhan . . .	*the small white stone is . . .*
Is ban a' chlach bheag,	*white is the small stone.*
Tha na clachan beaga ban,	*the small stones are white.*
Tha na clachan bana beag,	*the white stones are small.*
Tha na clachan beag, ban,	*the stones are small and white.*
Tha na clachan beaga, bana . . .	*the small white stones are . . .*

Upon examining these sentences it will be seen that in the first the adjective " small " comes before the verb " is " and " white " comes after " is " ; in the second they are reversed and in the third both adjectives come after " is." It is very important to note that in translating into Gaelic sentences like the above, that adjectives which in English follow the verb are not aspirated or modified in any way. In the fourth sentence we have both adjectives aspirated, which means that the sentence is incomplete, the qualification being left out.

322. The adjective is not modified when it qualifies the action of the verb, as :—**dean an sgian geur,** " make the knife sharp," Here the adjective does not agree with the noun, for it modifies not the noun but the verb, and the expression is equivalent to " sharpen the knife." But **to** express " take the sharp knife " we say, **gabh an sgian**

gheur wherein the adjective agrees with the noun, distinguishing that knife from others and consequently it is written in the feminine gender to agree with **sgian.**

323. A noun or adjective whose initial is **d, t, s ; l, n, r,** when preceded by a noun· or adjective terminating in **l** or **n** resists aspiration (par. 38).

324. When an adjective is used to describe the quality of two or more nouns it agrees with the one immediately next to it, as :—**fear agus bean mhath,** " a good man and woman." Here the adjective **mhath** agrees with **bean** the latter noun, but if the position of the nouns is reversed, **bean agus fear math,** " a good woman and man," the adjective **math** agrees with **fear.**

DECLENSION OF THE ADJECTIVE.

325. The adjective forms its cases in the singular number from the nominative singular according to the rules as given for the declension of nouns having the same vowel or diphthong or termination in the nominative.

326. Thus the general rule is to form the genitive by introducing an **i** after the last broad vowel, the feminine adding the terminal **e,** and the dative singular feminine the same as the genitive, but omitting the terminal **e.** Adjectives of two or more syllables generally make the genitive sing. feminine without the terminal **e.**

327. The nominative singular masculine and feminine are alike, but the feminine is aspirated ; the genitive singular masculine is always aspirated ; the genitive singular feminine is always plain and generally ends˙in **e** ; the nominative and dative singular feminine are aspirated both with and without the definite article ; the dative singular masculine is not aspirated when without the article but it suffers aspiration when the definite article is *attached ; the vocative singular and plural both masculine and feminine are aspirated.

---

* This is the only difference which combination with the article causes.

328. In the plural if the adjective is a monosyllable in a broad vowel an **a** is added, and if in a narrow vowel an **e** is added :

craobhan arda,	high trees.	**sruthan casa,**	swift streams.
orain bhinne,	sweet songs.	**daoine glice,**	wise men.
gillean mora,	big boys.		

329. Adjectives of more than one syllable have the plural the same as the nominative singular :

caileagan maiseach, handsome girls.
aithrichean dileas, faithful fathers.

330. Adjectives do not change for case or gender in the plural :

331. Some adjectives in **o** change the **o** into **ui** in the gen. sing.
Some adjectives in **ea, eu,** and **ia** change into **i** ,,
Some adjectives in **a** change into **oi** ,,

	Masc.	Fem.	Masc.	Fem.
Nom. and Acc.	**Mor**	**Mhor**	**Olc**	**Olc**
Gen.	**Mhoir**	**Moire**	**Uilc**	**Uilce**
Dat.	**Mor**	**Mhoir**	**Olc**	**Uilc**
Voc.	**Mhoir**	**Mhor**	**Uilc**	**Olc**

Common Plurals—**Mora** and **Olc(a).**

332. Examples of the Genitive Form of the Adjective :

Nom. Masc.	Gen. M.	Gen. F.
ard (*árdt*) high.	**aird**	**airde**
ban (*bpân*) fair.	**bhain**	**baine**
beag (*bpāk*) little.	**bhig**	**bige**
beairteach (*bpārshtyüch*) rich.	**bheairtich**	**beairtiche**
breac (*prāchk*) speckled.	**bhric**	**brice**
caol (*kŏll*) narrow.	**chaoil**	**caoile**
ceart (*kyârst*) right.	**cheirt**	**ceirte**
cian (*keeün*) foreign.	**chein**	**ceine**
crom (*krowm*) crooked.	**chruim**	**cruime**
crubach (*kroopüch*) lame.	**chrubaich**	**crubaiche**
dall (*tawll*) blind.	**dhoill**	**doille**
dearg (*tchârük*) red.	**dheirg**	**deirge**
direach (*tchyrüch*) straight.	**dhirich**	**diriche**
donn (*dtownn*) brown.	**dhuinn**	**duinne**
gann (*kâoonn*) scarce.	**ghoin**	**goine**
geal (*kyall*) white.	**ghil**	**gile**
geur (*kyur*) sharp.	**gheir**	**geire**
gian (*ghllan*) clean.	**ghloinn**	**gloinne**
glas (*ghlas*) grey.	**ghlais**	**glaise**
gorm (*gorüm*) blue.	**ghuirm**	**guirme**
lom (*llowm*) bare.	**luim**	**luime**

Nom. Masc.	*Gen. M.*	*Gen. F.*
maiseach (*mâ-shŭch*) pretty.	mhaisich	maisiche
mall (*mâ ool*) slow.	mhoill	moille
moch, early.	mhuich	muiche
mor big, great, tall.	mhoir	moire
olc (*awlk*) evil, bad, wicked.	uilc	uilce
searbh (*shârŭv*) bitter.	sheirbh	seirbhe
slan (*sllawn*) well.	shlain	slaine
taitneach (*tâtch-nyŭch*) pleasant.	thaitnich	taitniche
tearc (*dtchârŭk*) rare.	theirc	teirce
telnteach (*tchăn-tchŭch*) fiery.	theintich	teintiche
trom (*trowm*) heavy.	thruim	truime

333. Adjectives ending in a vowel, **ail, eil, idh,** or **chd,** are indeclinable.

NOUN AND ADJECTIVE WITHOUT THE ARTICLE.

334. The initial form of the adjective depends on the gender and termination of the noun with which it is joined, and on the presence of the article.

Masculine Noun.		*Feminine Noun.*	
gille mor, a big boy.		**craobh mhor,** a high tree.	
Singular.	*Plural.*	*Singular.*	*Plural.*
Nom. **gille mor**	**gillean mora**	**craobh mhor**	**craobhan mora**
Gen. **gille mhoir**	**ghillean mora**	**craoibhe moire**	**chraobh mora**
Dat. **gille mor**	**gillean mora**	**craoibh mhoir**	**craobhan mora**

cat glas, a grey cat.		**cearc dhubh,** a black hen.	
Nom. **cat glas**	**cait ghlasa**	**cearc dhubh**	**cearcan dubha**
Gen. **cait ghlais**	**chat glasa**	**circe duibhe**	**chearca dubha**
Dat. **cat glas**	**cait ghlasa**	**circ dhuibh**	**cearcan dubha**

335. It will be noticed from the above examples that the adjective is aspirated in the nominative and dative feminine, and in the genitive masculine singular.

336. Observe **cait ghlasa** and note that where the adjective qualifies a noun whose nominative plural is formed like the genitive singular the adjective is aspirated in the nominative and dative plural. It will be found that this class includes principally masculine nouns (pars. 243, 252).

337.   *Vocabulary.*

borb (*bporŭb*) adj. fierce.
boidheach (*bpoyŭch*) adj. pretty.

338. Read in Gaelic and translate into English :—

1. Tha clachan troma anns an achadh sin. 2. Tha an t-airgiod
gann a nis. 3. Tha an gille ban. 4. Bha na cailleagan ban. 5. Tha
cu beag an so. 6. Cha'n eil coin bheaga an sin. 7. Le slait gheir.
8. Ann am baile mor. 9. Casan cait dhuibh. 10. Cinn chat dubha.
11. Casan circe duibhe. 12. Tha casan dubha aig a' chaora.
13. Adhaircean fhiadh borba. 14. Ceann feidh bhuirb. 15. Anns
an luing bhig. 16. Siuil gheala luinge moire. 17. Ann am bailtean
mora. 18. Tha cearcan bana an sud. 19. Is e so leabhar gille mhoir.

339. Translate into Gaelic :—

1. The rich man was lame. 2. He had a little dog. 3. It was a little
black dog. 4. Was it a black terrier ? No. 5. Is a terrier a dog ?
6. A terrier is a small dog. 7. Was it not a white dog ? 8. There
was a brown dog at the door. 9. A bad little girl struck a little brown
dog yesterday. 10. She was a pretty girl. 11. A bad boy was
kicking a big horse. 12. A big horse was being kicked by a bad
little boy. 13. It is a bare house. 14. Was it a bare house with a
narrow door ? 15. He was a rich man. 16. A black hen's head.
17. A brown horse's foot. 18. A fierce cow in a big field. 19. A
sheep with black feet and a black head is there now.

LESSON XXVIII.

340.   NOUN AND ADJECTIVE WITH THE ARTICLE.

Examples.

an t-each donn *m.* the brown horse.

	Sing.	*Plur.*
Nom.	an t-each donn	na h-eich dhonna
Gen.	an eich dhuinn	nan each donna
Dat.	an each dhonn.	na h-eich dhonna, *or* na h-eachaibh donna

a' chreag bheag *f.* the little rock.

Nom.	a' chreag bheag	na creagan beaga
Gen.	na creige bige	nan creagan beaga
Dat.	a' chreig bhig	na creagan beaga

341. From the above examples notice that an adjective
qualifying a definite masculine noun in the dative case
singular is aspirated in addition to the aspiration of the
genitive shown in the previous example. (par. **334**).

342. Adjectives of quantity and of a partitive nature
qualify an indefinite noun in the genitive, but if the noun

is definite the preposition **de** and the dative case must be used (pars. 294, 302, 604b).

Beagan arain,	*a little bread.*
Beagan de'n. aran,	*a little of the bread.*
Moran sluaigh,	*many people.*
Iomadh de na bliadhnachan,	*many of the years.*
Beagan greine,	*little sunshine.*
Beagan de'n ghrein,	*little of the sunlight.*

343. Read in Gaelic and translate into English :—

1. Is fuar an la e. 2. An iad na h-cich mhora ? 3. Is iad. 4. Tha clachan troma anns an achadh so. 5. Tha an t-airgiod gann a nis. 6. Tha an t-each dubh trom. 7. Tha an cat breac leisg. 8. Tha na coin gheala mor. 9. Am bheil cearc air a' chreig bhig ? 10. Bha an duine og air briseadh na h-uinneige moire. 11. Tha a' bho bheag bhan a' tighinn dachaidh. 12. Tha a' chearc ghorm dall. 13. An robh an duine og air briseadh an doruis chaoil ? 14. Is dubh an dorus beag. 15. Tha neul glas air bharr na linne guirme. 16. Is boidheach an dath a tha air an t-sobhraich.

344. Translate into Gaelic :—

1. Have the bad boys been home yet ? No. 2. The pretty little girl was in that field this afternoon. 3. The right knife is sharp. 4. That man had the crooked stick. 5. Where was he with the crooked stick ? 6. He was (**bu**) a big man. 7. The house with the little narrow door is yonder. 8. That will not be the house with the big door. 9. The blind horse was being struck by the bad boys. 10. The young boy was at the big black house last night. 11. The bare trees are on the hill. 12. The trees are bare now. 13. Where is the little brown dog ? 14. The big black dog is with the man with the crooked stick.

345. Correct and translate :—

am bean mor ; an tigh bheag ; laimh geal ; mac an duine big ; ceann an lhoch ; beagan an h-aran ; lamhan an duine droch ; lamhan an ghille salacha ; mac an tailleir bhiga ; an duine mhath ; bean glic ; na clachan beage ; seann dhan.

346. Examination Questions :—

1. What is the general place of the Gaelic adjective qualifying a noun?
2. Are adjectives indeclinable in Gaelic as in English ?
3. How is the plural of an adjective generally formed ?
4. What is the difference of the nominative and genitive masculine ?
5. In what lies the difference between the nominative and genitive feminine ?
6. What happens when adjectives precede their nouns ?
7. Do all adjectives which precede their nouns aspirate the noun ?
8. Why not ? (give reasons).
9. What does the aspiration of an adjective indicate ?
10. When does the noun aspirate the adjective ?

LESSON XXIX.

THE VERBS **tha** AND **is** WITH AN ADJECTIVE.

347. There is always a difference in meaning between **tha** and **is** which we shall try to further illustrate by examples. One reason is that **tha** means " is now " and **is** means " is always " or " is " without any reference to time and circumstances. **Tha mi bacach** means " I am now lame," *i.e.*, at present. **Is bacach mi**—if we use **bacach** with the force of a noun—means " I am lame— I am a cripple " ; if **bacach** is used as a simple adjective then this form **is bacach mi** simply emphasises or draws special attention to the state or condition of " lameness," like saying " how lame I am!—it is lame I am—it is no slight lameness I have."

348. Compare the expressions (1) **tha mi bronach** and (2) **is bronach mi**. The first expression may be translated " I am sad," no particular emphasis being attached to any part of the sentence. The second expression is best translated " sad am I," in this case particular stress is laid on the fact of " sadness." The first phrase states with logical precision that the attribute " sad " belongs to the speaker, the second is a rhetorical device for calling attention to the existence or reality of the sadness. No. (1) is therefore the form to be used in everyday speech when the giving of information merely is the purpose of the speaker. No. (2) is the language of poetry, maxims, proverbs, and impassioned speech and is analogous to such inversions as " Great is Diana of the Ephesians," and the like in English, **Is mor Diana nan Ephesianach.**

DEFINITE NOUN (SUBJECT) and INDEFINITE NOUN AND ADJECTIVE (PREDICATE).

349. When a sentence contains a definite noun as the subject and an indefinite noun with an adjective as the predicate, we have three forms which we can use in Gaelic, according to the impression we wish to convey.

" James is a strong man " can be translated (1) **Tha Seumas 'na dhuine laidir**; the meaning of which is that " James has become—has grown to be—a strong man."

(2) **Is duine laidir Seumas** ; here we take James as we find him, and do not convey that he was at one time not so strong. He belongs to the species of strong men and is not an ordinary man. The emphasis in this sentence is on the **laidir**, and to make this emphasis more marked, the words are usually placed in a different order—(3) **Is laidir an duine Seumas** ; notice the use of the definite article **an**, a literal translation of the phrase being " Strong is the man James." In this construction we are much more impressed by his strength. Sentences of this latter form therefore are translated by detaching the adjective from the English predicate and making the noun follow it in the definite form.

350. In the affirmative question " Is James a strong man ? " we can only convey the idea of (1) quality, or (2) species ; we cannot say we are (3) impressed with his strength when we are merely inquiring about it. Neither can a negative sentence convey this third meaning. When, however, we have negative question forms, these do express feeling or impression about the subject and are equivalent to an exclamation. " Isn't James the strong man ? " is equal to saying " What a strong man James is ! " **Nach laidir an duine Seumas** ? The idea therefore of " feeling " and " impression " is confined to affirmative statements or negative questions.

It should be noted while we are talking of negative questions that sentences of " feeling " or " impression " like " How cold the water is ! " " How nice the house is ! " ; " How heavy the book is ! " ; " What a strong man James is ! " ; can all be translated in this manner by means of the negative question.

351. Translate into Gaelic using the verb **tha** and **Is** alternately :—

1. The dogs are clever. 2. Clever are the dogs. 3. The hero was brave. 4. Brave was the hero. 5. The bridge was shut. 6. Shut was the bridge. 7. The horse is swift. 8. Swift is the horse. 9. The primrose is pretty. 10. Pretty is the primrose. 11. The clouds are black. 12. Black are the clouds. 13. The wind is strong. 14. Strong is the wind. 15. The lamb is young. 16. Young is the lamb. 17. The dog is faithful. 18. Faithful is the dog. 19. I am happy. 20. Happy am I. 21. The brown dog is fierce. 22. Fierce is the brown dog.

LESSON XXX.

COMPARISON OF ADJECTIVES.

352. There are two kinds of Comparison, the one a comparison of equality, the other the comparison of inequality ; because all things are in some respect alike or unlike.

THE COMPARATIVE OF EQUALITY.

353. What we may term a comparison of equality is when two or more articles are compared as having an equal degree of the quality denoted by the adjective. In Gaelic the ordinary or positive form of the adjective is used, preceded by the conjunction **cho** and generally followed by **ri, ris, le,** etc. (pars. 633-4-5).

Tha ise cho glic riutsa, *she is as wise as you.*
Tha Iain cho ard ri Seumas, *John is as tall as James.*
Tha mo thigh cho ard ri ur tigh-se, *my house is as high as your house.*
Tha Seumas cho laidir ri Iain, *James is as strong as John.*
Tha e so cho geal ris an t-sneachda, *this is as white as snow.*

THE COMPARATIVE OF SUPERIORITY.

354. The comparative form of the adjective must be used when in comparing two objects, one object is said to possess more than the other of the quality mentioned.

355. The adjective has only one form for both comparative and superlative, and this form is the same as the genitive singular feminine in **e** final ; as

ban, fair. **baine,** fairer. **dubh,** black. **duibhe,** blacker.
trom, heavy. **truime,** heavier. **geal,** white. **gile,** whiter.

356. Further examples of the formation of the genitive singular feminine, which, as already stated, is the same as the comparative form of the adjective, will be found in par. 332.

357. The comparative adjective is not inflected for case or number, but suffers aspiration like any other adjective.

358. The comparison when made by the verb **is** is followed by **na,** " than."

Is gile mo lamhsa na do lamhsa,	*my hand is whiter than your hand.*
Is gile a' ghrian na a' ghealach,	*the sun is brighter than the moon.*
Is baine Seumas na Iain,	*James is fairer than John.*
Bu bhaine Seumas na Iain,	*James was fairer than John.*
Bu ghile e na sneachda,	*It was whiter than snow.*
An truime a' chlach so na i sin ?	*is this stone heavier than that ?*

359. When any other part of the verb **bi** (except **is**) is used in a comparative, we require to use a relative clause, the comparative adjective being preceded by **na's** (compounded of the relative phrase **an ni a is**, " the thing which is ") except in a past tense where **na bu** is used. Both forms being followed by **na** " than."

Tha Iain na's baine na Seumas,	*John is fairer than James.*
Bithidh Seumas na's airde na Iain,	*James will be taller than John.*
Bha Iain na bu bhaine na Seumas,	*John was fairer than James.*
Bha e na bu mhilse na a' mhil,	*It was sweeter than the honey.*
Tha e na's laidire a nis na bha e riamh,	*he is stronger than ever he was.*
Tha e na's fhearr na Iain,	*he is better than John.*

360. When translating an English adjective in the superlative degree we use the assertive form of the verb **is**, but we also put the sentence into a relative form. We use **as** the relative form of the verb **is** to precede the superlative when present time is spoken of, and **a bu** when past time is spoken of. The superlative relative requires the presence of the definite article in front of the nouns ; in this it specially differs from the comparative ; a proper noun is definite without the article. Thus :—" the tallest man " is translated **am fear as airde**," the man who is tallest." The superlative can be shown in the greatest degree of quality when comparing three or more objects by being followed with a prepositional phrase.

Is e Seumas as baine,	*James is the fairest.*
Is e Seumas as baine de'n teaghlach.	*James is the fairest of the family.*
B'e Seumas a bu bhaine de'n teaghlach	*James was the fairest of the family.*
Is e sud an tigh as motha anns a' bhaile,	*that is the biggest house in the town.*
Is e am fear as fhearr (note aspiration),	*he is the best man.*
Is i a' bheinn as airde anns an t-saoghal,	*it is the highest mountain in the world.*

361. Note for guidance :—

na's is the sign of the comparative.
as is generally the sign of the superlative.

Gaelic.	English.	French.
mor	great	*gros*
na's mo	greater	*plus gros*
as mo	greatest	*le plus gros*

THE COMPARATIVE OF INFERIORITY.

362. The comparison of inferiority is very similarly made with **na's** and the comparative **lugha** " less " = " least."

'S e Iain am fear as lugha de'n triuir.
John is the least of the three.

Tha a' ghealach na's lugha soillse na a' ghrian,
the moon has less light than the sun.

363. Intensive particles, such as **ro, glé, fior, air, leth, anabarrach**, are frequently placed before adjectives in their simple form, to increase their signification; as **ro mhath,** very good (too good) ; **anabarrach mor,** exceedingly great (par. 620-1).

A VERBAL ADJECTIVE.

364. Some monosyllabic adjectives admit of a verbal form compounded with the verb **is** and the prepositional pronoun formed from **de.** This is really not a second form of the comparative, as Stewart and other grammarians make out, being only an idiomatic combination which has nothing to do with the comparative adjective, as can be illustrated thus :—**is feairrde thu sin,** " thou art the better of that," can be resolved into **is fearr tu deth sin,** from which we can clearly see that **feairrde** is not a second form of the comparative (par. 604e). The final **e** changes into **id** or **ide**

B' fheairrde mi sin,
I was the better of that.

Nach bu mhisde e sin ?
was he not the worse of that ?

Is truimide am poca,
the bag is the heavier of it.

Is beag is mhisde thu sin,
it's little you are the worse of that.

Cha mhisde leam e 'bhi mar sin.
I do not think he will be the worse of being so (so=like that).

365. An abstract noun may be formed from the first comparative ; adding **ad** sometimes **eas**, as :—

baine, fairer.	**teotha**, hotter.	**daoire**, dearer.
baineas, fairness.	**teothad**, heat.	**daoiread**, dearness.

366. IRREGULAR ADJECTIVES.

Some of the commoner adjectives are irregular in the formation of their comparative form :—

Positive.	*Comparative.*
beag (*bpāk*) little.	**lugha** (*lōgh-ŭ*) less.
cumhang (*kooygh*), narrow.	**cuinge** (*kooyngŭ*).
duilich (*dtoolŭch*) difficult.	**duilghe** or **dorra** (*dtoolyŭ*)
fagus (*fagkŭs*) near.	**faisge** (*fāshkŭ*).
furasda (*foorastŭ*) easy.	**fhasa** (*assŭ*).
goirid (*gŏrytch*), **gearr** (*kyâr*) short.	**giorra** (*gyrrŭ*).
ionmhuinn (*eeun-vynn*) beloved.	**annsa** (*aunsā*) dearer.
leathan (*lyā-ŭn*) broad.	**leatha** (*lyā-ŭ*).
math (*ma*) good.	**fearr** (*fyârr*).
mor (*mōr*) great.	**mo** or **motha** (*mō-hŭ*)
olc (*awlk*) bad.	**miosa** (*myss-ŭ*) worse.
teth (*tchā*) hot.	**teotha** (*tcho-ŭ*).
toigh (*toyh*) loved, fond.	**docha** (*dochŭ*) fondest.
laidir (*llâtchŭr*) strong.	**treise, treasa** (*trāshŭ*), or **laidire** (*llātchyrŭ*).

367. *Vocabulary.*

Mor nf. Sarah.
teaghlach (*tchowlŭch*) nm. a family.
Glascho nm. Glasgow.
Alba (*Alŭpŭ*) nf. Scotland.
cuideachd (*kootchachk*) nf. a company.
sine (*sheenŭ*) adj. older.
faide (*fâtchŭ*) adj. longer.
Duneideann (*dunātchŭnn*) Edinburgh.

368. Read in Gaelic and translate into English :—

1. B'e Iain a b' airde de 'n teaghlach. 2. Is i so a' chraobh as motha anns a' choille. 3. Tha Seumas na's airde na Iain. 4. Bha Mor na bu lugha na Seumas. 5. Is i Mor as sine de 'n teaghlach. 6. A' chlach as truime anns an achadh. 7. An duine as beairtiche anns an Albainn. 8. Is lugha caora na bo. 9. Is miosa Mor na Seumas. 10. Bu treise Seumas na Iain. 11. Am miosa ań cu na cat ? 12. Is faigse a' chraobh so na a' chraobh sin. 13. Is gile do lamhsa na mo lamhsa. 14. Am bheil thu a' dol na's faide ? 15. B' fheairrde mi sin. 16. Am Iain as sine anns a' chuideachd ? 17. Is o Duneid eann as boidhche na Glascho. 18. Cha mhisde e sin. 19. Tha Seumas seań ach is i Mor as sine. 20. Tha an t-each sgith ach tha an cu na's sgithe. 21. Thainig an tuathanach agus bhris e casan nan con.

369. Translate into Gaelic :—

1. John is taller than James. 2. He is the eldest of the family. 3. He is not the eldest of the family. 4. Sarah is older than he. 5. Sarah will be the eldest of the family. 6. Is John not older than James ? 7. John is younger than James. 8. The sheep is smaller than the cow. 9. Is Edinburgh prettier than Glasgow ? 10. Edin-

burgh is smaller than Glasgow.   11. Glasgow is larger than Edinburgh but Edinburgh is the prettier.   12. The stones in this field are heavier than those in that field.   13. They are not the worse of that.   14. The highest trees are on that hill.   15. The biggest river in Scotland.   16. The highest mountain in Scotland.   17. The moon is not as bright as the sun.   18. What is better than gold ?   19. The worst boy in the school.   20. The shortest day in the year.   21. That is the biggest house in the town.

370. Examination Questions :—

1. What does the comparative express, and how many comparatives are ·there ?
2. How do you express a comparative of equality ?
3. What is to be observed when the preposition **de** is before a substantive in a comparative sentence ?
4. What is the positive ?
5. How do we translate the English termination " est " in a comparative ?
6. Mention three adjectives which form their comparative irregularly.

LESSON XXXI.

Numeral Adjectives.

371. Numerals, Cardinal and Ordinal, precede their nouns ; as **trì eich**, three horses ; **an ceathramh fear**, " the fourth man " ; except when the cardinal number is employed to designate a particular person ; as *Rìgh Tearlach a Dhà.* " King Charles the Second."

372. The cardinals have two forms, one form to be used with nouns—these become simple adjectives ; the other form is used without a noun and really become nouns themselves.   The following is a selected list of the former, illustrative of the various changes which take place when governing a masculine noun.

After **aon, da, fichead, ciad, mile**, and any multiple of these, the noun is in the singular form.   These numerals only seem to take the nominative singular—**fichead fear, ciad fear**.   They are in reality substantive nouns governing the genitive case, so that **fear** in **fichead fear** is not nominative singular but genitive plural without the aspiration.

1	man.	**aon fhear** (ŏn er).
2	men.	**da fhear** (dta er).
3	,,	**tri fir** (tree fyr).
4	,,	**ceithir fir** (kā-yr fyr).
5	,,	**coig fir** (ko-yk fyr).
6	,,	**se** or **sia fir** (shā or sheeü fyr).
7	,,	**seachd fir** (shachk fyr).
8	,,	**ochd fir** (ochk fyr).
9	,,	**naoi fir** (nooü fyr).
10	,,	**deich fir** (tchāych fyr).
11	,,	**aon fhear deug** (ŏn er tchāk).
12	,,	**da fhear dheug** (dâ er yāk) (2+10=12).
13	,,	**tri fir dheug.**
20	,,	**fichead fear** (feechütt fer).
21	,,	**aon fhear ar fhichead** (ŏn er āreechyütt).
22	,,	**da fhear ar fhichead.** (2+20=22).
23	,,	**tri fir ar fhichead** (tree fyr āreechyütt).
30	,,	**deich fir ar fhichead,** or **deich fir fhichead.**
31	,,	**aon fhear deug ar fhichead.**
32	,,	**da fhear dheug ar fhichead** (2+10+20=32).
33	,,	**tri fir dheug ar fhichead.**
40	,,	**da fhichead fear** (dta eechyütt fer).
41	,,	**da fhichead fear 's a h-aon** (ü hŏn).
42	,,	**da fhichead fear 's a dha** (ü ghâ).
50	,,	**da fhichead fear 's a deich,** or **leth chiad fear** (lyā-chyütt fer).
60	,,	**tri fichead fear** (tree feechyutt fer).
61	,,	**tri fichead fear 's a h-aon.**
62	,,	**tri fichead fear 's a dha.**
80	,,	**ceithir fichead fear** (4 twenties =4 score).
90	,,	**ceithir fichead fear 's a deich.**
100	,,	**ciad fear** (keeüt fer).
101	,,	**ciad fear 's a h-aon.**
150	,,	**ciad gu leth fear** (keeüt goo lyā fer).
200	,,	**da chiad fear** (da chyutt fer).
1,000	,,	**mile fear** (mylü fer).
1,915	,,	**mile fear, naoi ciad 's a coig deug,** or **mile, naoi ciad is coig fir dheug.**
14,000	,,	**ceithir mile deug fear.**
100,000	,,	**ciad mile fear.**
1,000,000	,,	**muillion fear** (moolyün fer).

373. Gu leth when used with the higher numerals signifies
" one half more "; **ciad gu leth,** " one hundred and a half,"
" 150 "; **mile gu leth,** " one thousand five hundred,"
" 1500," or " a mile and a half "; but with the smaller
numbers it means " one-half " only: **tri gu leth,** " three
and a half," " 3½ "; **lethchlach,** " half-a-stone "; **leth,**
one of a pair—**leth chas** " one foot."

NOTES ON THE NUMERALS.

374. Aon aspirates all consonants except **l, n, r ; d, t, s**.

Aon bhean,	*one woman.*	Aon duine,	*one man.*
Aon chraobh,	*one tree.*	Aon fhear,	*one man*
Aon eile,	*one other.*	Aon sam bith,	*anyone.*
M' aon chearc,	*my only hen.*	Gach aon,	*everyone.*
'San aon luing,	*in the same ship.*	Aon uair,	*once, 1 o'c.*

375. Da. (1) Aspirates all consonants except **l, n, r**.

(2) Takes a dual number of the noun, a form which closely corresponds to the modern dative singular aspirated.

Da righ,	*two kings.*	Da dhuine,	*two men.*
Da thigh,	*two houses.*	Da bhroig,	*two shoes.*
Da uair,	*twice, 2 o'c.*	Da chloich,	*two stones.*

(3) An adjective qualifying such a noun, whether it is masculine or feminine, is also aspirated. It is not inflected, remaining in the nominative case aspirated (or we might say the nominative singular feminine).

Da chloich bheag, *two little stones.* Da fhear dheug, *twelve men.*
Da bhradan mhor, *two big salmon.* Da each dhonn, *two brown horses.*

(4) In poetry the adjective sometimes takes the plural.

Da chirc mhora, *two large hens.* Da nighinn bheaga, *two little daughters.*

(5) If the numeral **da** with its noun and adjective is preceded by a preposition, both noun and adjective take the dative case singular.

Le da chloich bhig,	*with two little stones.*
Aig an da chaileig bhig,	*at the two little girls.*
Aig an da bhalach bheag,	*at the two little boys.*
Do dha nighinn oig,	*to two young daughters.*
Fo dha bhord fhada,	*under two long tables.*

(6) But when the noun after **da** is itself governed in the genitive by another noun, the government of the numeral **da** gives way to the stronger influence.

Buinn mo dha bhroige,	*the soles of my two shoes.*
Siuil an da luinge,	*the sails of the two ships.*
Barran da chluais duine,	*the tips of a man's two ears.*
Cul a da laimhe,	*the back of both her hands.*
Clann an da mhna,	*the children of both wives.*
Mal an da thighe,	*the rent of both houses.*
Ceann an da mheoir,	*the ends of the two fingers.*

376. Deug. (1) It is an adjective and always agrees with the gender of its noun.

(2) Of the numbers in which **deug** appears, namely 11 to 19, both inclusive, two of these, 11 and 12, take a singular noun. In 11, if the noun is masculine, **deug** remains unaspirated ; but if the noun is feminine **deug** suffers aspiration unless the noun ends in a dental or lingual (**d, t, s ; l, n, r**). In 12, the effect of **da** " two," which appears in this number, has been already shown.

Aon each deug	(m)	*eleven horses.*
Aon chat deug	(m)	*eleven cats.*
Da chu dheug	(m)	*twelve dogs.*
Da bhradan deug	(m)	*twelve salmon.*
Aon chluas deug	(f)	*eleven ears.*
Aon bhrog dheug	(f)	*eleven shoes.*
Da chirc dheug	(f)	*twelve hens.*
Da uair dheug	(f)	*twelve hours, 12 o'c.*

(3) The numbers 13 to 19 inclusive, take the noun in the plural. **Deug** is only aspirated in the case of nouns which introduce an **i** in their plural declension, generally masculine nouns (par. 336).

Tri fir dheug	(m)	*thirteen men.*
Tri cait dheug	(m)	*thirteen cats.*
Seachd doruis dheug	(m)	*seventeen doors.*
Coig bailtean deug	(m)	*fifteen towns.*
Naoi brogan deug	(f)	*nineteen shoes.*
Ceithir ba deug	(f)	*fourteen cows.*

(4) Notice that all the numbers 11 to 19 inclusive, place the noun between the digit and **deug**. **Deug** corresponds to the English termination " teen."

377. Ar fhichead. The cardinal numbers with a noun, from 21 to 30, require that noun placed immediately after the digit and before the termination **ar fhichead**. **Air,** or **ar,** is an aspirating preposition. **Ar** can be omitted.

Ceithir uain ar fhichead,	*twenty-four lambs.*
Tri brogan ar fhichead,	*twenty-three shoes.*
Tri brogan fichead*,	*twenty-three shoes.*
Ceithir uain fhichead,	*twenty-four lambs.*
Da chirc fhichead (ar fhichead)	*twenty-two hens.*
Deich cearcan fichead,	*thirty hens.*

* Note that plural nouns of more than one syllable ending in **n** used thus do not aspirate **fichead.**

378. When dealing with numbers above forty, the easiest way for translating is to take—First, the number of score, then the noun, and finally, the remaining odds.

> **fichead** " 20 =a score."
> **tri fichead**, " 60 =three score."

65 ;   **tri fichead agus a coig** " three score and five."
65 horses ;   **tri fichead each agus a coig.**
87 sheep ;   **ceithir fichead caora agus a seachd.**
123 men ;   **se fichead duine agus a tri** " six score men and three."

379. Ciad (ceud) is always aspirated after **aon, da, tri, ceithir** :—

> **tri chiad fear,**   " three hundred men."

THE CARDINAL NUMBER AS A NOUN.

380. When the cardinal number is used as a noun, the particle **a** is placed in front of the simple cardinal number ; this particle aspirates **aon, da,** and **ochd.** Twelve numbers are illustrated herewith. After " forty " both forms are alike. These nouns are feminine gender.

One,	**a h-aon** (*ü hŏn*).	seven,	**a seachd**
Two,	**a dha** (*ü ghâ*).	eight,	**a h-ochd**
Three,	**a tri** (*ü tree*).	nine,	**a naoi**
Four,	**a ceithir** (*ü kāhyr*).	ten,	**a deich**
Five,	**a coig** (*ü ko yk*).	eleven,	**a h-aon deug**
Six,	**a se, sia** (*ü shā, sheeü*)	twelve,	**a dha dheug**

Mharbh e a dha (*varv ā ü ghâ*),   *he killed two.*
Righ Seumas a h-aon,   *King James the First.*
Righ Tearlach a dha dheug,   *King Charles the Twelfth.*
Thainig e le a h-ochd,   *he came with eight.*
Chaidh iad le a h-aon deug air
    fhichead,   *they went with thirty-one.*

381. The cardinal numbers can also take the article :— **an aon** " the one " ; **an da** " the two " ; etc.

PERSONAL NUMERALS.

382. We have ten numerical nouns formed from the cardinal numbers used to refer to persons only. These, when followed by a noun, govern that noun in the genitive plural :—**ceathrar mhac** " four sons " ; **coignear bhan** " five women."

aonar,	one (person).	**seanar**	six (persons).
dithis,	two (persons).	**seachdnar,**	seven	,,
triuir,	three	,,	**ochdnar,**	eight	,,
ceathrar,	four	,,	**naonar,**	nine	,,
coignear,	five	,,	**deichnear,**	ten	,,

383. The numerical noun **aonar** is used in several ways idiomatically as follows, and generally means " alone " :—

Duine 'na aonar,	*a man all alone.*
Chaidh mi am aonar,	*I went alone* (am =*in my—one person*)
Rinn e so 'na aonar,	*he did this alone.*
Tha e leis fein,	*he is alone (with himself).*

384.   THE ORDINAL NUMBERS.

an ceud fhear, a' cheud fhear,	the first man.
an dara fear,	the second man.
an treas fear,	the third man.
an ceathramh fear,	the fourth man
an coigeamh fear,	the fifth man.
an seathamh fear,	the sixth man.
an seachdamh fear,	the seventh man.
an t-ochdamh fear,	the eighth man.
an naoidheamh fear,	the ninth man.
an deicheamh fear,	the tenth man,
an t-aona fear deug,	the eleventh man.
an dara fear deug,	the twelfth man.
an treas fear deug,	the thirteenth man.
am ficheadamh fear,	the twentieth man.
an t-aona fear fichead,	the twenty-first man.
an dara fear fichead,	the twenty-second man.
an treas fear fichead,	the twenty-third man.
an deicheamh fear fichead,	the thirtieth man.
an da fhicheadamh fear,	the fortieth man.
an da fhicheadamh fear 's a h-aon,	the forty-first man.
an da fhicheadamh fear 's a deich,	the fiftieth man.
an tri ficheadamh fear 's a h-aon deug,	the seventy-first man.
an ciadamh fear,	the hundreth man.
an se ficheadamh fear,	the hundred and twentieth man.
an se ficheadamh fear 's a tri,	the hundred and twenty-third man.
an mileamh fear,	the thousandth man.

an ceud is the only ordinal which aspirates the noun.

EXERCISES ON THE NUMERALS.

385.   *Vocabulary.*

sgillinn (*skylynn*) nf. a penny.
la, laithean (*llă yŭn*), nm., a day, days.
seachduin (*shachkŭn*) nm. a week.
mios (*myss*) nf. a month.
brog, -oige (*brawk*) nf. a shoe, of a shoe.
mionaid, -ean (*my natch*) nm. a minute, minutes.
uair, -ean (*ooŭr*) an hour, hours.
meadhon-la (*mă-on llă*) nm. mid-day.
cota m. (*koh ttŭ*) a coat.

E

tagaidh (*fåk-y*) v. fut. will leave.
theid (*hätch*) irr. v.f. will go.
thig (*heek*) irr. v.f. come *or* will arrive.
roimh (*roi*) prep. before.
pairc, pairce (*på yrk*) nf. a park, of a park.
saighdear (*så ytchür*) nm. a soldier.
cia meud ? cia mheud ? (*ky mätt*) how much, how many ?*

386. Read in Gaelic and translate into English :—

1. Bha ceathrar fhear agus coignear bhan air a' bhàta sin. 2. Bha da chiad uan agus ciad gu leth caora anns an fhang. 3. Tha an ceathramh gille agus tri coin air a' mhonadh. 4. Tha a h-aon de na coin crubach. 5. Bha seachd uain anns an fhang an de. 6. Bha da chaora an sin am feasgar so. 7. Tha tri fichead caora agus da fhichead uan anns a' phairc. 8. Tha da shlait bheag agus aon lion anns a' bhàta. 9. Cia meud iasg a bha anns an lion ? 10. Bha ochd ciad deug is a coig. 11. Tha da bhroig a' ghille anns an tigh. 12. Tha seachd laithean anns gach seachduin. 13. De 'n uair a tha e ? 14. Tha e deich mionaidean roimh dha uair. 15. Cuine a dh' fhalbhas an carbad-iaruinn ? 16. Falbhaidh e aig coig mionaidean deug ar fhichead an deidh naoi uairean roimh mheadhon la. 17. Tha deich leabhraichean agamsa ach is le m' athair an deicheamh fear. 18. Tha an treas fear sgith. 19. Cia meud duine tha anns a' bhaile ? 20. Is e sud an t-aona fear fichead. 21. Cia meud uan tha anns an fhang ? 22. Deich is tri fichead. 23. An robh na coin air a' mhonadh an de ? 24. Cia meud bha ann ? 25. Bha tri. 26. Bha na tri coin leis a' chiobair.

387. Translate into Gaelic :—

1. There are nineteen sheep in that field, and there are eleven sheep in this field. 2. How many sheep are in these two fields ? 3. Thirty sheep are in these two fields. 4. There are ten cows and two bulls in that park. 5. Three men and two boys are in that boat there. 6. They have four rods and two nets with them. 7. How many fish have they ? 8. The shepherd and his three dogs are on the hill. 9. He has eighty-five sheep on that hill and ninety on that hill. 10. His fourth dog is lame to-day. 11. When will the train leave here ? 12. The first train will leave at nine-thirty a.m. 13.

---

* **Cia meud?** " how much ? " or literally " what quality, size or amount." If to things for sale, it refers to price or value. If to man it refers to debt owed by him.

Cia meud a tha air an leabhar ?	*How much is on the book ?*
	What is the price for the book ?
Cia meud a tha air im ?	*What is the price for butter ?*
Cia meud a tha ort ?	*How much is on you ?*
	How much do you owe ?
Cia meud a tha aig mo thighearn' ort-sa ?	*How much owest thou unto my Lord ?* Luke xvi. 5.

Is there not one at eleven o'clock ? 14. The second train will go at twelve mid-day. 15. It is only nine o'clock at present. 16. My watch is fifteen minutes slow. 17. There are twenty shillings in the pound, and twelve pence in the shilling. 18. How many pence are in the pound ? 19. He had fifteen shillings and I had ten shillings. 20. How much had we ? 21. This little boy has two feet and two hands. 22. He has two shoes on his feet. 23. The third man has six boys.

388. Correct the following and translate :—

aon ba, aon buth, aon dhuinc, da casan, da daoine, da fichead, da miltean, da broige, tri cas, tri tasdan, aon deug fir, naoi deug earba, mile caoirich, tri mile fir, a cheud fear, an ceud clach, a ceud duine, seachd caoraidh deug.

389. Examination Questions :—

1. Why should we write **aon duine** and not **aon dhuine** ?
2. Why should we not translate " men " in the plural in **da dhuine** ?
3. What is wrong with **da shgillin ; da broige ; da choise.**
4. Why should we not say **coig tasdain dheug** ?
5. Is **deug** always aspirated ?
6. Does **da** always aspirate and cause aspiration ?
7. What is the difference in **a dha** and **an da** ? Why are both not aspirated ?
8. What does **a' cheud** do that no other ordinal number does ?

LESSON XXXII.

THE PERSONAL PRONOUN.

390. Personal pronouns agree with the noun for which they stand in gender number and case, and are as follows :

Singular.

	Simple.	Emphatic.	
1st,	**mi** (*mee*)	**mise** (*meeshŭ*)	I, me.
2nd,	**thu** (*oo*)	**thusa** (*oosŭ*)	thou, thee.
3rd,	**e** (*ă*)	**esan** (*essŭn*)	he, him, it.
	i (*ee*)	**ise** (*eeshŭ*)	she, her, it.

Plural.

	Simple.	Emphatic.	
1st,	**sinn** (*sheeñn*)	**sinne** (*sheennyŭ*)	we, us.
2nd,	**sibh** (*sheev*)	**sibhse** (*sheev-shŭ*)	you
3rd,	**iad** (*eeŭtt*)	**iadsan** (*eeutt-sun*)	they, them.

391. Each personal pronoun may be declined and each may take the emphatic form through all the cases.

1st PERSON SINGULAR **mi** I.

Nom.	**mi** I.	**mise** I.	**mi-fein** myself.
Gen.	**mo** my.	**mo ... sa** my.	**mo ... fhein** my own.
Dat.	**dhomh** to me.	**dhomhsa** to myself.	**dhomh fhein** to myself.
Acc.	**mi** me.	**mise** myself.	**mi ... fhein** myself.

1st PERSON PLURAL **sinn** we.

Nom.	**sinn** we.	**sinne** we.	**sinn-fein** ourselves.
Gen.	**ar** our, of us	**ar ... ne** our	**ar ... fein** our own.
Dat.	**dhuinn** to us	**dhuinne** to us.	**dhuinn-fhein** to ourselves.
Acc.	**sinn** us.	**sinne** us.	**sinn-fhein** ourselves.

392. **Mi** and **mise** are aspirated after **bu** and **cha** in the tenses of the verb **is**.

393. **Tu** when nominative to a verb is always aspirated except with the verbs **is** and **bu** and sometimes with the relative future and subjunctive tenses of the active voice. In the accusative it is always aspirated.

bu tu   it was thou.   **buailidh tu e**, you will strike him. **bhuail iad thu**, they struck you.   **bhuail thu e**, you struck him.

394. The 3rd person singular pronoun used to be more inflected than we now have it. Nom. **se**, " he " ; Acc. **e** " him." It is still heard in this nominative form in a few instances to mark a distinction, as :—**bhuail se e**, " he struck him " ; **chuala si e** " she heard him."

395. The pronoun **sibh** " you " is frequently used in the singular number instead of **thu**, when addressing a person senior in age or in polite conversation, as :—**Ciamar tha sibh** ? " How are you ? "

396. As there is no difference in Gaelic between the nominative and objective cases, the position in the clause must fix this, as :—**bhuail e mi**, " he struck me " ; **bhuail mi e**, " I struck him."

397. The pronouns have all an emphatic form which is most frequently used with the verb **is**.

398. The word **fein** or **fhein**, corresponding to the English words " self" and " own," adds still more emphasis, as : —**mi fein**, " I myself " ; **sibh fein**, " you yourselves " ; **iad fein**, " themselves " ; **mo shluagh fhein**, " my own people " ; **mo chu fhein**, " my own dog."

399. Read in Gaelic and translate into English :—

1. Bha e fliuch an de. 2. Tha duine aig an dorus, tha e sgith. 3. Tha na gillean a' dol do'n bhaile. 4. Tha iad a' dol ann an diugh. 5. Bithidh mi anns a' bhaile am maireach. 6. Thilg* e clach agus bhuail e mi. 7. Bhuail thu e. 8. Nach do bhuail thu e ? 9. Ciamar tha sibh ? 10. Tha mi gle sgith. 11. Is e so an cu. 12. Cha'n e. 13. Is e sin cat. 14. Cha leam-sa e. 15. Bha sinn an sin sinn-fein an raoir. 16. Chunnaic mi esan agus a' chaileag anns an dorus. 17. Nach robh iad-san anns an tigh ? 18. Am bheil iad aig an dorus ? 19. Tha iad aig an dorus. 20. Nach eil iad-san aig an dorus ? 21. Cha'n eil. 22. Am bi iad anns a' bhaile ? 23. Cha bhi.

400. Translate into Gaelic :—

1. I will be in town to-morrow. 2. It is wet now. 3. The boy was at the door. 4. You struck him last night. 5. He was there yesterday. 6. Did you strike him ? 7. I threw* a stone and it struck him. 8. The stone struck the girl. 9. She was at the door. 10. They went to the town to-night. 11. They are going to-morrow. 12. We will be there the day after to-morrow. 13. Were you at home last night ? 14. I was. 15. You will be at home to-morrow. 16. I said she will not be there. 17. I was there myself last night. 18. I was not there to-day. 19. You said that you would be going this evening. 20. This book is mine and that is the boy's. 21. It was there yesterday.

LESSON XXXIII.

PREPOSITIONAL PRONOUNS.

401. All the personal pronouns unite with the prepositions, each compound forming a single word. In each case the preposition and the pronoun amalgamate in such forms as to be considerably and in some cases completely disguised.

402. These prepositional pronouns are of constant occurrence in the language—scarce a sentence in which they are not met with. They are therefore of great importance and the learner is well advised to get most of the more commonly used forms off by heart.

403. Each of these prepositional pronouns takes an emphatic increase or suffix -se, -sa, -san, -ne, and the whole word thus formed is called the emphatic form.

---

* thilg (*heeleek*) v. threw.

THE PREPOSITIONAL PRONOUNS.

404.

Prepositions.	Singular. mi me	tu thee	e him	i her	Plural. sinn us	sibh you	iad them
Aig, *at*	agam, *at me*	agad	aige, *at him*	aice, *at her*	againn	agaibh	aca
air, *on*	orm	ort	air	oirre	oirnn	oirbh	orra
ann, *in*	annam	annad	ann	innte	annainn	annaibh	annta
a, as, *out of*	asam	asad	as	aiste aisde	asainn	asaibh	asda
bho, o, *from*	bhuam, uam	bhuat	bhuaithe	bhuaipe	bhuainn	bhuaibh	bhuapa
de, *of, off*	diom, dhiom	diot, dhiot	deth, dheth	dith dhith	dinn, dhinn	dibh, dhibh	diubh dhiubh
do, *to*	domh, dhomh	duit, dhuit	da, dha	di, dhith	duinn, dhuinn	duibh, dhuibh	daibh dhaibh
fo, *under*	fodham	fodhad	fodha, foidhe	foidhpe	fodhainn	fodhaibh	fopa
gu, gus, *to, till*	chugam	chugad	chuige	chuice	chugainn	chugaibh	chuca
le, leis, *with*	leam	leat	leis	leatha	leinn	leibh	leo
mu, *about*	umam	umad	uime	uimpe	umainn	umaibh	umpa
ri, ris, *to*	rium	riut	ris	rithe	ruinn	ribh	riutha
roimh, *before*	romham	romhad	roimhe	roimpe	romhainn	romhaibh	rompa
thar, *over*	tharam	tharad	thairis air	thairis oirre	tharainn	tharaibh	tharta
troimh, *through*	tromham	tromhad	troimhe	troimpe	tromhainn	tromhaibh	trompa
eadar, *between*	—	—	—	—	eadarainn	eadaraibh	eatorra
Emphatic forms -sa, -san, -se, -ne.	agamsa etc.	agadsa etc.	aige, san etc.	aicese etc.	againne etc.	agaibhse etc.	acasan etc.

405. The dative of the pronoun, i.e. :—the prepositional pronoun must be used for " me," " him," " her," " us," " you," " them," when the meaning is " to me," " to him," etc. This can easily be seen by the sense.

Thoir dhomh freagairt,	*give me an answer.*
Thoir dhomh leabhar,	*lend me a book.*
Thug sibh uam-sa an leabhar sin.	*you have taken from me that book.*
Thoir dhaibh an t-airgiod,	*give them the money.*
Bheir mi dhuit e,	*I will give it you.*
Thoir dhomh deoch,	*give me a drink.*
Dh'innis e sgeul dhomh-sa,	*he told me a story.*
Cuir chugam litir,	*send me a letter.*

406. Read in Gaelic and translate into English :—

1. Tha leabhraichean againn. 2. Tha eagal orm. 3. Thug mi aran da. 4. Cuir uait an leabhar agus innis dhuinn sgeul no seinn oran. 5. Cuir toidhpe do chota. 6. Bha eagal mor orra. 7. Thubhairt mi rithe. 8. Falbh leis do 'n bhaile. 9. Cuir dhiot do chota fliuch. 10. Tha an t-uisge ann. 11. Theid mi leibh anns a' mhaduinn. 12. Thainig mi leo an raoir. 13. Thoir dhomh do lamh. 14. Slan leibh. 15. Is le Seumas an leabhar sin. 16. Tha leabhar aig Seumas. 17. Thug iad uaibh na leabhraichean so. 18. Chuir i oirre a cota agus thainig i le m' mhac do 'n mhonadh.

407. Translate English into Gaelic :—

1. Do not be afraid. 2. I was not afraid and I will not be afraid. 3. The man was angry to-day. 4. You were angry last night. 5. I do not know him and he does not know me. 6. This house is mine. 7. He has a house. 8. I have a house, but it is not my own house. 9. If we had bread we would not be hungry. 10. Are you not hungry? 11. I am hungry. 12. Is it raining ? 13. Was there rain yesterday ? 14. It will be wet here to-morrow, it was wet there to-day. 15. There is rain. 16. They have the books. 17. Tell them the story. 18. Do not put under me your hat. 19. I came before you last night. 20. You came between John and James. 21. They will be out of town to-day. 22. I will be with them in town the day after to-morrow. 23. We will go to the town now.

LESSON XXXIV.

POSSESSIVE PRONOUNS.

408. The possessive pronouns or possessive adjectives, which are merely the genitives of the personal pronouns, are as follows :—

	Singular.			**Plural.**		
	(before a consonant)	(before a vowel)		(before a consonant)	(before a vowel)	
1.	**mo** (*mŏ*)	m'	my.	**ar** (*ăr*)	ar n-	our.
2.	**do** (*do*)	d' ; t'*	thy.	**ur** ; **bhur**	bhur n-	your.
3.	**a** (*ŭh*)	'	his.	**an** (*ŭn*)	an	their.
	a (*ŭh*)	a h-	her.	**am** (before b f m p)		their.

* For note see following page.

409. These possessive pronouns are adjectival and precede their nouns. They cause aspiration of all aspirable consonants in the 1st and 2nd singular, and in the 3rd singular masculine.

Mo chathair,	*my chair.*	M' athair,	*my father.*
Do chu,	*thy dog.*	*D' fhalt (*dalt*),	*your hair.*
A mhac (*vachk*),	*his son.*	'Athair (*a'ür*),	*his father.*
A mac,	*her son.*	A h-athair,	*her father.*
Ar n-athair,	*our father.*	Bhur n-athair,	*your father.*
An gille,	*their boy.*	Am bàta,	*their boat.*

410. Observe that while the masculine a "his" aspirates a following consonant it does not aspirate a vowel, and again that **a** "her" aspirates a following vowel but does not aspirate a consonant.

411. The possessive pronouns do not attach the emphatic terminations as do the personal pronouns. If emphasis is to be shown the emphatic increase is attached to the noun which is qualified by the possessive, or if one or more adjectives are present it is attached to the last adjective.

>Is e so mo leabhar-sa,   *this is my book.*
>A cat beag-se.   *her little cat.*

412. **Fein** combines with the possessive as with the personal pronoun, but here it means "own"; like the emphatic termination it is placed after the noun or last adjective if any are attached.

>Mo mhac math fein,   *my own good son.*

413. In English there are distinct forms of the possessive pronouns which can stand without nouns, "mine," "thine," "his," "hers," etc. In Gaelic we have no forms corresponding to these. When they are in the predicate after the verb "to be" we use in Gaelic the prepositional pronouns formed from **le** "with" (belonging to)† (par. 188).

>This book is hers,   *tha an leabhar so leatha-se.*
>That hat is mine,   *tha an ad sin leam-sa.*
>These shoes are yours,   *tha na brogan sin leibh-se.*

---

* Before vowel and **f**+vowel nouns **do** is often hardened to an original **t** and instead of **d' fhalt** we hear **t' fhalt**; **t' athair** "thy father"; except when preceded by a preposition ending in a vowel **air t' each** "on your horse" but **do d' each** "to your horse."

† cf. French idiom :—
>*Ce livre est à moi.*   "This book is mine" (=belongs to me).

414. The possessive pronouns may be replaced by the prepositional pronouns formed from **aig** ; " my dog " **an cu agam.**

415. Thcsc possessives are used with the verbal nouns to denote a passive meaning :

Chaidh e g' a mharbhadh,   *he went to his death.*
                                    lit. *he went to his killing.*

416. Read in Gaelic and translate into English :—

1. Tha ar n-eich anns an stabull. 2. Am bheil d' each an sin ? 3. Cha'n eil. 4. Tha e anns a' phairç. 5. Tha m' athair aig an dorus, ach tha mo mhathair anns an tigh. 6. Am bheil do chu an so ? 7. Tha. 8. Tha m'fhalt fliuch a nis. 9. Is e so mo chu-sa. 10. Tha an gille aig a' bhaile. 11. Bha a mac an sin an de. 12. Cha bhi e an so am maireach. 13. Tha na brogan so leam-sa. 14. Is le Seumas an leabhar. 15. Theid thu leam. 16. Bha mo chathair briste. 17. Thilg e clach, bhuail i mo chas agus ghearr si i.

417. Translate into Gaelic :—

1. My mother is at the door. 2. Is your dog there ? 3. No, my dog is in the house. 4. My father is here now. 5. His son is not here. 6. Her son will be in the town to-morrow. 7. He is not there now. 8. Their boat struck a rock. 9. They had to come out of her. 10. They went to their death. 11. That hat is yours. 12. This house is theirs. 13. That is her coat. 14. I will go with you. 15. The book belongs to James. 16. I threw a stone and it struck his foot.

418. Correct these and translate :—

Mo falt, mo h-athair, do cu, do cas, an fear, am chu, ur thigh, mo brog-se, do suil-sa, ar bhàta-san, am n-athair, am mhac, bhur h-athair.

419. Examination Questions :—

1. What is the place of the possessive adjective ?
2. Do possessives agree with the nouns they specify ?
3. How do we express " my chair," " your chair," " his chair," " her chair " ?
4. **Cathair** is feminine ; now apply the same possessives to the masculine noun **falt** " hair."
5. Where do we put the emphatic increase when used with the possessive ?
6. How do we translate the English possessive pronouns " mine," " thine," " yours," " hers " ?
7. When do we translate " his " by **a** and when should we use **leis** ?

PREPOSITIONAL POSSESSIVE PRONOUNS.

420. There are two prepositional possessive pronouns in common use formed from the prepositions **ann** " in "

E*

and **aig** " at." These are used in idiomatic phrases with the verbal nouns. These prepositional possessive pronouns have the same influence over the nouns which may follow them as the simple possessives exercise.

421. **Ag.**

1st	'**gam**,	at my.	'**gar**,	at our.
2nd	'**gad**,	at thy.	'**gur**,	at your.
3rd	'**ga**,	at his, *or* at her.	'**gan**,	at their.

422. **Ann.**

	Singular.		*Plural.*	
1st	'**nam**,	in my.	'**nar**,	in our.
2nd	'**nad**,	in thy.	'**nur**,	in your.
3rd	'**na**,	in his, *or* in her.	'**nan**,	in their.

423. These prepositional possessives are used when in English the personal pronoun follows the participle or verbal noun (pars. 571-2).

Tha an dealg so gam chiurradh.   *this pin is hurting me*
Tha sibh 'ga chaireadh,   *you are mending it* (*at its mending*).

424. The other prepositions are also used with the possessive, but they do not enter into such close union with them as **aig** and **ann** do ; the elision of a final vowel being the only change effected.

LESSON XXXV.

IDIOMS OF THE VERB **bi** ;   **bi** WITH **ann.**

425. We have previously shown that the verbs **tha, bha, bheil,** etc., signify existence connected with locality, state, condition, and that they take the preposition or particle **ann** to strengthen them in that statement.

426. When the predicate is an appellative denoting something which belongs to the subject, the general term is limited by placing before it the prepositional possessive pronoun corresponding to the nominative.

Tha e 'na gharradh,   *he is in his garden.*
Tha e 'na thigh,   *he is in his house.*
Tha e 'na bhàta,   *he is in his boat.*

427. In these expressions the general term is limited to a particular instance of that which is denoted by it, viz. : —that which belongs to the subject. Thus the subject is in the locality denoted by the appellatives " garden," " house," etc., and particularly by the restricted definition " his garden."

428. The same idiom is used to declare the condition of the body or mind—physical, mental, or moral.

Tha e 'na shlainte,	*he is well (in his health)*
Tha e 'na chabhaig,	*he is in haste (in his haste).*
Tha e 'na chiall,	*he is in his senses.*

The state which is defined by the term " health," " his health," or " the health which is peculiar to him."

429. We have already seen the relationship which connects men and things with a large portion of their conditions and belongings.   As things or states were seen to affect us and to become related to us because they were " at us " or " with us " or " on us " so now *vice versa* things or states affect us and become related to us all the more because we are " in " them.   They are grafted as living branches into the tree of our personality ; or rather our personality is merged in them.

430. The same idiom is used to declare a man's outward attitudes.

Tha e 'na chadal,	*he is asleep (in his sleeping).*
Tha iad 'nan seasamh,	*they are standing (in their standing, in their posture of standing).*
Tha e 'na laighe,	*he is lying (he is abed).*

431. Precisely the same idiom is used to express actual existence or what is predicated of or declared of the nominative case.   Actual existence being a concrete term, the predicate by which it is expressed is a concrete term and not an abstract term.   This is the strangest and most peculiar idiom yet noticed.

A man's office, trade, or relationship :—

Bha Iain 'na sheoladair,	*John was a sailor (in his sailor).*
Tha e 'na shaor,	*he is a joiner (in his joiner).*
Tha e 'na mhinistear,	*he is a minister (in his minister).*
Tha e 'na dhuine,	*he is a man (in the state denoted by the term man, " manhood ")*

Tha e 'na athair do'n teaghlach, *he is a father to the family.*
(lit. : *he is in his father ; in his relation of father*).
Tha e 'na sheirbhiseach do Iain, *he is a servant to John.*
(lit. : *he is in his servant, in his relation of servant to John*).

432. Further examples of its use to declare a man's reputation, character, personal attributes, nationality, etc.

Tha e 'na ghaisgeach,	*he is a hero (in his hero)*
Tha i 'na sgoilear,	*she is a scholar (in her scholar).*
Tha e 'na fhirean,	*he is a just man (in his true one).*
Tha e 'na dhuine uasal,	*he is a gentleman (in his man honourable).*
Tha e 'na bhreugair,	*he is a liar.*
Tha e 'na chealgair,	*he is a cheat.*
Tha e 'na ghealtair,	*he is a coward.*
Tha an leanabh 'na ghille,	*the child is a boy (in his boy).*
Tha e 'na choigreach,	*he is a stranger.*
Tha e 'na Shasunnach,	*he is an Englishman,* or
Cha'n eil ann ach Sasunnach,	*there is not in him but an Englishman.*
Bha i 'na mnaoi ghlic,	*She was (in her) a wise woman.*
Bha an duine 'na amadan,	*the man was a fool (in his fool).*
Tha e 'na aon-fhear (par. 383)	*he is alone (in his one-man).*
Tha e 'na thruaghan,	*he is miserable (in his miserable one).*

433. Prof. Masson gives a helpful definition of this last idiom, that by converting the adjective descriptive of a man's abstract condition into a personal noun, it takes that personal noun, and so to speak plants the man in the middle of it. Thus while as in English, we say, **tha an duine balbh** " the man is dumb," yet by means of this idiom, we concrete and animate the man's abstract quality of dumbness, and, planting him in the heart of our creation, we say, **tha an duine 'na bhalbhan** " the man is in his dumb one," or as, owning the influence of this Gaelic idiom, we would say vulgarly, " he is a dummie."

434. Another similar Gaelic idiom in very common use may be illustrated here. We have shown that the man can exist " in his carpenter " ; that the subject can exist in a quality ; but in Gaelic a quality can also be said to exist in a subject. The " carpenter " can exist in the man, as well as the man " in his carpenter."

Is e saor tha annad, (lit.) *it is a carpenter that is in you.*
Cha'n eil innte ach a' ghlaoic, *she is but a silly woman.*

435. Read in Gaelic and translate into English :—

1. Tha e 'na oglach. 2. Tha e 'na chabhaig. 3. Tha mi 'nam gharradh. 4. Tha mi 'nam thigh. 5. Tha iad 'nam bàta. 6. Tha sinn 'nar cadal. 7. Tha mi 'nam laighe. 8. Bha e 'na chiall. 9. Tha e 'na mhinistear. 10. Tha e 'ga bhualadh. 11. Tha i 'ga bualadh. 12. An robh each 'gad bhreabadh ? 13. Cha robh, bha e 'ga bhreabadh-san 14. Tha thu 'nad dhuine math. 15. Tha thu 'nad bhreugair. 16. Bha e 'na dhroch dhuine.

436. Translate into Gaelic :—

1. My horse is in the field but his is in his garden. 2. Her brothers are in your father's house. 3. They were on their ship. 4. James was a sailor. 5. They say John is a joiner. 6. She was striking him and he was striking her. 7. I was a stranger. 8. He is in his boat. 9. I am standing. 10. He was asleep in his house. 11. You are in haste. 12. I am well. 13. She was a cheat. 14. The boy was a fool. 15. He was a coward. 16. That man was a gentleman.

LESSON XXXVI.

437. THE RELATIVE PRONOUN.

a	(*üh*)	who, whose, whom, which, that
an	(*ün*)	which, that (dative after a preposition) **becomes**
am	(*üm*)	which, that (dative) before **b, f, m,** or **p.**
na	(*nüh*)	what, that which.
nach	(*nach*)	who not, which not, that not, but.

438. As the relative **a** has no inflection for case, the construction or context must determine whether the relative is nominative to the verb which follows it, or is governed by it in the accusative, as :—**an gille a bhuail mi** may mean either " the boy who struck me " or " the boy whom I struck."

439. The relative **a** is the same for each case.

Nom. and Acc. **a** " who " ; *Gen.* **a** " whose " ; *Dative* **a** " whom."

440. After all the cases the verb is aspirated and has a special form used in the future ending in **as** or **eas** (par. 510).

Am fear a thuit,	*the man who fell.*
An gille a tha dubh,	*the boy who is black.*
Am mac a bha fuar,	*the son who was cold.*
Am fear a bhitheas fuar,	*the man who will be cold.*
Am fear a bhitheadh fuar,	*the man who would be cold.*
An gille a dh'ith an t-aran	*the boy who ate the bread.*
Am fear a thogas a' chìs,	*the man who collects the tax.*
A' chìs a thogas am fear,	*the tax which the man collects.*
An duine a dh'fhosgail an dorus,	*the man who opened the door.*

441. The genitive of the relative **a** is distinguished by the presence of a possessive pronoun thus :—" the boy whose book I took," **an gille a thug mi a leabhar** (" the boy of whom I took his book ")

An duine a fhuair thu a chuid,   *the man of whom you received his property.*

Sud a' bhean a bha sinn anns an tigh aice,   *yon is the woman in whose house we were.*

Am fear a thainig a mhac gu baile,   *the man whose son came home.*

442. The dative is usually strengthened by a preposition.

Na daoine a dh'fhuirich thu aca,   *the men with whom you stayed.*
An te a tha thu suirdhe oirre,   *the girl whom thou art courting.*

443. In Gaelic the relative is frequently used adverbially in an explanatory way as in the phrase :—**Cia mar a tha sibh ?** " How are you " (**lit.** " How is it that you are ") (par. 450-1).

444. The only change for case in the relative **a** is in the dative after a preposition, where it takes the form of **an**, changing the **n** into **m** before **b, f, m,** or **p**. Prepositions which take an **s** before the definite article take it also in this position. The relative drops the **a** following vowels ; in some places is represented by an apostrophe and sometimes all trace of it is omitted.

An obair ris an robh mi,   *the work at which I was.*
An tigh anns am bi sinn,   *the house in which we shall be.*
Am bord air am bitheadh e,   *the table on which it would be.*
An t-eilean far am bheil iad,   *the island where they are.*
A' chiste air an do chuir mi e,   *the chest on which I put it.*
An cupan as an ol mi,   *the cup out of which I shall drink.*
An gille bho'n d'thug mi a leabhar.   *the boy from whom I took his book.*
   the boy whose book I took.

445. The relatives **an, am, a', 'n,** when coming immediately after a preposition and before a verb must not be mistaken for the article or the verbal interrogative particle.

446. The relative negative **nach** gives little trouble and may be illustrated in a few sentences. It is followed by the dependent form of the verb.

Am fear nach cuala mi,	*the man who did not hear me.*
Am bord air nach bitheadh e,	*the table on which it would not be.*
An tigh nach do thog mi,	*the house which I did not build.*
An obair ris nach robh mi,	*the work at which I was not.*
Thubhairt e nach bitheamaid,	*he said that we would not be.*

447. Na " what " follows the construction of a relative, but has never any antecedent expressed. It is used like " that " and " what " in English (with an idea of totality).

Chuala mi na thubhairt thu,	*I heard (all of) what you said.*
Phaidh Iain na cheannaich e,	*John paid what he bought.*
Fhuair mi na dh'iarr mi,	*I got what I asked.*
An e sin na tha agad ?	*Is that all you have?*
Tha mi coma air son na chaill mì,	*I care not for what I lost.*

448. THE VERB is IN RELATIVE SENTENCES.

The Relative Forms of the Verb **is** are :—

Present **is, as** : Past **a bu** : Neg. **nach.**

is and **as** aspirate verbs with initial **f** followed by a vowel.
bu aspirates all aspirable consonants except a **d** or **t**.

449. These forms are usually found with the comparative and superlative of adjectives and sometimes with the positive.

Is tu am fear as fhearr,	*you are the best man.*
(lit. :	*you are the man who is best).*
Bu mhise am fear a bu fhearr,	*I was the best man.*
Tir nach beag,	*a land which is not small.*
Am fear is aithne dhomh,	*the man whom I know.*
Am fear is mo a tha ann diubh,	*the biggest man there is of them.*
Am fear is righ an Albainn,	*the man who is king in Scotland.*
Ciod is crioch araid do'n duine ?	*what is the chief end of man?*
A' bheinn as airde anns an t-saoghal.	*the highest mountain in the world.*
B'i Mairi a b'airde de'n teaghlach	*Mary was the tallest of the family.*

450. An English sentence containing a nominative case, verb and adjective, is often translated into Gaelic in a relative sentence. Take **tha mi tinn** " I am sick " ; this can be reproduced in Gaelic in a peculiar idiom and one very often heard in Highland English as the effect of adopting the Gaelic idiom.* The Gael can lay special

---

* French :
Qui est-ce qui vient de vous parler ?   Who has just spoken to you ?
   (*lit.* who is it that comes to you speak) ?
Qu'est-ce que vous dites ?   What do (*lit.* What is it that) you say ?

stress on the adjective by bringing it forward to the beginning of the sentence, thus :—**is tinn a tha mi** " I am (very) sick," " it is sick that I am," and so in the negative question **nach tinn a tha e** ? " is it not sick that he is ? "

451. Similarly " it is I who am here," " it was I who was there." In these English sentences when the second verb is, in the past tense the introductory verb is also in the same tense. In Gaelic the introductory verb generally is in the present tense, though the second verb may be past or future tense.

Is mise a tha ann,	*I am here=It is I who am here.*
Is mise a bha ann,	*I was there=It (is) was I who was there.*
Nach tu a bha ann ?	*Is it not you that was there ?*
Is mise a bhitheas ann,	*It is I who will be there.*

452. **Gu'n**, which is a relative conjunction is a contraction for **gu** " to, unto, with " and **an** the dative case of the relative **a.** It is used to signify a wish or idea and implies that a sentence which is not expressed precedes the clause it introduces.

(Is e mo mhiann-sa) gu'm bu slan a chi mi thu.
(It is my wish) that I may see you well.
B' fhearr leam gu'n tigeadh tu.
I wish that thou would'st come (lit. : *I wish to that thou would'st come=I wish to the effect that you would'st come*).

453. Similarly, the other prepositions combine with the relative :—

do'n	" to whom, to which."
mu'n	" about whom, before that."
fo'n	" under whom, under which."
o'n	" from whom, from that."

454. Read in Gaelic and translate into English :—

1. Is e am fear a dh'ith an t-aran. 2. Is e an gille a bha fuar. 3. An duine a thug thu bhuaithe a bhàta. 4. Cia mar a tha thu? 5. Is e an gille a bhuail mi. 6. An obair ris an robh thu. 7. Thubhairt e gu'n robh mi tinn. 8. An cupan as an ol thu. 9. Am bord air nach bi e. 10. Chuala mi na thubhairt iad. 11. An d'thubhairt iad gu'n robh iad fuar ? 12. C'aite am bheil an gille a fhuair an sgian ? 13. Nach eil e anns an stabull ? 14. Co bha anns an dorus ? 15. Is e so am fear nach gabh a' bhean. 16. Am fear nach cuala mi. 17. An tigh anns an robh e. 18. Co bha leis na gillean anns an achadh ? 19. Bha na fir leis na gillean.

455. Translate into Gaelic :—

1. That man paid what he got. 2. Who is he ? 3. What is it ?
4. He is the man who has the horse. 5. I slept in the house in which
he was. 6. Who has that horse in the field ? 7. Who lost the knife
in the house ? 8. Who is it that lost this knife in my house ? 9. We
saw the boy who was in the boat. 10. I was there. 11. It is my wish
that you may see me well. 12. He will be the best man. 13. The
highest mountain in Scotland. 14. What is the chief end of man ?
15. That is not the house where we were. 16. That is the man who
opened the door.

LESSON XXXVII.

456. Interrogative Relative Pronouns.

Co ? (*ko*) who is ? ; **co e** ? who is he ? ; **co i** ? who is she.

The Gaelic verb **Is** is completely eclipsed, but is still
understood after the interrogative relative.

co dhiubh ? (*ho yoo*) which of them ? (properly of two).
co aca ? (*ko ach-kü*) which of them ? among them ? (of many).
co leis ? (*ho lāsh*) whose ? (lit. : whom with ?).
co sam bith (*ko süm be*) whoever, whatever (who in the world).
ciod ? (*küt*) what is ? **ciod e so** ? what is this ?
cia ? (*ky*) what ? which ? how ?
cia meud ? (*ky mätt*) how many ? how much ?
de ? (*tchā*) what ? (from **ciod**) **de tha so** ? what is this ?

457. The English interrogative possessive " whose " is
translated into Gaelic by the idiom \" whom with " *
(par. 188, 413 and note).

Co leis an leabhar so ?   *whose is this book ?*
Is leam-sa e,   *It is mine (with me).*

458. Co and **ciod** when occurring in the middle of a
phrase are affirmative and not interrogative. **Ciod** is often
followed by the relative **a** when affirmative, though this
latter can be sometimes understood.

Cha n'eil fios agam co (a is) iad,   *I do not know who they are.*
Chunnaic mi co (a) bha anns an   *I saw who was in (at) the door.*
    dorus.
Tha fios agam ciod a ni feum da,   *I know what will do good to him.*

459.   *Vocabulary.*

mu, conj. (*moo*), about.
labhairt vn. (*llāv-ürtch*) speaking.
seoladair (*shyollüttür*) a sailor.
maileid, nf. (*māllatch*), a bag.

caileag, nf. (*kālük*), a girl.
rinn, v. irr. p. (*roynn*), did.
sgeul, nm. (*skāll*), a story.
theich, v. p. (*hāych*), ran away.

---

* French :   *A qui est ce livre ?*   Whose (*lit.* : to whom) is this **book ?**

460. Read in Gaelic and translate into English :—

1. Co leis so ? 2. Nach eil fios agaibh co e ? 3. Bha am bàta,air an robh sinn, air a bhriseadh. 4. Sin an t-achadh anns nach eil craobh. 5. Co aig am bheil an t-airgiod ? 6. Co leis an t-airgiod ? 7. Bha am fear o'n d'fhuair sinn am bàta 'na sheoladair. 8. Ciod e mu'm bheil sibh a' labhairt ? 9. Cheannaich mi an t-each nach do cheannaich sibh-se. 10. Thug mi an leabhar so do dhuine aig nach robh airgiod. 11. Co e rinn so ? 12. De tha so ? 13. Is e so cu. 14. Ciod e sin ? 15. Is i a' mhaileid sin a bha aig a' chaileig. 16. Co air bith thug i do'n chaileig ? 17. Co bha leis na gillean anns an achadh ? 18. Bha na fir leis na gillean. 19. Co bhris an uinneag ? 20. Co aca rinn sin ? 21. Is e Calum no Iain a bhris i.

461. Translate into Gaelic :—

1. Who is he ? 2. I do not know who he is. 3. Do you know who is at the door ? 4. Who is it ? 5. The boy who broke the window is here now. 6. The girl whom you saw ran away. 7. Who did it ? 8. Which of them did it? 9. What is it ? 10. James gave it to me, but a man broke it. 11. He went into the house in which his sons were. 12. He bought the boat from a sailor who had no money. 13. The man from whom I got the story was a soldier, who was not young. 14. The man who struck me ran away. 15. Who was he ? 16. I did not know him. 17. The boat of which you were speaking is on the shore. 18. Whose was it ? 19. It would be the fisherman's boat. 20. Which of them said that ? 21. Whoever said it ran away. 22. What is this ? 23. It is a bag they gave me. 24. Which of them gave you that ? 25. Whose is this ? 26. Is it not yours ? 27. No.

LESSON XXXVIII.

THE DEMONSTRATIVES.

462. The demonstratives are mostly used as adjectives to distinguish one or more objects from others spoken of, and point out their distance from and proximity to the speaker. They do not aspirate in any position, nor do they cause aspiration to other words.

so   (*shoh*)   this, these, here.
sin   (*shin*)   that, those, there.
sud   (*shoott*)   yon, yonder, that, there (used as a pronoun).
ud   (*oott*)   yon, yonder, that, there (used after a noun).

463. They are used as adjectives limiting a noun or pro noun as regards time or place. They are indeclinable for person or number and always follow the noun. The latter must always be preceded by the definite article.

An duine so,   *" this man "* (the man here=close at hand).
An duine sin,   *" that man "* (the man there =some distance away)
An duine ud,   *" yon man "* (the man yonder =much further away)

464. They may be used as a pronoun or attached to a pronoun :—

Tha so math,	*this is good.*	Chi mi sin,	*I see that.*
E so,	*this one, this person.*	I sin,	*that one.*
Sin agad e,	*there you have it.*	Sin ri radh,	*that is to say.*
Sud an t-aite,	*yonder is the place.*	Sud e,	*yonder he is.*

465. They may be used after the prepositions :—

An so,	*here.*	Gun sin,	*without that.*
Uaithe so,	*from here, hence.*	Mar sin,	*so that, like that.*
Mar so,	*thus, in this manner.*	Mar sud,	*like yon.*

466. A euphonic **a** appears when they are used after a preposition ending in an **s**.

As a sin,	*out of that.*	Leis a sin,	*with that.*
		Gus a so,	*until this, up till now.*

467. Used adverbially preceding a definite noun, these demonstratives become indistinguishable from adverbs of place. The verb **is** is generally understood though omitted (par. 161).

So a' bheinn,	*this is the hill=here is the hill.*
Sin am baile,	*that is the town=there is the town.*
Sud na tighean,	*yonder are the houses.*
Sin iad a' tighinn,	*there they are coming ; that is them coming.*

468. You must always distinguish carefully between the demonstrative " that " and the relative " that."

Bhuail mi an t-each sin,	*I struck that horse.*
Sin an t-each a bhuail mi,	*that is the horse that I struck.*
Is e an t-each sin a bhuail mi;	*It is that horse that I struck.*

469. Read in Gaelic and translate into English :—

1. Tha a' bho so dubh.   2. 'S ann dubh a tha a' bho so.   3. 'S i bo dhubh a tha an so.   4. De tha so, a Mhairi ?   5. Is e so maide mor. 6. C'aite an robh a' bhean ud ?   7. Bha i anns an tigh sin.   8. Tha am fear so fliuch.   9. Tha am fear sin 'na bhàta.   10. De tha sin ? 11. Is e sin cu.   12. De tha sud ?   13. Is e sud bàta.   14. Cha'n e sud bàta.   15. Sin ri radh gu'm bheil mi 'nam bhreugair.   16. Sin agad e.   17. Leis a sin bhuail mi e.   18. Tog sin.

470. Translate into Gaelic :—

1. This dog is black.   2. That dog is not black.   3. This is a white cow.   4. Yon cow is not white.   5. What is that ?   6. Who is this ?

7. It is that man.　8. This boy is wet.　9. He says that he was there.
10. With that I will go home.　11. What is that you have ?　12. I do
not know this dog.　13. This is not the book I found last night.
14. That is they coming from the town.　15. That is the town on
the hill there.

471. Examination Questions :—

1. Do demonstratives in Gaelic agree with the nouns which they
　　serve to demonstrate ?
2. When may we term the demonstrative an adjective ?
3. Give an illustration.
4. When are demonstrative pronouns so called ?
5. How are they used ?
6. When do we translate " that " by **sin** and when by **a** ?
7. How are they used ?
8. What is the similarity between the Gaelic translation of " this "
　　" that," and " here " " there " ?

LESSON XXXIX.

472.　　INDEFINITE PRONOUNS, ETC.

cach, the rest, the others ;　**am measg chach,** among the rest.
cach-a-cheile (*kach-ŭ-chālŭ*), one another, each other.
cuid (*kootch*), a share, some (followed by the genitive of nouns, but if
　　the noun is definite, the preposition **de**, " of," is used before
　　the article, and the noun is put in the dative) :—**cuid chlach,**
　　" some stones " ;　**cuid de na clachan,** " some of the stones " ;
　　tha cuid ag radh, " some are saying."
cuid na's mò, a greater share ; more ;　**cuid na's mò de na clachan,**
　　" more stones."
cuid as mò, the greatest share, most ;　**cuid as mò de na clachan,**
　　" most of the stones."
cuid-eiginn (*kootch-ākin*), some one (some certain one), somebody.
cuid-fein, own ;　own share.　**mo chuid fein,** " my own."
eile (*ālŭ*), other (follows noun).　**fear eile,** " another man."
eiginn, some, any (follows noun).　**fear eiginn,** " some man."
feadhainn (*fyāghynn*), some people.　**feadhainn eile,** " others."
fein (*fān*)　(*a*) after a pronoun or prepositional pronoun means " self."
　　　　mi-fein, " myself " ;　**sinn-fein,** " ourselves."
　　　　(*b*) after a noun preceded by a possessive pronoun means
　　　　　" own " ;　**mo thigh fhein,** " my own house."
　　　　(*c*) after the prepositional pronoun **le** " with," " by," **fein**
　　　　　means " alone "—**bha mi leam fein,** " I was alone."

　　Cuid in these expressions signifies any indefinite number of a
whole and **cach** (or **an corr**) all the rest of it.
　　Cuid as a noun is fem. and very irregular, see declension, par. 282.
　　Thoir do chach e,　　　　*give it to the rest.*
　　Thoir dhomhs' an corr,　　*give me the remainder.*

ge b'e (*ga*) ⎱ Whoever (is followed by the relative pronoun **a**,
ge b'e neach ⎰ " who ")—**ge b' e neach a chluinneas**, " whoever
(*lit.* whoever he was) will hear."

ge b' e ni. Whatever (is followed by the relative pronoun **a** " who ")
—**ge b' e ni a rinn sibh**, " whatever you have done."

ge b' e aite, wherever (is followed by the relative **a**).

gach, each, every ; **gach fear** (m), **gach te*** (f) " each one."

gach uile, every ; **gach uile fhear**, " every man."

gin (*geen*), some one ; **cha robh gin an so**, " there was no one here."

iomadh (*yeemy*), many a ; **iomadh bliadhna air ais**, " many a year
back." **iomadh uair**, many a time.

iomlan (*eem-llan*), the whole. **an t-iomlan dhiubh**, the whole of them.

moran, many (followed by the genitive—**moran sluaigh**, " many
people," " many of people."

neach, some one, any one, an individual.

neach sam bith, any one ; **neach air bith**, anyone at all.

sam bith, any (follows noun) ; **duine sam bith**, " any man."

The following pronouns are followed by the preposition
de, " of " and the dative case of the noun.

uile (*oolü*),	all, every.	**uiread** (*oorütt*)	so much.
na h-uile,	the whole, all.	**a leithid so** (*lyätch*)	such.
a h-uile,	everyone.	**a leithid eile,**	such another.

473. *Vocabulary.*

bheir (*vār*) irr. v.,	will give.
theid (*hätch*), irr. v.,	will go.
ni (*nye*) irr. v.,	will do.
leanaidh (*lyăny*) v.,	will follow.
ni, -thean, nm. (*nyee*),	a thing, things.
cearr (*hyâr*), adj.	wrong.
obair (*opür*) nf.	work.

474. Read in Gaelic and translate into English :—
1. Cia meud craobh tha anns a' gharradh ? 2. De tha thu ag radh ?
3. Bha na gillean anns a' phairc an de agus thilg iad clachan air
cach-a-cheile. 4. Co bhris an uinneag ? 5. Bha na h-uile a' briseadh uinneag 6. Co air bith tha an so a nis, bithidh mi an sin an
nochd. 7. Tha cuid ag radh gu'm bheil mi bochd. 8. Cha 'n eil
fios againn. 9. Cuin a dh' fhalbh thu ? 10. Tha sinn 'nar tigh fein.
11. Chaidh gach fear d'a thigh fein. 12. Tha chuid as mo de na
clachan mora anns an achadh sin. 13. Tha na h-uile de na clachan
beaga anns an achadh sin eile. 14. Ge b'e ni a rinn sibh ni fir eile.
15. Bha mi leam fein air a' bhàta. 16. Cha robh gin an sin. 17.
Theid moran sluaigh an sin a nis. 18. Bha na h-uile shluagh anns

---

* **Fear** (m) in the sense "one" is applied to all nouns masculine
whether signifying persons or things, and **te** (f) "one" is similarly
applied to all nouns feminine. **te air bith** any woman; **te elginn**
some woman; some one (f); **te eile** another one (f).

a' phairc. 19. Theid gach fear dachaidh. 20. Co e an duine sin.agus ciod e 'obair ? 21. Tha cuid ag radh gu'm bheil e 'na shaor. 22. Cuin a dh' fhalbh e ? 23. Airgiod no or cha'n eil agam, ach an ni a tha agam bheir mi dhuit.

475. Translate into Gaelic :—

1. Some of the stones in this field are big, but the others are small. 2. There are more big stones in that other field. 3. Most of the stones here are big. 4. I have big stones in my own field. 5. All the stones in your own field are small. 6. I will be in his house to-night, but I will go to my own house to-morrow. 7. Some say that he was alone. 8. There was no* one there last night. 9. Many people were there yesterday, but everyone had gone away. 10. It is many a year back since many people were here. 11. What is that ? 12. Whatever you will do others will do also. 13. Wherever you will go the rest will follow. 14. Most of these windows are broken. 15. Every window is broken now. 16. Which of the men will go ? 17. Anyone of them is ready. 18. Some say he is a joiner. 19. Everyone is saying it now. 20. They are all wrong. 21. I did not know I was wrong. 22. What will you give for this dog ? 23. That dog is not yours, it is my own dog.

476. " No " in these sentences* is translated by using an indefinite pronoun preceded by a dependent form of the verb and the negative **cha.** Observe the following examples where : " no " and " none " = " not any " " not one " ; " nobody " by " not anyone " ; " nothing " by " not anything " ; " never " by " not ever."

Cha'n eil a h-aon gun choire,	*there is none without fault.*
Cha'n eil dad an so,	*there is nothing here (not anything).*
Cha'n eil neach sam bith an sin,	*there is nobody there (not anyone).*
Cha robh a h-aon aig an tigh,	*there was nobody (no one) at home.*
Cha'n abair mi dad,	*I will say nothing (not anything).*
Cha'n fhaca mi riamh e,	*I never saw him.*
Cha toigh leam neach ach thusa,	*I love nobody but you.*

LESSON XL.

THE VERB.

477. The Gaelic verb is very different from the English verb in form and structure, and is very closely allied to the Greek verb. The whole of the tenses of our Gaelic verb are formed from its root, which is the 2nd singular imperative, the order of command, as :— **tog,** lift (thou) ; **buail,** strike.

478. From this root, the conjugation of verbs is effected by prefixing particles, by occasionally aspirating an initial consonant, or by affixing a termination. Sometimes all these operate together, sometimes the particle and aspiration only, and sometimes the aspiration alone.

479. All verbs in the Gaelic language are regular, and have their tenses formed in exactly the same fashion, except the ten irregular verbs which agree to no rule, and of which a list is given, showing all their parts complete. Every verb is regular in the imperative mood.

480. There are two voices, an active and a passive. The active voice is that form of a verb which shows that the subject of the sentence stands for the doer of the action expressed by the verb. The passive voice is that form of a verb which shows that the subject of the sentence stands for the object of the action expressed by the verb.

481. Compare the two statements : **bhuail mi** and **bha mi buailte.** The same word is the subject of each sentence—the nominative to each verb. But in the first statement, the subject **mi** stands for the doer of the act of **buailte**, while in the second statement, the subject **mi** stands for the object, or receiver, of the act of **buailte.** In the first sentence, the verb is said to be in the active voice ; in the second, it is said to be in the passive.

482. A sentence may be changed from the active to the passive form, by turning the object into the subject, and the subject into the object.

Act., *they struck the table.* bhuail iad am bord.
Pass., *the table was struck by them.* bhuaileadh am bord leotha.

483. The Gaelic verb has only two time tenses, viz., the past and the future, and it has another which, for want of a better name, may be called the subjunctive, translated by the addition of the word " would," as, " he would go."

484. The indicative mood is so called because it simply points out a connection or agreement between a subject and predicate. In Gaelic it has two forms, an independent and a dependent. Many grammarians show an interro-

gative and conditional form but all these are merely the dependent form used with the respective qualifying particles which effect this change of meaning.

485. The independent or absolute form simply makes a statement and is used in affirmative propositions only, as :—**bhuail mi**, " I struck "; **bha mi a' bualadh**, " I was striking."

486. The dependent or conjoint form is used in negative, interrogative, and conditional clauses after the particles except **ma** (par. 494).

487. The subjunctive makes a statement, but it generally does this in a hesitating and uncertain manner. It expresses a condition, motive or wish. Used in its simple form it corresponds to the English tense formed by the auxiliary " would."

488. The imperative mood expresses a desire, whether purpose, command, or request, as :—**buaileam**, " let me strike " ; **na h-abair facal**, " speak not a word."

489. The infinitive is hardly in the strict sense a mood at all, being properly the verb used as a substantive or verbal noun denoting the energy of the verb. These verbal nouns enter largely into the composition of the compound tenses, both active and passive. Preceded by the preposition **ag, a',** " at," they express continuous or progressive action in combination with the verb **bi**. As only the verb **bi** has a present tense, all other verbs mark present time by this means (par. 192). Preceded by the preposition **air** in a similar idiom they express a completed action.

Infinitive,　　　　**a bhualadh**,　" to strike."
Compound present tense, **a' bualadh**,　" striking " (*lit.*, at striking).
Compound perfect tense, **air bualadh**,　" struck " (*lit.*, after striking).

490. The verbal adjective is used with the substantive verbs **bi, tha, bheil,** etc., to express a form of the passive voice, as :—

　　　Tha an dorus fosgailte,　　　*the door is open.*

491. Observe that in the various tenses of the Gaelic verb (with the exception of the subjunctive and imperative) the termination of the verb throughout all the persons of

the same tense is the same in the singular and plural numbers. Hence the person of the verb is only known by its nominative.

492. The use of one sign to convey one idea is advanced in a book on speech recently published. The author says, " It is more logical to say **I is, thou is, he is,** than **I am, thou art, he is,** since logic demands that we should always use the same sign to indicate the same idea."* Again we have **I love, they love,** but **he loves.** The **s** in **loves** does not signify anything, **he loves** signifies no more than if we should say **he love.**

493. The verb **bi**, already given on page 16 and subsequent pages in all its details, is a good guide to the whole construction of a verb, and if carefully studied will help the pupil very materially to grasp and understand the various changes in the tense. It is as regards the future, subjunctive, and imperative a regular verb.

The Verbal Particles.

494. The nature and effect of these will be already known to the student from their use with the verb **bi** in the earlier chapters, the following is a résumé.

do   The particle **do** (par. 498)

an ?   Interrogative particle. Preceding a verb changes its meaning to ask a question. The **n** changes to **m** before **b, f, m**, and **p** ; causes eclipsis. **An** has the effect of interrogation though the verb itself be omitted.

An tog sibh ?	*will you lift* ?
Am buail sibh ?	*will you strike* ?
An do bhuail mi an dorus ?	*did I strike the door* ?
An teid (*tchătch*) thu leam ?	*will you go with me* ?
Am mi an duine ?	*am I the man* ?
cf. Cha'n aithne dhomh an teid thu,	*I don't know whether you will go.*
Gach aite an teid thu,	*each place where you go.*

cha   " not." **Cha** simply negatives the meaning of the verb and is used in all the tenses except in the imperative, where we use **na** instead. **Cha**† aspirates the con-

---

* The Philosophy of Speech, by George Willis (1919).

† The initial aspiration of **cha** is due to a lost particle **ni, no.** In Old Gaelic we can trace it in **nicon, nocha, no chon,** etc., literally " not that." In the modern language the actual particle of negation

sonants **g, c, m, p,** and **b** excepting the verb **bu;**
d, t, and **s** resist aspiration.   **Cha'n** always aspirates
f verbs, and the **n** is also retained before a vowel.

Cha'n fhosgail mi an dorus,	*I shall not open the door.*
Cha seinn mi,	*I shall not sing.*
Cha do thog mi,	*I did not lift.*
Cha'n iarr mi,	*I will not ask.*
Cha ghabh mi tuille,	*I will not take more.*
Cha mhi,	*it is not I.*
Cha bu tu,	*it was not you.*

na The imperative negative particle, it being used only
in the imperative mood to make an imperative prohibition, as :—**na treig a' Ghaidhlig,** "forsake not the
Gaelic." ; **na buail,** "don't strike."

nach The interrogative negative particle, as it asks a
question in a negative manner, as :—

Nach do thog iad a' chlach ?	*did they not lift the stone ?*
Nach do bhristeadh i ?	*was it not broken ?*

ma Conditional particle "if"; it is used with the past
independent and the future relative tenses of all verbs,
and in the present and past independent tenses of
the verb **bi**.   It aspirates all consonants and requires
dh' before all vowels, as :—

Ma bhuaileas iad,	*if they will strike.*
Ma dh' iarras sibh,	*if ye will ask.*
Ma tha mi,	*if I am.*
Ma bhuail mi,	*if I struck.*

na'n Conditional particle "if." Complementary to **ma.**
It is used where ***ma** is not used :—the past dependent
and subjunctive tenses of all verbs, and the past
dependent of the verb **bi—robh.**   It does not cause
aspiration. The **n** changes to **m** before **b, f, m,** and **p.**

Na'n robh mi,	*if I was.*
Na'n tiginn,	*if I would come.*
Na'n do bhuail e,	*if he did strike.*
Na'n d'ol mi,	*if I drank.*
Na'm bitheadh e,	*if he were.*
Na'n do ghlacadh e,	*if he would be caught.*

---

has been lost and **cha** and **cha'n** remain in appearance a negative
but etymologically introductory of a dependent clause.   That the
n of **cha'n** is organic is evident when it is still retained before vowels,
and also from the fact that **cha** does not aspirate **d, t,** or **s.**

* For note see following page.

mur Conditional negative particle " if not." It is used in all the tenses, of the dependent form, as :—

Mur glac mi,	*if I will not catch.*
Mur glacteadh iad,	*if they were not caught.*
Mur (an) do bhuail mi,	*if I did not strike.*

ged (a) Conditional particle " though " " although." It is used with the independent forms of the verb **bi—tha, bha,** and with the independent forms of all other verbs in the past, subjunctive, and future relative tenses. It aspirates all aspirable consonants and requires **dh'** before vowels (**ged a** being **ge +do**; it is **do** which causes aspiration). This **a** is a euphonic particle and not necessarily the relative, though it claims the rights of the relative as regards the form of the verb which follows it in the future.

Ged a tha mi,	*though I am, although I am.*
Ged a bha mi,	*though I was.*
Ged a thogas mi,	*though I will lift.*
Ged a dh' iarras mi,	*though I will ask.*

ged nach Conditional negative particle " though not," " although not," used thus :—

Ged nach do bhuail e,	*though he did not strike.*
Ged nach glacar an duine,	*though the man will not be caught.*

gu'n A relative conjunctive particle serving to introduce a dependent clause. Its antecedent may or may not be expressed (par. 452). The **n** changes to **m.**

Thubhairt e gu'n do thog e iad,	*he said that he lifted them.*
Gu'm buail mi an dorus,	*that I shall strike the door.*

nach A negative relative conjunctive particle " that not," " who not," serving to introduce a dependent negative relative sentence.

Thubhairt e nach do thog e iad,	*he said that he did not lift them.*
An duine nach do thuit,	*the man who did not fall.*

---

*Synopsis of what may be called the " Conditional Mood."

	Consonant verb, **bi** be	Cons. verb (f+ vowel) **faisg** squeeze.	Vowel verb, **ol** drink.
Pres. Indpt.,	**ma tha mi**		
Past Indpt.,	**ma bha mi**	**ma dh'fhaisg mi**	**ma dh'ol mi**
Past Dept.,	**na'n robh mi**	**na'n d'fhaisg mi**	**na'n d'ol mi**
Fut. Rel.,	**ma bhitheas mi**	**ma dh'fhaisgeas mi**	**ma dh'olas mi**
Subjunctive,	**na'm bithinn**	**na'm faisginn**	**na'n olainn**
	if I am, was, *etc.*	*if I squeezed,* *etc.*	*if I drank,* *etc.*

495. It will be noticed that **nach** has three different meanings, but no ambiguity need arise, as if it is the interrogative negative it comes at the beginning of the clause or sentence without an antecedent ; if the conjunctive negative it follows a verb ; and if the relative negative it follows its noun.

Nach buail sibh ?   *will you not strike ?*
Thubhairt e nach do bhuail e,   *he said that he did not strike.*
'S e sin an duine nach do thuit,   *that is the man who did not fall.*

FORMATION OF THE TENSES.

496. The changes on the termination are made to one model and by the same rules, but in order to illustrate the initial changes it may be convenient to arrange all verbs into three classes according as they begin with a consonant, a vowel, or an **f**, as vowels are unaspirable, and **f** when aspirated is silent, and thus the verb would in this case begin with a vowel sound, and must be treated accordingly. Their chief difference consists in the use of the particle **do** which aspirates the verb, and which is itself aspirated and contracted **dh'** and **d'**.

LESSON XLI.

THE PAST TENSE, ACTIVE VOICE.

497. In Gaelic, the past tense may fulfil more than one function. It may take the meaning of the aorist, the perfect, and even the pluperfect tenses as we know them in English.

498. The formation of the past tense is invariably (except in the case of the ten irregular verbs and the substantive verb) effected by taking the bare root preceded by the verbal particle **do** and appending the personal pronouns. Aspiration of an aspirable consonant of a root is caused by this particle. When the verb is used in an affirmative independent sentence the particle **do** is omitted before a verb beginning with a consonant ; but the aspiration remains ; thus from **buail** we would have **do bhuail mi** or usually **bhuail mi, bhuail thu,** etc.

499. But if the root verb begin with a vowel, the particle is not omitted as otherwise there would be no difference between it and the future dependent tense, for aspiration of a vowel cannot otherwise be shown. The aspiration is thrown back on the. particle **do** and its vowel is elided. Thus the past tense of **innis** " tell " is **dh'innis mi** " I told." As already stated a root with initial **f** is treated as if it began with a vowel, thus, **fag** " leave " becomes **dh'fhag mi** (*ghâk*) " I left."

1. **bhuail mi**	**dh'innis mi**	**dh'fhag mi**
2. **bhuail thu**	**dh'innis thu**	**dh'fhag thu**
3. **bhuail e**	**dh'innis e**	**dh'fhag e**
etc.	etc.	etc.

500. In the dependent tense forms, the particle **do** is retained before the consonants ; contracting to **d'** before vowel and **f** verbs ; causing the latter to also aspirate.

Cha do bhuail mi, Cha d'innis mi (*tchynnish*), Cha d'fhag mi (*dtak*)
I did not strike. I did not tell. I did not leave.

Further ex. :—

Nach do thuit a' chraobh ?	*did the tree not fall ?*
An do mharbh an duine am fiadh ?	*did the man kill the deer ?*
An d'ol an cat am bainne ?	*did the cat drink the milk ?*
Nach d' iarr sibh (*tchyür*),	*did you not ask ?*
Cha d' fhas e mor (*dtâs*),	*he did not grow big.*
Cha d' iarr e orm,	*he did not ask me.*

PAST TENSE, PASSIVE VOICE.

501. Consonant verbs aspirate the root and affix **adh** (**eadh**) ; vowel verbs prefix **dh'** and affix **adh** ; **f** verbs combine both methods by prefixing **dh'** aspirating and affixing **adh**. The termination **eadh** stands merely by orthographical rule for **adh** (pars. 33-4-5).

Bhuaileadh mi Dh' innseadh dhomh, Dh'fhagadh mi (*ghâk ügh*)
I was struck. I was told. I was left.

502. The dependent tenses are formed by prefixing **do, d',** and affixing **adh** (**eadh**).

Cha do bhuaileadh mi,	*I was not struck.*
Cha d' innseadh dhomh (*tchynnshügh*),	*I was not told.*
Cha d' fhagadh mi (*dtâkugh*),	*I was not left.*
Nach do bhriseadh e ?	*Was it not broken ?*
An do bhuaileadh e ?	*Was he struck ?*
Nach d' fhagadh e air a' bhord ?	*Was it not left on the table ?*

503.   *Vocabulary.*

tuit (*ttooytch*), fall.   **ith** (*ee*), eat.
tog (*tok*), lift.   **bris** break.
leugh (*llyā*), read.   **fas** (*fâs*), grow.
chunnaic irr. v. (*choonnyk*), saw.

504. Read in Gaelic and translate into English :—

1. Bhuail mi an dorus.   2. Dh' innis e, sgeul.   3. Dh' fhag mi an leabhar.   4. Cha do leugh mi an leabhar.   5. Cha do bhris e an uinneag.   6. Nach do bhris an duine an uinneag ?   7. Cha do bhris. 8. Is e an gille a bhris an dorus.   9. Chunnaic mi an duine a' dol dachaidh.   10. Cha d' fhag e an leabhar anns an tigh.   11. Dh' fhagadh an leabhar leis a' ghille.   12. Dh' innseadh iad sin.   13. Nach d' fhagadh e air a' bhord ?   14. Thuit an leabhar air an lar. 15. Dh' ith an gille an t-aran a dh' fhagadh air a' bhord.   16. Bhuail-teadh mi anns a' cheann.   17. Bhuail mi dorus an tigh   18. Bhriseadh an dorus mor.   19. Thogadh an t-ord mor.   20. Dh' fhag mi a' chlach.   21. Dh' fhas an gille mor.   22. Thuit an t-each. 23. Nach do thuit an t-each ?   24. Cha do thuit.

505. Translate English into Gaelic :—

1. I told a story.   2. He struck the door.   3. I left the book on the table.   4. I did not read the book.   5. When did you leave it ? 6. I left it on the table in the house last night.   7. It was the big book.   8. I did not break the window.   9. The window was broken by a big man who left this hammer here.   10. Was it not some bad boys who broke this window ?   11. Was it not broken with that hammer ?   12. The door fell and it broke.   13. Did I tell a story ? 14. You told a story to them.   15. You did not tell (to) us a story. 16. Did you read that book ?   17. Did he break the window ?   18. The window was struck with the stone. 19. The bread has been eaten by that boy.   20. The young man has eaten some bread.   21. Did the boy not eat the bread ?   22. The boy lifted it from the table. 23. It fell on the floor.   24. Was the dog not struck by the boy ? 25. The boy struck the dog with a stick.   26. Have you asked him ? 27. I asked the little boy this morning.   28. If the boy did not, strike it, who did ?

506. Write in your note book the complete past tense of the verbs **tuit**, **ith**, and **fas**. Repeat the same verbs with the particles **cha**, **nach**, **na'm**, and **mur**.

LESSON XLII.

FUTURE TENSE.

507. In the future tense of the active voice the verb has three forms—the independent, the dependent, and the relative.

508. The independent form is made by adding **idh** to the root (**aidh** to correspond to a broad vowel).

cuiridh mi,	I will put.	**olaidh mi,**	I will drink.
cuiridh thu,	you will put.	**olaidh thu,**	you will drink.
cuiridh e,	he will put.	**olaidh e,**	he will drink.
etc., etc.		etc., etc.	

509. The dependent form is the same as the simple root verb with the addition of the particles.   No aspiration except after **cha.**

an cuir mi ?	shall I put ?
cha chuir mi,	I shall not put.
ged nach freagair mi,	although I will not answer.
an ol mi ?	shall I drink ?
cha'n ol sinn,	we shall not drink.
nach buail mi,	that I shall not strike.
gu'm buail mi,	that I shall strike.
mur (am) buail mi,	if I shall not strike.

510. The relative future as the name we give it implies is generally used after the relative pronoun, which whether present or understood causes aspiration of the root verb. The relative future ending is **as**, or **eas** to correspond to a narrow vowel.   The aspirated particle **dh'** is retained before vowels and **f** (pure) but it has now no effect save for euphony having lost all trace of a time distinction.

511. Examples of the use of the relative form.   It is used after a relative pronoun (including an adverbial relative) which as in English is often understood, or after the conjunctive particles **ma** " if " ; **o, o'n** " since."

ma chuireas mi,	**ma dh' olas mi,**	**ma dh' fhagas mi,**
If I will put.	If I will drink.	If I will leave.

Am fear a thogas mi,	*the man whom I will lift,* or *the man who will lift me.*
Ma ghlacas mi e,	*if I will catch him.*
Ma dh' olas e am bainne,	*if he will drink the milk.*
Am fear a ghlacas iad,	*the man whom they will catch,* or *the man who will catch them.*
Am fear nach glac iad,	*the man whom they will not catch,* or *the man who will not catch them.*
Mu na h-uile ni a shaoileas iad,	*concerning everything they can think of.*
Cuin a bhuaileas mi ?	*when shall I strike ?* (lit., *what is the time such as that I shall strike at ?*)

An uair a bhuaileas mi,	*whenever I shall strike.*
Cha dean iad ach na bhios ceart,	*they will not do but what is right.*
'N uair a thachras so,	*whenever this happens.*
'N uair a smaointicheas tu,	*whenever you think.*

512. The future relative is used when **an uair a** " the hour in which " (**a** being the adverbial relative) indicates indefinite frequency.

513. It may be appropriate here to notice a usage of the future in Gaelic where in English we employ the present. When an action or state is represented as being habitual or uniform, involving, for instance, such an idea as that expressed by the term " law of nature," then Gaelic uses the future, thus, **eiridh a' ghrian** " the sun rises," literally " the sun will rise." An event that happens indefinitely often the inference is that it will happen again, the uniformity of nature is involved.

With possibly the exception of the verb **bi** and another* there is no present tense. in Gaelic† and there are many other languages similarly placed. Time . being like space, continuous and uninterrupted, it is divisible in idea only. Present time does not exist any more than a mathematical point can be composed of parts. What we call present time is only the intermediate limit which the mind fixes between the past and the future. Every portion of time that we can mention—a year, a month, a week, an hour, a minute—is composed of past and future time. When we say " this hour " the whole hour is not present at once, it is obvious that a part is past and a part future. Again, if we connect actions with the division of time, it is obvious that actions can only be of the past and future. " I write a letter." The whole act of writing the letter is not present at once, it is composed of the part written and the part to be written, that is of past and future action. Although you have just read these lines, you use the past tense in saying so. These are illustrative sentences of the invisible line which separates past and future time, the present must be the realisation of, or won from the future. Gaelic uses the future form in this manner for the expression of the continuous present, movable and always moving into the future.

FUTURE : PASSIVE VOICE.

514. The future passive of all verbs is formed alike by adding **ar (ear)** to the root.

Togar a' chlach,	*the stone will be lifted.*
An togar i ?	*will it be lifted ?*

---

* **chi mi** " I see " or " I will see."
† Except in the progressive form, Lesson XXI.

Nach ithear an t-aran ?	*will the bread not be eaten ?*
Brisear an uinneag,	*the window will be broken.*
An olar an t-uisge ?	*will the water be drunk ?*
Cha bhuailear mi,	*I shall not be struck.*

515. Read in Gaelic and translate into English :—

1. Cuiridh mi an t-aran air a' bhord. 2. Cha chuir mi an sin e. 3. Ma chuireas togaidh-se e. 4. An do thog iad na clachan ? 5. Ma thogas iad na clachan bithidh iad sgith. 6. Buailidh am balach beag an dorus. 7. Buailidh sinn an dorus le ord. 8. Buailear dorus an tighe. 9. Buailidh mi an t-cach. 10. Nach buail thu an t-each sin ? 11. Ma dh' fhagas mi an cu am buail thu e ? 12. Am fear a thogas mi. 13. Thubhairt e gu'm buail e am bord. 14. Togaidh mi a' chlach so. 15. Brisear na clachan. 16. C'uine a dh' fhagas thu am baile ? 17. Fagaidh mi am baile am maireach. 18. Cha 'n innis mi cuin a dh' fhagas mi so. 19. Is e am fear nach oladh am bainne. 20. 'Nuair a thachras sin an innis thu dhomh e ? 21. An ithear an t-aran ? 22. Cha'n ithear ach olar an t-uisge. 23. An ol thu am bainne so ? 24. Cha bhrisear an uinneag.

516. Translate into Gaelic :—

1. Will I put the bread on the table ? 2. There is bread on the table. 3. I will not put it where he will lift it. 4. They will strike the door with a stick. 5. Will they not break the door ? 6. They will not lift these stones. 7. If they do not lift these stones they will be left there. 8. I will not lift the stones. 9. The stones will not be broken. 10. John will break that window if he will throw stones. 11. The window will be broken. 12. I will put the stones away. 13. We shall not strike the window. 14. He is the man who will not drink water. 15. Will he drink milk ? 16. No. If he will not drink milk who will drink it ? 17. The cat will drink it. 18. It will not be drunk by the cat. 19. That milk will not be good. 20. If you will put it on the table someone will drink it.

LESSON XLIII.

Subjunctive Tense.

517. The first person of this tense is a synthetic form and is one of the few instances where it has not been superseded by the form of the third person. The remaining persons are indicated by one form with the addition of the pronoun.

518. The first person singular of consonant verbs aspirates the root and adds the termination **ainn (inn)**. the first person plural aspirates and adds **amald (eamaid)**. The termination for the other persons is **adh (eadh)**. Vowel

F

verbs prefix **dh'** ; and **f** verbs prefix **dh'** and also aspirate the root.

Sg.	1.	**thogainn,** I would lift.	**dh' innsinn,** I would tell.
	2.	**thogadh thu**	**dh' innseadh thu**
	3.	**thogadh e**	**dh' innseadh e**
Pl.	1.	**thogamaid**	**dh' innseamaid**
	2.	**thogadh sibh**	**dh' innseadh sibh**
	3.	**thogadh iad**	**dh' innseadh iad**

519. The changes on the terminations **ainn, eadh,** etc., stand merely by the orthographical rule.

520. The subjunctive is regularly aspirated (the result of a particle which is now lost) except after certain conjunctive particles (par. 494). Observe also the appearance of the aspirated particle **do** before vowels which would seem to be merely for euphonic reasons as it has now no other signification, it disappears after the conjunctive particles.

521. Examples of the dependent form with the particles.

an togainn ?	would I lift ?
nach togainn ?	would I not lift ?
na'n togainn,	if I would lift.
cha thogainn,	I would not lift.
mur togainn,	if I would not lift.
mur innsinn,	if I would not tell.
cha'n innsinn,	I would not tell.
an innsinn ?	would I tell ?

Thubhairt e gu'n togainn e,   *he said that I would lift it.*
Chunnaic mi an leabhar nach   *I saw the book which I would not*
   togainn,   *lift.*

522. We use the future relative with the conjunctive particle **ma** where the fulfilment of a possible event is contemplated. We use the subjunctive with **na'n** when the case supposed is to be regarded as remotely probable or almost impossible, and also where the contrary of an actual past event is supposed and the different result contemplated.

Na'n saoilinn ; chitheadh tu mi,   *If I thought so : you would*
                                    see me.

SUBJUNCTIVE TENSE—PASSIVE VOICE.

523. The passive voice of the subjunctive is formed in **tadh (teadh)** for all the persons of all verbs, with aspiration of an initial consonant, **do** being prefixed in the case of

verbs beginning with a vowel or **f**, except after certain of the particles. This **do** has no time signification, and is only retained where euphony seems to require it.

bhuailteadh mi.	I would be struck.
thogtadh mi,	I would be lifted.
dh' iarrtadh e,	he would be asked.
dh' innsteadh dhuit,	you would be told.

524. After the particles in the dependent tense no aspiration or **dh'** is used.

an togtadh e ?	would he be lifted ?
cha thogtadh mi,	I would not be lifted.
an iarrtadh e ?	would ho be asked ?
cha'n iarrtadh sinn,	we would not be asked.

525. Read in Gaelic and translate into English :—

1. Bhuailinn an dorus. 2. Bhuaileadh esan an dorus. 3. Bhuaileamaid an dorus le clachan. 4. Bhuailteadh an gille mor le maide. 5. Bhrisinn an uinneag leis an ord. 6. Cha thogainn an t-ord. 7. Dh'innsinn air an duine. 8. Cha'n innsinn air a' ghille. 9. Thogadh iad na clachan agus thuiteadh iad air an t-sraid. 10. Ciod a dh' innsinn do 'n duine anns a' mhaduinn ? 11. Chunnaic mi an duine a' leughadh an leabhair. 12. Cha leughadh an duine sin an leabhar so. 13. Na'n togadh thu e, cha'n innsinn e do 'n duine. 14. Chuirinn an leabhar air a' bhord. 15. Cha'n fhagainn e air an lar. 16. Thubhairt e gu'n tigeadh e leam. 17. Nach ithteadh an t-aran air a' bhord ? 18. Cha'n ithteadh. 19. Dh' olainn am bainne na'n fagadh i e. 20. Bhriseadh Calum na clachan leis an ord throm. 21. Nach buailinn an dorus le cloich ? 22. Na'm buailinn sa an dorus am buaileadh thusa e. 23. Thubhairt e gu'm buailinn an dorus leis na clachan sin. 24. Is e am fear nach buaileadh an gille.

526. Translate English into Gaelic :—

1. I would not throw that stone. 2. The one who would throw that stone (he) would be very strong. 3. I would leave the stones there if they would not lift them. 4. The man who would not lift the book. 5. We would break the stones if you would let us. 6. If you threw a stone you would break the window. 7. The window would not be broken. 8. Would the sheep be on the hill this morning ? 9. He would lift the stone and would throw it at the boy. 10. The boy would be struck with the stone. 11. That man would strike the boy with a stick. 12. He said that he would not strike the boy. 13 Would you strike the boy ? 14. Yes.

LESSON XLIV.

THE IMPERATIVE.

527. The Imperative admits of only one tense form, and the only particle applicable is the negative, which in this case is **na** not **cha**.

ACTIVE VOICE.

528. In the imperative, the pronouns are amalgamated with the verb in the 1st and 2nd persons, both singular and plural, and only in the 3rd person are pronouns added.

529. All verbs are regular in the imperative. The 1st singular adds **am (eam)** to the root. The 2nd singular is the root of the verb, and requires no pronoun, though for emphasis, the emphatic pronoun **thusa** may be used. The 3rd singular is formed by adding **adh (eadh)** to the root and attaching the pronoun or noun. The 1st plural adds **amaid (eamaid)** to the root. The 2nd plural adds **aibh (ibh)** to the root. The 3rd plural is formed by adding **adh (eadh)** to the root and attaching the noun or pronoun.

Sg.	1.	**togam**	let me lift.	**cuiream,**	let me put.
	2.	**tog,**	lift (thou).	**cuir,**	put (thou).
	3.	**togadh e,**	let him lift.	**cuireadh e,**	let him put.
Pl.	1.	**togamaid,**	let us lift.	**cuireamaid,**	let us put.
	2.	**togaibh,**	lift ye.	**cuiribh,**	put ye.
	3.	**togadh iad,**	let them lift.	**cuireadh iad,**	let them put.

530. These are negatived by **na** thus making an imperative prohibition in the 2nd person, **na buail** " don't strike." It does not cause aspiration.

PASSIVE VOICE.

531. The imperative passive of all verbs is formed by adding **tar (tear)** to the root of the verb. The pronouns are used in all persons, no amalgamation taking place.

togtar sinn,	let us be lifted.
buailtear mi,	let me be struck.

The terminations throughout vary according to the orthographical rule.

532. Read in Gaelic and translate into English :—

1. Buail an dorus. 2. Buail an dorus mor le maide. 3. Bhuaileadh iad an dorus mor. 4. Buailtear iad leis na clachan mora. 5. Tog ord agus buail an uinneag. 6. Druid an uinneag. 7. Tog a' chlach

sin. 8. Na buail an dorus. 9. Na druid an uinneag. 10. Na fag an t-slat. 11. Na briseadh e an uinneag. 12. Ithear an t-aran an nochd. 13. Fagar an t-aran air an lar. 14. Fagamaid an t-ord anns an tigh. 15. Na treig* a' Ghaidhlig. 16. Na treig mi. 17. Cuiream an t-aran air falbh. 18. Na cuir an t-aran air falbh. 19. Olam am bainne. 20. Buailtear an t-arbhar. 21. Na cuir an cu air falbh. 22. Togtar an cat agus cuirear air falbh e. 23. Thogtadh an tigh mor air a' chreig. 24. Cuir sgian an fhir sin air a' bhord agus na bris i.

533. Translate into Gaelic :—

1. Strike the big window with a hammer. 2. Let us break the window with stones. 3. Strike the door with your stick. 4. Lift that stone and throw it at that dog. 5. Let that dog alone. 6. Don't strike it. 7. Let me put that stone in my pocket. 8. Let us go away now. 9. Put this stone on the table. 10. Don't put it there. 11. Do not forsake* me. 12. Forsake not the Gaelic. 13. Eat that bread but do not drink the milk. 14. Ask that man there. 15. Let us ask him for bread. 16. Lift that dog. 17. Don't lift that dog, it is not ours. 18. Let me tell (to) you a story. 19. Tell us a long story. 20. Put the bread away now. 21. Do not eat this bread. 22. Leave that bread on the table. 23. Build (**tog**) your house on a rock.

LESSON XLV.

THE PARTICIPIAL ADJECTIVE.

534. Nearly all Gaelic verbs have a participial or verbal adjective, formed by adding **te** or **ta** to the root verb, as— **briste** " broken " ; **togte**, " lifted " ;\ this verbal adjective must not be confused with the verbal noun. When qualifying the noun it is a pure adjective. It is indeclinable for number or person, but suffers aspiration as any other adjective. Notice that some of these adjectival forms are exceptions to the orthographical rule (pars. 33-4-5).

> **bàta briste** (*bprystchü*),   a broken boat.
> **caora fheannte** (*y aunntchü*), a skinned sheep.
>
> Tha an sgian briste,   *the knife is broken.*
> Tha an sgian bhriste togte, *the broken knife is lifted.*

535. When the root verb ends in **t** only an **e** is added, when ending in **th**, the **h** is rejected and an **e** is added.

> **lot** wound, **loite** wounded ; **bath** drown. **baite** drowned.

---

* **treig** v. (*treek*) forsake.

536. A whole series of compound tenses of a passive form is formed from the combination of the verb **bi** in all its inflections and the verbal adjective.

Am bheil an dorus fosgailte ?	*is the door open ?*
Bha an dorus duinte,	*the door was shut.*
Bitheam dearbhte,	*let me be proved or tested.*
Cha robh mi leonta an de,	*I was not wounded yesterday.*
Tha mi sgithichte leotha,	*I am done or worn out with them.*

537. Adjectival participles of past time are followed as in English by **le** " with " before the name of the instrument or agent.

Buailte le claidheamh (*bpooāyltchü*),	*struck with a sword.*
Leonta le Seumas (*llyontü*),	*wounded by James.*

THE INFINITIVE.

538. The present infinitive is translated by aspirating the verbal noun and prefixing **a**, as :—**a bhi** (**bhith**), " to be "; **a bhualadh** " to strike "; and usually follows the noun instead of preceding it as in English, as :—**Thubhairt e rium an rop a tharruinn**. " He told me to pull the rope " (p. 147).

539. The infinitive of verbs commencing with a vowel take **a dh** before the verbal noun and verbs in **f** followed by a vowel take **a dh** before the verbal noun aspirated, as :— **ol** " drink "; **a dh' ol** " to drink "; **fag** " leave "; **a dh' fhagail** " to leave " (par. 606).

540. *Vocabulary.*

ceangailte adj. (*kengyltchü*), tied.
fuasgailte adj. (*fooasgyltchü*), liberated.

541. Read in Gaelic and translate into English :—

1. C'aite am bheil am bàta ? 2. Tha am bàta briste. 3. Tha an t-aran ithte. 4. Tha an uinneag briste. 5. Bha an sgian briste. 6. Tha an dorus mor fosgailte. 7. Tha an uinneag druidte. 8. Tha a' chlach sin briste. 9. Bha a' chlach mhor sin trom. 10. Am bheil a' chlach dhubh briste ? 11. Bha an dorus briste leis an ord. 12. Bha sgian a' bhalaich math ach tha i a nis briste. 13. Bha an cu ceangailte ris a' bhord an raoir. 14. Bha e fuasgailte 'sa mhaduinn. 15. Bithidh an dorus fosgailte. 16. B'ann duinte a bha an dorus. 17. Am bheil an dorus fosgailte ? 18. Cuin' a bha an tigh togte ?

542. Translate into Gaelic :—

1. Is this boat broken ? 2. No, that is the broken boat. 3. The window is broken. 4. The big door was open last night. 5. It will

not be open to-night. 6. Leave it shut now. 7. The window is shut. 8. Open the window and shut the door. 9. That man's knife was good but it is broken now. 10. The knife will be left on the table to-night. 11. If it is lifted to-night it will not be left there again. 12. Is the big stone broken ? 13. All the stones will be broken. 14. If the biggest stone is not broken yet it will be broken to-day. 15. It was lifted from the floor. 16. Will the big stone be good ? 17. Will you be putting it on the table ? 18. We will be breaking it on the floor. 19. Was the dog tied to the table this morning ? 20. He was tied to the chair this morning. 21. I will liberate him now. 22. He will be liberated immediately.

543. PARADIGMS OF THE REGULAR VERB.

We illustrate a complete paradigm of three regular verbs, exhibiting the initial forms and terminations of all the simple tenses at one view. The imperative and subjunctive have been given in full. In the other tenses, the pronoun only changes, the verb being the same for all persons, sing. and plural.

Imp. Root.	**tog**	**ol**	**fill**
Translation.	lift.	drink.	fold.

PAST TENSE (Preterite).

Active indept.	‡thog mi (*hok*)	‡dh'ol mi (*ghawl*)	‡dh'fhill mi (*y yll*)
,. *dept.*	do thog mi	d'ol mi (*tawl*)	d'fhill mi (*diyll*)
Passive indep.	thogadh mi	dh'oladh mi	dh'fhilleadh mi
,, *dept.*	do thogadh mi	d'oladh mi	d'fhilleadh mi

FUTURE TENSE (Habitual Present).

Independent,	togaidh mi	olaidh mi (*awly*)	fillidh mi (*fylly*)
Dependent,	*tog mi	*ol mi (*awl*)	*fill mi
Relative,	thogas	dh'olas	dh'fhilleas (*y yllüs*)
Passive,	*togar mi	*olar mi	*fillear mi

SUBJUNCTIVE TENSE (Active Voice).

‡*Independ.*	1	thogainn	dh'olainn (*ghawlin*)	dh'fhillinn
,,	2	thogadh thu	dh'oladh thu	dh'fhilleadh thu
,,	3	thogadh e	dh.oladh e	dh'fhilleadh e
,, *pl.*	1	thogamaid	dh'olamaid	dh'fhilleamaid
,,	2	thogadh sibh	dh.oladh sibh	dh'fhilleadh sibh
,,	3	thogadh iad	dh'oladh iad	dh'fhilleadh iad
Depend., sg.	1	*togainn	*olainn	*fillinn
		(etc.)	(etc.)	(etc.)

SUBJUNCTIVE TENSE (Passive Voice).

Independent,	thogtadh mi	dh'oltadh mi	dh'fhillteadh mi
Dependent,	*togadh mi	*oltadh mi	*fillteadh mi

For notes see following page.

IMPERATIVE MOOD.

Active	1	*sing.*	togam	olam (*awlŭm*)	filleam
,,	2	,,	tog	ol	fill
,,	3	,,	togadh e	oladh e	filleadh e
,,	1	pl.	togamaid	olamaid	filleamaid
,,	2	,,	togaibh	olaibh	fillibh
,,	3	,,	togadh iad	oladh iad	filleadh iad
Passive,			togtar mi	oltar mi	filltear mi
Infinitive pres.			a thogail	a dh'ol	a dh'fhilleadh
,,	*fut.*		ri togail	ri ol	ri filleadh
Participle pres.			a' togail	ag ol	a' filleadh
,,	*past*		air togail	air ol	air filleadh
Participial adj.			togte	olte	fillte.

*These dependent forms are used with all the particles, as shown in par. 494.   **Cha** aspirates all these dependent forms where the initial of the verb is **g, c, m, p,** and **b** (excepting **bu**) ; **cha'n** aspirates initial **f** + vowel verbs (see **cha,** par. 494).

‡ These independent forms are also used after the conditional affirmative particles :—**ma** and **ged a**

ma thog mi if I lift.   **ma thogadh mi,** if I was lifted.

LESSON XLVI.

544. Conversational Exercise :—Questions and Answers.

There is in Gaelic no affirmative word corresponding to the English " yes," or negative " no."   A question is put by the interrogative form of the verb and the answer must be made by the affirmative or negative form of the verb correspondent in tense to the form used in putting the question.

ciod e ?	(*kut ā*)	what is it ?
is sgian i	(*iss skeeun y*)	it is a knife.
co leis i ?	(*ko llāsh y*)	whose is it ?
cha'n eil fios agam	(*chan yāl fyss akum*)	I do not know.
nach leat-sa i ?	(*nach lettsha y*)	is it not yours ?
c'aite am bheil i ?	(*ka-chüm vāl y*)	where is it ?
tha i 'nam sporan	(*ha y nam sporan*)	it is in my purse.
an gabh thu so ?	(*ung gav oo sho*)	will you take this ?
cha ghabh	(*cha ghav*)	No—I will not.
thoir ort	(*hoir orst*)	away with you.
an d'fhag e i ?	(*un dak ā y*)	did he leave her ?
dh'fhag	(*ghak*)	yes—he did.
an do thog thu e ?	(*un do hok oo ā*)	did you lift him ?

thog	(hok)	yes—I did.
cha do thog	(chat tdo hok)	no—I did not.
an leig sinn as e ?	(ün-leik-shynn ass•ā)	shall we let him go ?
leigidh. cha leig	(llāky, cha-leik)	yes. no.
an do phos e ?	(un do fos ā)	did he marry ?
cha do phos	(cha do fos)	no—he did not.
am pos thu mi ?	(um pos oo mee)	will you marry me ?
posaidh	(poss-y)	yes—I will.
cha phos	(cha foss)	no—I will not.
an leat so ?	(un lāhtt shoh)	is this yours ?
is leam, 's leam	(iss lyām, slyām)	yes—it is.
an tusa a th'ann ?	(ün toosü ü hānn)	is this you ?
's mi. cha mhi	(smee, chav-vee)	yes—no.
co tha so ?	(ko ha sho)	who is this ? —here ?
tha mise	(ha mish-ü)	I am—it is I.
am bheil thu sgith ?	(um vāl oo skee)	are you tired ?
tha mi gle sgith	(ha mee klā skee)	I am very tired.
an ol thu so ?	(ün awll oo sho)	will you drink this ?
olaidh, cha'n ol	(awlly chan-awll)	yes—no, I will not drink.
an d'ol thu e ?	(un dawll oo ā)	did you drink it ?
dh' ol. cha d' ol	(ghawll, chat-awll)	yes—no.
cia meud uair tha e ?	(ky mātt ooür ü hā ā)	what time is it ?
tha e da uair	(ha ā dtā ooür)	it is two o'clock.
de'n uair a tha e ?	(tchänn ooür ü hā ā)	what o'clock is it ?
leth-uair an deidh uair	(lyā ooür ün tchā ooür)	half-past one.
cia an uair ?	(kā ün ooür)	what hour ? = when?
mu dha uair	(mü ghā ooür)	about two o'clock.
eadar a h-aon agus a dha	(ātür ü hōn āghus ü ghā)	between one and two
an uair mu dheireadh	(ün ooür mü yārügh)	the last time.
a' cheud uair	(ü chyütt ooür)	the first time.
aon uair	(ōn ooür)	one o'clock, once.
uair sam bith	(ooür süm by)	any time.
uair a rinn mi sin	(ooür ü rynn my shyn)	once I did that.
b'idh mi falbh	(by my fallüv)	I will be going.
tha mi a' dol dachaidh	(ha mee ü dawl tachy)	I am going home.
greas ort, ma ta	(grāss orst, mü ta)	haste you, then.
slan leat	(sllawn lett)	farewell.
an la chi's nach fhaic	(ün llā ü chy snach āychk)	the day I see you and the day I don't.

545. In English, as an answer to a question in which the verb is fully expressed, the mere sign of the tense suffices, the rest being understood from the question put, as :—
" did you go to town to-day ? " answer " I did."   To the reply " I did," the verb " go " is understood. In Gaelic, no such suppression as this can occur, we must enunciate the whole verb as in the examples shown in this exercise.

F*

IRREGULAR VERBS.

Verb Root / Translation	beir / bear.	cluinn / hear.	dean / do.	rach / go.	ruig / reach, arrive.
PAST TENSE.					
Active Ind.	rug mi (*rook*)	chuala mi (*chooulu*)	rinn mi (*rynn*)	chaidh mi (*chāy*)	rainig mi
„ Dep.	do rug mi	*cuala mi	do rinn mi	deachaidh mi	do rainig mi
Passive Ind.	rugadh mi	chualadh mi	rinneadh mi	†chaidheas	raineadh mi
„ Dep.	do rugadh mi	*cualas (*rel*)	d'rinneadh mi	†deachas	raineas
FUTURE TENSE (Habitual Present).					
Active Ind.	beiridh mi	cluinneadh mi	ni mi (*nny*)	theid mi (*hātch*)	ruigidh mi
„ Dep.	*beir mi	*cluinn mi	dean mi	teid mi (*tchātch*)	ruig mi (*rooyk*)
Relative	bheireas	chluinneas	ni mi	rachas, theid mi	ruigeas
Passive Ind.	beirear mi	cluinntear	nithear mi	†theidear	ruigear mi
„ Dep.	*beirear mi	*cluinntear	deanar mi	†teidear	ruigear mi
SUBJUNCTIVE (Active Voice).					
Ind. 1 *sing.*	bheirinn	chluinninn	dheanainn	rachainn	ruiginn
„ 1 *plur.*	bheireamaid	chluinneamaid	dheanamaid	rachamaid	ruigeamaid
„ 2, 3 *s. & p.*	bheireadh thu	chluinneadh thu	dheanadh thu	rachadh thu	ruigeadh thu
Dep. 1 *sing.*	*beirinn	*cluininn	deanainn	rachainn	ruiginn
„ 2, 3 *s. & p.*	*beiridh thu	*cluinnidh thu	deanadh thu	rachadh thu	ruigeadh thu
SUBJUNCTIVE (Passive Voice).					
Independent	bheirteadh mi	chluinnteadh mi	dheantadh mi	†rachainn	ruigteadh mi
Dependent	*beirteadh mi	*cluinnteadh mi	deantadh mi	†rachtadh	ruigteadh mi
IMPERATIVE.					
Active 1 *sg.*	beiream	cluinneam	deanam	racham	ruigeam
„ 2 „	beir	cluinn	dean	rach	ruig
„ 3 „	beireadh e	cluinneadh e	deanadh e	rachadh e	ruigeadh
„ 1 *pl.*	beireamaid	cluinneamaid	deanamaid	rachamaid	ruigeamaid
„ 2 „	beiribh	cluinnibh	deanaibh	rachaibh	ruigibh
„ 3 „	beireadh iad	cluinneadh iad	deanadh iad	rachadh iad	ruigeadh iad
Passive	beirtear mi	cluinntear mi	deantar mi	†trachtar leam	ruigtear mi
Infin. *pres.*	a bhreith	a chluinntinn (f)	a dheanamh (m)	a dhol (m)	a ruigsinn (f)
„ *future*	ri breith	ri cluinntinn	ri deanamh	ri dol	ri ruigsinn
Partic. pres.	a' breith	a' cluinntinn	a' deanamh	a' dol	a' ruigsinn
Partic. past	air breith	air cluinntinn	air deanamh	air dol	air ruigsinn
Partic. adj.	beirte	cluinnte	deante		ruigte

IRREGULAR VERBS.

Verb Root / Translation.	thoir, tabhair / give.	thig / come.	abair / say.	faic / see.	faigh / get, find.
Past Tense.					
Active Ind.	thug mi (*hook*)	thainig mi	thubhairt mi	chunnaic mi	fhuair mi (*hoo-ur*)
,, *Dep.*	*d' thug mi	d'thainig mi	d'thubhairt mi	*faca mi	d'fhuair mi (*dtooir*)
Passive Ind.	thugadh mi	†thaineas	†thubhairteadh	chunnacas	fhuaradh mi
,, *Dep.*	d' thugadh mi	†d'thaineas	†d'thubhairteadh	*facas	d'fhuaradh mi
Future Tense (Habitual Present).					
Active Ind.	bheir mi (*vār*)	thig mi (*heek*)	their mi (*hār*)	chi mi (*chee*)	gheibh mi (*yōu*)
,, *Dep.*	toir mi (*ītor*)	tig m. (*tcheek*)	abair mi (*apur*)	*faic mi (*fāchk*)	*faigh mi (*fāy*)
Relative	bheir mi	thig mi	their mi	chi mi	gheibh mi
Passive Ind.	bheirear mi	†tigear	†theirear	chithear mi	gheibhear mi
,, *Dep.*	toirear mi	†tigear	†abairear	*faictear mi	*faightear mi
Subjunctive (Active Voice).					
Ind. 1 *sing.*	bheirinn	thiginn (*heekynn*)	theirinn	chithinn	gheibhinn
,, 1 *plur.*	bheireamaid	thigeamaid	theireamaid	chitheamaid	gheibheamaid
,, 2, 3 *s. & p.*	bheireadh thu	thigeadh thu	theiread thu	chitheadh thu	gheibheadh thu
Dep. 1 *sing.*	toirinn	tiginn	abairinn	*faicinn	*faighinn
,, 2, 3 *s. & p.*	tugadh thu	tigeadh thu	abaireadh thu	*faiceadh thu	*faigheadh thu
Subjunctive (Passive Voice).					
Independent	bheirteadh mi	†thigeadh	†thearteadh	chitheadh mi	gheibheadh mi
Dependent	tugtadh mi	†tigteadh	†abairteadh	*faicteadh mi	*faighteadh mi
Imperative.					
Active 1 *sg.*	thoiream	thigeam	abaiream	faiceam	faigheam
,, 2 ,,	thoir *or* tabhair	thig	abair	faic	faigh
,, 3 ,,	thoireadh e	thigeadh e	abairteadh e	faiceadh e	faidheadh e
,, 1 *pl.*	thoireamaid	thigeamaid	abairearaid	faiceamaid	faigheamaid
,, 2 ,,	thoiribh	thigibh	abairibh, abraibh	faicibh	faighibh
,, 3 ,,	thoireadh iad	thigeadh iad	abaireadh iad	faiceadh iad	faigheadh iad
Passive	thoirear mi	†thigtear	†abairear, abrar	faictear mi	faigheadh mi
Infin. pres.	a thoirt (f)	a thighinn (m)	a radh (m)	a dh'fhaicinn	a fhaighinn
Partic. pres. future	ri toirt	ri tighinn	ri radh	ri faicinn	ri faighinn
Partic. pres.	a' toirt	a' tighinn	ag radh	a' faicinn	a' faighinn
,, *past*	air toirt	air tighinn	air radh	air faicinn	air faighinn
Partic. adj.	tugte		raite	faicte	faighte

LESSON XLVII.

THE IRREGULAR VERBS.

546. In Gaelic grammar there are ten verbs classed as irregular because they do not conform to the one uniform type of conjugation now known. To these in consistency must be added the substantive verb **bi**.‡ From a closer study it will be found that these verbs are rather defective than irregular. They are perfectly regular in their numbers and persons. Their irregularity consists only in this, that they want certain tenses which they borrow from certain other verbs which are in themselves quite regular.

547. Irregular verbs are always very troublesome to the learner, but we have only **ten** in Gaelic. There are over two hundred irregular verbs in English, and nearly four hundred in French.

The preceding table illustrates these ten irregular Gaelic verbs in all their simple tenses.

‡ Synopsis of the irregular verb **bi** be (thou).

	Independent.	*Dependent.*	*Impersonal forms.*	
Present,	tha	bheil, eil	thatar	bheilear, eilear
Past,	bha	robh	bhatar	robhtar
Future,	bithidh	*bi	bitear	*bitear
Rel. Future,	bhitheas (bhios)		bhitheas	
Subjunctive,	bhithinn (*par.* 79)	*bithinn	bhiteadh	*biteadh
Infinitive,	bith *being* ;	a bhi, bhith *to be* ;	air bhi *have been.*	

Also the various forms of the assertive verb **is** and its past tense **bu**. These are also used with the tenses of the verb **bi** to express existence emphatically. **Is mi a tha** " It is I who am "—" I am indeed " ; **cha mhi a bha ann** " it is not I who was in it, there—I was not there."

NOTES ON IRREGULAR VERBS, pages 138, 139.

The dependent forms are used after the particles (par. **494**).

† These being intransitive verbs have no passive, the forms shown are impersonal or relative.

These independent forms are also used after the conditional affirmative particles **ma** and **ged a**.

    ma chuala mi, if I heard.   **ma chualas mi**, if I was heard.

* These forms are used with the particles as shown in par. **494**. They are aspirated by the negative particle **cha**. Verbs in **l, n, r, d, t s**, resist aspiration.

cha do rinn mi	I did not do.
cha do chuala mi,	I did not hear.
cha chluinnear mi,	I shall not be heard.
cha chluinn mi,	I will not hear.

Notes on Verbs.

548. A verb is said to be impersonal when it is used in its third person singular passive without a nominative expressed to indicate that an object is undergoing some operation. A progressive passive tense is thus formed which is similar to the Latin, but which has no analogy to the passive in English, French, etc. A series of tenses is formed from the impersonal forms of the verb **bi**; with the pronoun **le**; used as a future passive.

Thatar a' cur an t-sil,	*the seed is being sown.*
Bhatar a' togail an tighe,	*the house was being built.*
Thathas a' togail an tighe,	*they are building the house.*
	the house is being built.
Bithear a' togail na cruaiche,	*let the stack be built.*
Thatar ag radh,	*it is said, people are saying.*
Cha'n eilear ag radh,	*it is not said.*
Cluinnear leam fuaim na gaoithe,	*(methinks) I hear the sound of the wind.*
Buailear leam,	*it shall be struck by me. I strike*
Chithear, chiteadh,	*(one) sees, might see.*

549. As in English many simple verbs require a preposition after them to make their sense complete. These prepositional verbs always take their object in the dative case after the preposition. If a pronoun is the object it becomes a prepositional pronoun. The verbs assume different meanings according to the pronoun used.

Leig as mo lamh,	*let go my hand.*
Ghabh e air a bhi gu tinn,	*he pretended to be sick.*
Ghabh iad air ; orm,	*they beat (punished) him ; me*
Gabh air a' chu	*strike the dog.*
Gabh ris,	*acknowledge, confess.*
Gabh a null ; a nuas,	*go over ; come down.*
Eisd ris an duine,	*listen to the man.*
Abair ri Tomas bualadh,	*tell Thomas to strike.*
Cuir an clo,	*put in type, print.*
Cuir an aghaidh,	*put against, oppose.*

550. The irregular verb **beir** means " bear " or " bring forth "—**rug i mac** " she bore a son "; **rug a' bho** " the cow calved." But with the preposition **air** it conveys the further meanings of " catching," " overtaking," etc.

Rug mi air Domhnull,	*I caught Donald.*
Beir air Iain ; beir orm,	*catch John, catch me.*
Rug mi air an each,	*I caught the horse.*
Cha bheir mi air an nochd,	*I will not catch him to-night.*
Beiridh mi orra am maireach,	*I will catch them to-morrow.*
Ruigidh mi air an ord,	*I will reach for the hammer.*
An ruig thu air a' chraoibh ?	*can you reach the tree ?*

551. Thoir or tabhair means " give*, take, bring," etc., dependent on the preposition used. Note the following :—

Thoir a nall,	*reach or fetch here.*
Thoir air falbh ; thairis,	*take away ; give over.*
Thug e aran do Sheumas,	*he gave bread to James.*
Thug e a steach an cu,	*he brought in the dog.*
Thug e am peann leis,	*he took the pen with him.*
Thug e sgillinn air paipeir,	*he gave a penny for a paper.*
Thug e air Mairi suidhe,	*he made Mary sit.*
Thug sibh uam-sa mo chlann	*you have taken from me my children.*
Thug mi air,	*I compelled him.*

552. Read in Gaelic and translate into English :—

1. Thubhairt e gu'n robh mise air falbh.   2. Cha d'thubhairt ach tha e ag radh gu'm bheil thu-sa a' falbh.   3. Ma thubhairt e sin bha e cearr.   4. Ged nach abairinn ni sam bith ris bhriseadh e an dorus.   5. Ged a theirinn ris gu'n robh e cearr, theireadh esan gu'n robh e fhein ceart.   6. Beir air an duine is gheibh thu sgian.   7. Beiridh mi air ma gheibh mi sgillinn.   8. An do rug thu air ? · 9. Cha do rug ach beiridh mi air am maireach.   10. Thubhairt an ciobair nach fhaighinn caora no uan.   11. Mur faigh mise tigh m' athar fagaidh mi an duthaich.   12. Cha'n fhaigh thu sin gu brath.   13. Co fhuair an t-iasg so ?   14. Am faigh mise iasg ?   15. Chunnaic mise duine dubh ach cha 'n fhaca tusa duine gorm a riamh.   16. Ged nach fhaca sinn am bàta chunnaic sinn na h-iasgairean.   17. Tha mise ag radh gu'm faic duine sam bith a' ghealach.   18. Tha mi a' faicinn gu'm bheil thusa gle mhath.   19. An cluinn duine dall ceol ?   20. Cluinnidh duine dall ceol ged nach fhaic e am fear-ciuil.   21. Ma cluinneas mise ceol bithidh mi sona.   22. An d' thug thusa an leabhar do 'n ghille ?   23. Cha d' thug.   24. An d' thainig na gillean eile ?   25. Cha d' thainig ach tha iad a' tighinn anns an fheasgar.   26. Nach tig thu do 'n bhaile mhor.   27. An deachaidh na fir do 'n bhaile ?   28. Cha deach, ach theid iad do 'n choille an diugh.   29. Mur teid iad do 'n choille an diugh cha teid iad an nochd.   30. Ma ruigeas mi anns a' mhaduinn an toir thu dhomh deoch bhainne ?   31. Tha mi a' dol a dheanamh bhrog.   32. Ni mi sin is cha bhi mi fada 'ga ruigsinn.   33. Am bheil thu a' dol a dh' iasgach an nochd ?   34. Tha ; na'n ruigeamaid an abhainn roimh choig uairean dheanamaid iasgach math.   35. Ni mi sin is cha bhi sinn fada 'ga ruigsinn.   36. An dean thu so ?   37. Ni.   38. Co e, a rinn so ?   **39.** Rinn mise e agus ni mi e a ris.

553. Translate English into Gaelic :—

1. He did not get it yesterday, but he got it to-day.   2. What will he get to-morrow ?   3. The boat has been found.   4. I went home

---

* According to the English dictionary the verb " give " in English has over 100 different meanings, primary, secondary, and from the aid of prepositions.

and saw my father. 5. When I go home I will see the land I was born in. 6. Let it be done now. 7. He did not do it, but if you asked him he would do it. 8. He will not go away yet. 9. Did he not go home yesterday ? 10. No, but he will go home to-morrow. 11. Give me that and I will give you this. 12. Where did you find it ? 13. If you will catch him I will give you a shilling. 14. I would not catch a black cat for any money. 15. The white cow calved yesterday. 16. I heard you in the house last night. 17. Will you see the farmer to-day ? 18. If I do not, I will see him to-morrow. 19. If I should see him to-night I will get milk from him. 20. Let me see, it is a very dark night and he will not come. 21. When will he come to the town ? 22. He will go to the town to-morrow. 23. Leave that and do this. 24. When did she arrive home last night ? 25. That man came to our house to-day and he will come again to-morrow. 26. He did not go fishing yesterday. . 27. This is the man who made the boat. 28. Let us go and see it. 29. You will get a book at our house if you will go. 30. Will I get it ? 31. Give me that book. 32. A noise was heard here last night. 33. Where were you born ? 34. I was born in Glasgow, but I have Gaelic. 35. Did he do that ? 36. Will he do it for me ? 37. Yes.

LESSON XLVIII.

The Verbal Noun.

554. The verbal noun in Gaelic corresponds to the infinitive, participle and gerund in English grammar. In Gaelic it is in all respects a noun denoting action or energy of the verb. Verbal nouns are used in conjunction with the verb **bi** to form the present tense of Gaelic verbs which is thus a compound present tense. Other compound tenses are also formed. They are generally preceded by a preposition which marks the ⟨ time of the action, thus **bualadh** " striking " ; **a' bualadh** " a-striking," literally " at striking "—(**a' ag, aig** " at ") ; **air bualadh** " after striking."

tha mi a' bualadh, I am at striking ; I am striking, *or* I strike.

555. By adding a terminal **adh, ail,** etc. (which corresponds to " ing " etc. in English) to the root of a Gaelic verb a word partaking of the quality of noun and verb will be formed. Thus by adding **adh** to **trus** " gather " we have **trusadh,** which as a noun signifies " a gathering " ; and again when preceded by the preposition **aig (ag)** acquires the verbal signification of " gathering." These are properly termed participles, participating as they do in the qualities of more than one part of speech.

556. Verbal nouns are always nouns. They may be governed by prepositions qualified by adjectives, used (many of them) in the plural number, followed by a genitive case, and so on. They can never govern an accusative or objective case as verbs can. They are generally of the masculine gender and are declined through the cases as other nouns.

trusadh (m) a gathering.

N.	**trusadh**	a gathering.	**trusaidheam**	gatherings.
G.	**trusaidh**	of a gathering.	**trusadh**	of gatherings.
D.	**(air) trusadh**	(on) a gathering	**(air) trusaidhean**	(on) gatherings
V.	**A thrusaidh**	O gathering.	**O thrusadha**	O gatherings.

FORMATION OF THE VERBAL NOUN.

557. In English there is no rule for the formation of a noun of action. It may be identical with the simple root, or it may be formed by adding one of a variety of endings : " restraint," " prohibition," " growth," " departure," " gathering,"·etc.

558. So in Gaelic there is no rule for the formation of a verbal noun. It may be identical with the root verb, or it may add one of a variety of endings, as:—**adh, eadh, amh, ail, inn** ; some contract while others again are totally different.

559. The general rule is to add **adh (eadh)** to the root verb.

breab	(*bprăp*)	kick.	**breabadh**	(*bprăp-ŭgh*)	kicking.
bris	(*bprys*)	break.	**briseadh**	(*bprysh-ugh*)	breaking.
taom	(*ttŏm*)	pour.	**taomadh**	(*ttŏm ŭgh*)	pouring.

560. A number add **adh** to a contracted root.

buail	(*booal*)	strike.	**bualadh**	(*booal-ŭgh*)	striking.
duisg	(*dooshk*)	awake.	**dusgadh**	(*dooskŭgh*)	awakening.
fosgail	(*foskŭl*)	open.	**fosgladh**	(*fosklŭgh*)	opening.
innis	(*ynnysh*)	tell.	**innseadh**	(*ynnshŭgh*)	telling.

561. A number use the root as the verbal noun.

fas	(*făs*)	grow, growing.	**ol**	(*awl*)	drink, drinking.
falbh	(*fallŭv*)	go, going.	**ruith**	(*rooyh*)	run, running.
snamh	(*snav*)	swim, swimming.	**seinn**	(*shăynn*)	sing, singing.

562. A number leave out the last small vowel and substitute a broad.

caidil	*(katchyl)*	sleep.	**cadal**	*(ka ttŭll)*	sleeping.	
caill	*(ka yll)*	lose.	**call**	*(ka ooll)*	losing.	
ceangail	*(kyangŭl)*	tie, bind.	**ceangal**	*(kyangul)*	tying.	
cuir	*(koor)*	put, sow.	**cur**	*(koor)*	putting, sowing.	
iasgaich	*(y asküch)*	fish.	**iasgach**	*(y asküch)*	fishing.	

563. Many verbs ending in **air** add a **t**.

labhair	*(llavür)*	speak.	**labhairt**	*(llavürtch)*	speaking.
tachair	*(ttachür)*	meet.	**tachairt**	*(ttachürtch)*	meeting.
freagair	*(frākür)*	answer.	**freagairt**	*(frākürtch)*	answering.

564. Many monosyllable verbs add **sinn**.

creid	*(krātch)*	believe.	**creidsinn**	*(crātchynn)*	believing.
ruig	*(rooyk)*	reach.	**ruigsinn**	*(rooykshynn)*	reaching.
treig	*(trāyk)*	forsake.	**treigsinn**	*(ttrākshynn)*	forsaking.

565. A number of monosyllables add **tinn**, which becomes **tuinn** when the root verb is broad.

cinn	*(kynn)*	grow.	**cinntinn**	*(hyntchyn)*	growing.
cluinn	*(klooynn)*	hear.	**cluinntinn**	*(clooyntchynn)*	hearing.
seall	*(shaool)*	see, look.	**sealltuinn**	*(shaultyn)*	looking.

566. A number add **ail** or **eil** to the root verb.

gabh	*(gav)*	take.	**gabhail**	*(gavül)*	taking.
tog	*(tok)*	lift, build.	**togail**	*(tokül)*	lifting.
fag	*(fâk)*	leave.	**fagail**	*(fâkül)*	leaving.
tilg	*(cheeleek)*	throw.	**tilgeil**	*(cheeleekül)*	throwing.

567. A few verbs form their verbal nouns irregularly.

marcaich	*(markāch)*	ride.	**marcachd**	*(marcachk)*	riding.
thig	*(heek)*	come.	**tighinn**	*(tchy ynn)*	coming.
seas	*(shās)*	stand.	**seasamh**	*(shāssüv)*	standing.
gluais	*(glooash)*	move.	**gluasad**	*(gloo as üd)*	moving.
iarr	*(eeür)*	ask.	**iarraidh**	*(eear-y)*	asking.
suidh	*(soo-y)*	sit.	**suidhe**	*(soo-y ü)*	sitting.
tuit	*(tootch)*	fall.	**tuiteam**	*(tooh tchüm)*	falling.

568. In vocabularies and dictionaries, the verbal noun, when not regularly formed, is usually given as well as the root verb.

GOVERNMENT OF THE PARTICIPLE.

569. A transitive participle takes its noun object in the genitive case, after the participle.

Bha an gille ag itheadh arain,　　*the lad was eating bread.*

Arain is the genitive case of **aran**, after **ag itheadh**. Literally the sentence is : The lad was at the eating **of bread**.

Tha an t-each a' breabadh an doruis,　*the horse is kicking the door.*

570. A transitive participle takes its noun object in the accusative case when that object is qualified by another noun in the genitive.

Tha an t-each air briseadh cas a' bhalaich,	*the horse has broken the boy's foot.*

571. When the object of a transitive participle is a personal pronoun, we use in Gaelic the possessive pronoun and a preposition in a combined form. Such a combination is called a prepositional possessive pronoun (par. 423). In such positions the participle becomes a pure substantive noun, hence the name, verbal noun.

Tha e 'gam bhualadh,	*he is striking me (at my striking).*
Cha bhi mi 'ga dusgadh,	*I will not waken her (at her awakening)*

572. When the intransitive participles " sitting," " standing," " sleeping," etc., convey the idea of state as they generally do they are rendered by the verbal noun preceded by the verb **bi** in any of its forms and the prepositional possessive pronouns formed from **ann** " in " (pars. 420-3, 430).

Tha e 'na shuidhe,	*he is sitting.*
Bithidh e 'na chadal,	*he will be sleeping.*
Bithidh i 'na cadal,	*she will be sleeping.*

573. When another verb than **bi** is used the infinitive takes the place of the participle, but in such cases state is not conveyed.

Chaidh e a chadal,	*he went to sleep.*
Thainig e a laighe,	*he came to lie down.*

574. An absolute clause or the beginning of a narrative is often expressed in Gaelic by the participle preceded by the prepositions **air, an deidh,** etc., with the preposition **do** " to " immediately following and preceding the noun, which it places in the dative case ; preceding a pronoun the preposition **do** becomes compounded with the pronoun. These may be rendered in English by " when," " after," " on," or by the past participle preceded by " having."

Air do'n luing seoladh,	*when the ship sailed,* or *the ship having sailed.*
Air do'n t-samhradh tighinn,	*when summer comes after summer comes. on summer coming. summer having come.*
Air dhomh tighinn air m'ais,	*on my coming back. after I come back.*

GOVERNMENT OF THE INFINITIVE.

575. One verb governs another in the infinitive.

Tha sinn a' dol a bhualadh,   *we are going to strike.*

576. The object of a transitive infinitive expressing purpose stands after the infinitive in the genitive case.

Thainig mi a bhualadh an doruis,   *I came to strike the door.*
Chaidh mi a dh' ol an uisge,   *I went to drink the water.*

577. If the object be a pronoun, the possessive pronoun or an emphatic personal takes its place. We use the preposition **gu.**

Tha e a' dol g'ur bualadh,   *he is going to strike you.*
Thog e lamh g'a bhualadh,   *he raised a hand to strike him.*
Feumaidh Iain mise 'phaidheadh,   *John must pay me.*

578. When the object to a transitive verb does not denote purpose it stands before the infinitive in the accusative case. All those compound expressions which do duty for verbs come under this rule as the infinitive and its noun are really the subject of these sentences, the predicate being the noun or adjective which immediately follows **is.**

Is toigh leam an leabhar a leughadh*   *I wish or desire to read the book.*
Dh'iarr e orm an dorus a dhunadh,   *he asked me to shut the door.*

* *cf.* Is toigh leam leughadh an leabhair,
     The reading of the book (by another) is a pleasure to me.

579. In a few instances, principally intransitives, the infinitive sign is not required and no aspiration takes place.

Feumaidh mi suidhe,   *I must sit.*
Cha'n fheum thu seasamh,   *you must not stand.*

580. Those verbs which require a preposition after them to complete their sense take their object after the infinitive. The object is governed in the dative case by the preposition. A pronoun object becomes a prepositional pronoun.

Chaidh mi a bhreith air an each,   *I went to catch the horse.*
Cha deachaidh mi a bhreith air,   *I did not go to catch him.*
Theid mi a bhreith orra,   *I will go to catch them.*

581. **ri**, signifying " to," has the effect of changing the sense to that of future passive (par. 607).

Tha an leabhar ri fhaicinn,   *the book is to be seen.*
Tha iad ri tighinn,   *they are to come.*

582. In English a noun of action can usually be substituted for the infinitive, and in translating it with the possessive pronoun it is better to do so. Consider the effect of " my to come " with " my coming."

Is fhearr suidhe goirid na seasamh fada,
> *It is better to sit short than to stand long.*
> *better short sitting than long-standing.*

Bonnach a mhealladh na cloinne,
> *A bannock for deceiving of* (not *to deceive*) *the children.*

Thainig orm falbh,
> (*It came on me to go*) *I was obliged going.*

Bha mi am shuidhe,
> (*I was in my to sit*) *I was* (*in my*) *sitting.*

583. Read in Gaelic and translate into English :—

1. De tha e a' deanamh ?   2. Tha e a' seinn a nis.   3. De bha e a' deanamh ?   4. Bha e ag iasgach anns an t-sruth.   5. De bha iad a' togail ?   6. Bha iad a' togail tighe.   7. Caite am bheil e a' dol ?   8. Tha e a' dol g'ur bualadh.   9. Thog e cas g'a bhreabadh.   10. Thainig e gu mo phiuthar 'fhaicinn.   11. Tha mi a' dol g'a bhualadh.   12. Dh' iarr e orm an dorus a dhunadh.   13. De bhitheas e a' deanamh ?   14. Bithidh e a' ruith dachaidh.   15. Tha mi a' tighinn dachaidh a nis.   16. De tha thu ag iarraidh ?   17. Am bheil d' athair a' dol a dh' iasgach ?   18. Thainig a' chaileag bheag a dh' fhrosgladh an doruis.   19. Tha an gille mor a' trusadh nan clachan.   20. Bha na daoine a' labhairt ri cach-a-cheile.   21. Tha an ciobair a' dol dachaidh anns a' mhaduinn.   22. Bha na fir 'nan suidhe.   23. Tha e 'na shuidhe.   24. Tha mi am sheasamh an so.   25. Thog e lamh g'ar bualadh.   26. Tha e a' togail an uird mhoir.   27. Tha an gille a' briseadh na cloiche.

584. Translate into Gaelic :—

1. The little girl will be opening the door.   2. What is he doing now ?   3. He is fishing in the stream.   4. What is that man doing ?   5. He is going to strike the boy.   6. What is that other man doing ?   7. He is coming to kick the dog.   8. I will lift my left hand to strike him.   9. He is breaking my stick.   10. He was eating bread this morning.   11. He will be going home now.   12. Will the boy be running away ?   13. The men were sitting at the door.   14. What were you saying ?   15. The little boy was gathering stones.   16. What were you asking ?   17. Will your father be going fishing this evening ?   18. The boy is breaking stones with a hammer.   19. He will be striking us with the stones.   20. We were breaking them.   21. James is putting bread on the table.   22. They were running home.   23. What are you building ?   24. I am building a small house.   25. John is striking the door.   26. He came to see my sister last night.   27. I will be striking him.   28. He has not been drinking water.   29. Who says that ?

LESSON XLIX.

SYNOPSIS OF A GAELIC VERB.

585. When the verb is alike in the three persons of both numbers as is the case in most of the tenses, it will be enough to show the 1st person singular only, as a sufficient guide to all the other persons. The remaining persons can be formed by changing the pronoun. The following shows the independent form. By the aid of the prepositions **a'**, **ag**, and **air**, we have nearly as complete a set of tenses as can be formed in English.

INDICATIVE ACTIVE.

Pres. Progres.		Tha mi a' bualadh	*I am striking (at striking).*
,,	*Perfect,*	Tha mi air bualadh,	*I have struck (after striking).*
,,	*Perfect (contin.)*	Tha mi air bhi a' bualadh,	*I have been striking (I am after being striking).*
Fut. Indef.		Buailidh mi,	*I shall strike.*
,,	*Progress.*	Bithidh mi a' bualadh,	*I shall be striking.*
,,	*Perfect,*	Bithidh mi air bualadh,	*I shall have struck.*
,,	*Perfect (contin.)*	Bithidh mi air bhi a' bualadh,	*I shall have been striking (after being striking).*
Past Indef.		Bhuail mi,	*I struck.*
,,	*Progres.*	Bha mi a' bualadh,	*I was striking (a-striking).*
,,	*Perfect,*	Bha mi air bualadh,	*I had struck (after striking).*
,,	,, *(cont.)*	Bha mi air bhi a' bualadh,	*I had been striking.*

INDICATIVE PASSIVE.

Pres. Defin.,		Tha mi buailte,	*I am struck.*
,,	*Progres.*	Tha mi 'gam bhualadh,	*I am being struck.*
,,	*Perfect,*	Tha mi air mo bhualadh	*I have been struck.*
Fut. Indef.,		Bithidh mi buailte,	*I shall be struck.*
		Buailear mi,	*I shall be struck.*
,,	*Perfect,*	Bithidh mi air mo bhualadh,	*I will have been struck. (I will be after my striking).*
Past Indef.,		Dhuaileadh mi	*I was struck.*
		Bha mi buailte,	*I was struck.*
,,	*Progres.,*	Bha mi 'gam bhualadh,	*I was being struck.*
,,	*Perfect,*	Bha mi air mo bhualadh	*I had been struck.*
Subjun. Active		Bhithinn a' bualadh,	*I would be striking.*
		Bhuailinn,	*I would strike.*
		Bhithinn air bualadh,	*I would have struck.*
,,	*Passive*	Bhithinn 'gam bhualadh	*I would be struck.*
		Bhithinn buailte,	*I would be struck.*
		Bhuailteadh mi,	*I would be struck.*
		Bhithinn air mo bhualadh,	*I would have been struck. (would have been after my striking)*

Exercise—Write a similar synopsis of the verbs, **ol** and **fag**.

LESSON L.

DEFECTIVE VERBS.

586. There are a number of verbs which are deficient or defective, being used in one tense or part of a tense only. The following are the more commonly used forms of these verbs.

arsa, ars', orsa, ors', said, quoth.

Used in the past tense only:

Arsa mise,   *said I.*   Ars' esan,   *said he.*

theab (*hăhp*) had almost, had nearly, was like.

Used in the past tense only, affirmative, negative, etc. :

Theab mi tuiteam,   *I nearly fell.*
An do theab e tuiteam,   *did he almost fall.*
Ged nach do theab mi tuiteam,   *though I was not like falling.*

feuch (*făch*) behold, see ; **feuchaibh** behold ye.

These are the only forms. **feuch** " to show " is not defective.

tiugainn (*tchookynn*) ; **tiugainnibh** ; come away.

Used in these persons of the imperative only :

Eirich agus tiugainn O !   *rise and let us come away !*
Tiugainnibh,   *come along.*

trothad (*trho-üt*) ; **trothadaibh** ; come here ; come hither.

is (*iss*) is, are, etc. ; **bu** was, were, etc.

The assertive form of the verb **bi** ; used in the present and past tenses only (see Lesson XVII.).

AUXILIARY VERBS.

587. The idea of possibility, permission, duty, necessity, as conveyed by the English verbs " may," " might," " must," " ought," etc.

We have in Gaelic two regular verbs **faod** (*föd*) and **feum** (*făm*) which are used with the verbal nouns of other verbs and have the same force as English " may " and " must," etc.

faodaidh mi (*föd-y*) I may.
dh'fhaodainn (*ghödynn*) I might.
gu'n d'fhaodainn that I might.
dh'fhaodadh e it might
am faodainn ? might I ?
cha d'fhaod mi, I might not have,
am faod mi ? may I ?

feumaidh mi (*făm-y*) I must.
dh'fheumainn (*yămynn*) I would need.
dh'fheum (*yăm*) I would need have.
an d'fheum mi ? (*dyăm*) had I to ?
cha d'fheum mi, I must not.
am feum mi ? must I ?

151

Further examples with the infinitive :—

Faodaidh mi falbh am maireach,	*I may go to-morrow.*
Am faod mi falbh ?	*may I go ?*
Ma dh'fhaodas mi falbh (*yŏdüs*),	*if I may go.*
Dh'fhaod mi falbh,	*I might have gone.*
Na'n d'fhaod mi falbh,	*if I might have gone.*
Ma dh'fheumas e falbh (*yămüs*),	*if he must go.*
Faodar a bualadh (*fŏdür*),	*she may be struck.*
Feumar a bualadh (*fămür*),	*she must be struck.*
Feumaidh tu a bualadh,	*you must strike her.*
Faodaidh e a' chlach a bhualadh,	*he may strike the stone.*

COMPOSITE PREPOSITIONAL VERBS.   PRE VERBS.

588. There is a very important class of idioms in connection with the verbs **is** and **bu** and the preposition **le** " with." These idioms relate to the action of the will, intellect, the memory, the fancy, and at times the passions.

English verbs such as " I choose " ; " I desire " ; " I disregard " ; " I pity " ; " I am fond " ; " I prefer " ; " I love " ; " I remember " ; " I wonder " ; " I am surprised." It seems " right," " wrong," " poor," " just," " bad," " painful," and many others of kindred meaning are thus rendered into Gaelic.

is miann leam (*mee-ün*),	I wish, or desire (it is a wish with me)
is toigh leam (*toi*),	I love (it is love with me).
is eol leam (*yol*),	I know (it is knowledge with me).
is coma leam,	I don't care for (it is indifference with me).
is cuimhne leam (*koo ynü*),	I remember (it is memory with me).
is fearr leam (*fyărr*),	I prefer (it is better with me).
is deise leam (*tchăshü*),	I think it is pretty *or* it seems easier to me.
is annsa leam, (*aunnsü*),	I prefer (it is more dear with me).
is miosa leam (*meesü*),	I pity (it is worse with me).
is maith leam (*mah*),	I like. I am glad (it is good with me).

An object to these verbs is placed next after the pronoun ; **Is toigh leam Mairi** " I love Mary—I am fond of Mary." They are also used with all the verbal particles (494) **Ma 's toigh leam Mairi** " If I do love Mary," etc.

589. Here is an example of this last idiom in a very simple sentence. **Is maith dhomh e ach cha mhaith leam e** (*lit.*), " It is good for me but it is not good with me." Here the first clause may be translated literally, but the second is

152

idiomatic and signifies " I do not like it " (though, perhaps, it is good for me).

Many of these idioms are used in comparison, thus :—Is fearr leam or na airgiod " I prefer gold to silver."

590. The preposition **do** " to " and the prepositional pronouns formed from it also combine with the verbs **is** and **bu** in representing a number of English verbs, as :—**is urrainn do** " can "; **is urrainn domh** " I can "; **is aithne do** " know."

is aithne[1] domh,	I know.	is mithich[3] domh,	it is time for me.
is eudar[2] domh,	I must.	is eiginn[4] domh,	I must.
is urrainn[5] domh,	I can.	is urrainn duinn,	we can.
b' urrainn domh,	I could.	b' urrainn duinn,	we could.
is coir dhomh,	I ought.	is eudar dhomh,	I must.
bu choir dhomh,	I ought.	b' eudar dhomh,	I was obliged (had to).

[1] *anü ;* [2] *ādür ;* [3] *my ych ;* [4] *ākynn ;* [5] *oor ynn.*

591.   EXERCISES.

Vocabulary.

gus, prep. to, till.   **air ais,** adv., back.

592. Read in Gaelic and translate into English :—

1. Faodaidh tu suidhe ach cha'n fhaod thu seasamh. 2. Am faod mi seasamh air an lar? 3. Am feum thu dol air ais ? 4. Feumaidh thu. 5. Ma dh' fheumas mi dol dachaidh cha till mi. 6. Co a dh' fhaodas tighinn ? 7. Ma dh'fheumas sibh, feumaidh sibh. 8. Cha'n urrainn duinn tilleadh. 9. Is coir duibh tighinn. 10. Is aithne dhomh gur coir dhuinn tighinn ach cha'n urrainn dhuinn. 11. Theab mi tuiteam an trath so. 12. Cha'n urrainn dhuibh fhaotainn a nis. 13. Cha'n aithne dhomh de a thachras. 14. Is eudar dhuinn a bhi samhach. 15. Feumaidh sibh a bhi 'nur seasamh. 16. Is coir do na caileagan a bhi sàmhach. 17. Deanadh e na's urrainn da. 18. Nach b'urrainn sibh an tigh fhaicinn ? 19. Cha b'urrainn daibh a bhi ann aig seachd uairean. 20. Eirich agus tiugainn O ! ars' esan.

593. Translate into Gaelic :—

1. I must go if I cannot stay. 2. May I not stay longer ? 3. No. You must go. 4. You ought not to say that. 5. I know that I ought not. 6. Do you know what it is ? 7. No. You ought to know (*fios a bhi agaibh*). 8. Do you like milk or do you prefer beer. 9. I do not like beer. 10. You may go now. 11. Must I go now ? 12. Yes. 13. He had to stay till the morning. 14. If he had to go

he ought to have told us.   15. You may stay if you wish, but I know
you ought to go.   16. He did not do what he could.   17. He ought
to have done what he could.   18. If he does not do what he can, he
ought not to be here.   19. He could not see, but he could speak.
20. You ought to tell what you know.   21. I might see you in the
evening.

LESSON LI.

594.   THE PREPOSITION.

aig, at,
air, on, upon.
anns (*awns*) in.
ann an, in a.
anns an, in the.
a, as, out of.
bho, o, from, out of.
de (*tchā*) of.
do, to, into.
eadar (*ātŭr*) between.
gun, without.

fo (*foh*) under, below.
gu, gus (*goo, goos*) to, towards.
le, leis, with, by.
re (*rā*) during, for.
ri (*ree*) **ris**, at, to, against.
mu, about, around.
roimh (*roye*) before.
thar (*har*) over, across.
troimh (*troee*) **trid**, through.
mar (*mŭr*) like.
chun, thun, to, towards.

anns, as, gus, leis, ris, are the forms used before the article
or relative pronouns.

595. Most simple prepositions govern the dative case,
so that when we have an indefinite noun following a preposition we have :—

> The dative singular masculine like the nominative
> singular.
> The dative singular feminine like the genitive feminine
> with the omission of the final **e**.
> The dative plural masculine like the genitive singular.
> The dative plural feminine adds **an** or **ean** to the
> nominative singular.

596. But when the noun is definite and we have the preposition followed by the definite article, aspiration takes
place in the dative case singular, both masculine and
feminine.   Definite nouns with an initial **d, l, n, r, s, t**, do
not aspirate (par. 38).

Indefinite.		*Definite.*	
air bord,	on a table.	**air a' bhord,**	on the table.
air gruaidh,	on a cheek.	**air a' ghruaidh,**	on the cheek.
ann am baile,	in a town.	**anns a' bhaile,**	in the town.

Indefinite.		_Definite._	
ann an dorus,	in a door.	**anns an dorus**,	in the door.
ann an cathair,	in a chair.	**anns a' chathair**,	in the chair.
a tigh,	out of a house.	**as an tigh**,	out of the house.
le bata,	with a stick.	**leis a' bhata**,	with the stick.
ri duine,	to a man.	**ris an duine**,	with the man.

597. **Gun** "without"; **do** "to"; **fo** "under"; **bho, o** "from"; **mar** "like" "as"; **mu** "about"; **troimh** "through"; **roimh** "before"; **de** "of" aspirate in the dative singular both definite and indefinite nouns as well as conforming to the rule aforementioned.

598. Observe that an indefinite noun beginning with **d, t, s**, aspirates, but when the same noun is definite it resists aspiration as the effect of following the dental **n** of the article.

Indefinite.		_Definite._	
de cheo,	of mist.	**de'n cheo**,	of the mist.
do chill,	to a grave.	**do'n chill**,	to the grave.
fo bhord,	under a table.	**fo 'n bhord**,	under the table.
mar chraoibh,	like a tree.	**mar a' chraobh**,	like the tree.
mu phairt,	about a part.	**mu 'n phairt**,	about the part.
o mhod,	from a court.	**o 'n mhod**,	from the court.
roimh ghunna	before a gun.	**roimh 'n ghunna**	before the gun.
troimh thir,	through a land.	**troimh 'n tir**,	through the land.
fo dhorn,	under a fist.	**fo 'n dorn**,	under the fist.
do shuil,	to an eye.	**do 'n t-suil**,	to the eye.

599. The simple Gaelic preposition is capable of being used very extensively. The most peculiar of its uses is to form a compound with the pronouns, of which we give a complete list. The contents of this table should be familiar to every would-be-learner of Gaelic (par. **404**).

600. **eadar** "between" governs the accusative case which is the same as the nominative in Gaelic.

Eadar fear agus bean, _between man and wife._
Eadar a' chlach agus a' chraobh, _between the stone and the tree._
mar governs the accusative case when the noun is definite.

THE PREPOSITION **ann** " IN."

601. **ann an, ann am.** Observe the duplication of the preposition **ann** here, it is used in this form before an indefinite noun both singular and plural and may be called an emphatic form. (See also the particle **ann** (Lessons **16, 35**).

602. **ann an** " in " before a definite noun, which in turn is qualified by another noun in the genitive, may give the student some trouble. It has always been a stumbling block to learners. The duplication is common in all writing, but good Gaelic writers are coming to avoid it more and more.

Ann an comhairle nan aingidh,	*in the counsel of the wicked.*
Ann an slighe nam peacach,	*in the way of sinners.*
Ann an lagh an Tighearna,	*in the law of the Lord.*
Ann an tigh-a-mhinisteir,	*in the minister's manse.*
An ait a mhic,	*in the place of his son.*

ann an in these sentences is this duplicated or emphatic preposition **ann** " in " and must not be mistaken or confused with the article and preposition **anns an, anns a'**, " in the." A definite noun qualified by a definite noun never takes the article (par. 212, 289, 290). Don't be misled by the English idiom.

603. **anns an** " in the " is often contracted

Singular	'S an tir (*for* anns an tir),	*in the land.*
Plural,	'S na h-aitibh sin,	*in these places.*

IDIOMATIC USES OF THE PREPOSITION " OF."

604. The preposition " of " is one which has many applications and meanings, both in English and Gaelic. We will endeavour to classify the more common uses as follows :—

(a) Source, origin, cause, possession.
(b) Class, rank, or a partitive reference.
(c) " Of " has the meaning of " among," " on," " from," " taking from," etc.
(d) " Of " expressing a property, quality, or attribute.
(e) A verbal form " the better of it," etc.

(a) " Of " coming between two English nouns is not translated into Gaelic. We employ the genitive case as that case in Gaelic, as in certain other languages, gives the idea of source, origin, cause, possession, etc. (par. 212, 289).

(b) " Of " may mean class, rank, or have a partitive reference, when it is rendered by **de** (same as the French **de**) ; whenever it follows numerals ; adjectives of the comparative and superlative degree ; partitives ; nouns denoting fullness, abundance or scarcity. The noun following **de** being in the dative (pars. 302, 342).

Airde de 'n teaghlach,	*the tallest of the family.*
Cuid de na fir,	*some of the men.*

Before a noun or adjective beginning with a vowel or an **f** followed by a vowel **de** is written **dh'** ; thus :—**dh' fhear** " of a man " ; **dh' aon inntinn** " of one mind." In current practice the favourite mode of showing aspiration where **de** is used before **f** or a vowel, appears to be **a dh'**, which is a duplication of the preposition, thus :—**a dh' fhear ; a dh' àon inntinn**.

Armailt mhor de dhaoinibh agus a dh' eachaibh,
A great army of men and of horses

Again observe, we say, **pios iaruinn**, where **iaruinn** is in the genitive ; **pios de iarunn** or **pios de dh' iarunn—iarunn** being the dative after the preposition **de**.

(c) " Of " may have the sense of the genitive plural of the personal pronouns when it follows words denoting a part. It may mean " some of us," " how many of us," " among," " on," " from," as :—**gach fear againn** " each man of us " ; **cia agaibh** " which of you " ; **cia aca** " which of them " (not **dinn** " of us " ; **dibh** " of you " etc). **Cia aca is fearr leat** ? " Which of them do you like best ? " = " which do you prefer ? " But this is peculiar to the plural of these prepositional pronouns only, compare, " he spoke of him," *i.e.* " on him " as " on a subject," **labhair e air** ; " he spoke of us " **labhair e oirnn**.

" Of = from ". **Fear o Ghlaschu,** " a man from Glasgow " = " a man of Glasgow " = " a Glasgow man." **Rinn se e uaithe fein** " he did it of himself " (*lit.* " from " = " it proceded from him as the originator.")

" Of, off " in the sense of " taking from " ; " of " possession ; motion " out of."

Thug e 'n diollaid de'n each,	*he took the saddle off the horse.*
Tha gu leor agam dheth,	*I have enough of it.*
Gearr sliseag de'n mhulachaig,	*cut a slice from the cheese.*
Mac do dh' Alasdair,	*a son to (of) Alexander.*
Thainig an t-eun as an ubh,	*the chicken has come out of the egg.*
As an uisge,	*out of the water.*

(d) When " of " expresses property, quality, or attribute, " of " has no equivalent in Gaclic. In the absence of any preposition the noun remains in the nominative case (par. 304).

Fear is mor neart,	*a man of great strength.*
Fear is mo ciall,	*a man of the greatest sense.*

(e) An idiomatic application of " of " in phrases like **is truimide am poca** " the bag is the heavier of it." **Truimide** being a verbal form compounded of **truime** " heavy " and **deth** " of it " (par. 364).

" Perhaps," " probably," " likely " are translated by **moide** (compounded of **mo** " greater " from **mor** " great " and **de** " of it " ; *i.e.* " greater probability of it ") (par. 364).

Cha mhoide gu 'n thainig e,   *very likely he has not come.*
Cha mhoide gu 'm bheil thu slan, *perhaps you are not quite well.*

605.   THE PREPOSITION **air.**

We have already given phrases where **air** is used idiomatically.

1st—**air** is used to express any quality of mind or body ; **tha acras orm** " I am hungry " (Lesson XV.) ; rest :— **air a' bhord** " on the table."

2nd—**air** means " in." The words denoting measure and weight are followed by **air** :—

Mile air fad,	*a mile in length.*
Slat air airde,	*a yard in height.*
Punnd air chudthrom,	*a pound in weight.*

3rd—Buying and selling. **Air** stands for " for," in this sense it is placed before the noun of price or the thing priced. " What is the price for that coat ? " is translated into Gaelic **ciod tha air a' chota sin**? or **cia an luach tha an cota sin** ? as if the price were marked on the article. To buy a thing for or at a certain price is to buy it on that price, as :—**fhuair e an leabhar sin air tasdain** " he got that book for (on) a shilling " (see note page 98)

606.   THE PREPOSITION **do** " TO."

Do is used as a preposition with the infinitives of verbs. It has been changed in its form probably as the effect of aspiration to **a** in connection with infinitives beginning with a consonant; thus instead of being written **do bhi** " to be " it is now the common practice to write **a bhi**, and so with the other consonant infinitives. With infinitives beginning with a vowel or **f** followed by a vowel the form of the preposition is **a dh'**; thus, **a dh' ol** " to drink " ; **a dh' ltheadh** " to eat " ; **a dh' fhagail** " to leave " ; but, **a fhreagairt** " to answer," where **f** is followed by a consonant (par. 538).

607.　　　The Preposition **ri** " to."

Ri signifying " to," " towards " has when placed instead of **ag** before the verbal noun, the effect of changing its signification into that of a future tense of the passive voice, thus :—**ri fhaicinn** " to be seen." **Ri** has also the effect of " at," " against," " during," " in," etc.

　Tha e ri brogan,　　*he is (at) making shoes.*

608.　　　The Preposition **gu** " to."

Gu signifies that the motion terminates at the object, as :—**gu tigh an duine** " to the man's house " (and no further); **gus an dorus** " to the door " (and no further); **gu Glaschu**, " to Glasgow "; **gu tuath**, " to north." Before the verbal noun **gu** intimates the beginning of motion, as :—**tha iad gu falbh** " they were about going," " on the point of going." The same particle is used as an adverbial prefix to convert adjectives into adverbs and then corresponds to the English suffix " ly " :—**gu mor** " very great," " greatly "; **gu h-olc** " badly." " For," " during," **gu brath, gu siorruidh** " for ever." **Gus** the form used before the article governs the accusative case. (pars. 452, 577).

609.　　　The Preposition **gun** " without."

Gun signifies " without " ; before a noun it corresponds to the English affix " less " ; is equivalent to a negative.

Gun eolas,	*without knowledge.*	Gun airgiod,	*without money.*
Gun chiall,	*senseless.*	Gun churam,	*careless.*

　Dh'aithn e dhomh gun sin a dheanamh,
　　　　　he ordered me not to do that.

610.   THE PREPOSITIONS **aig**, and **le**.

For idioms with the preposition **aig**, " at " see Lesson
XII.   For the preposition **le** " with," " in possession,"
etc. see Lesson XX.

611. Read in Gaelic and translate into English :—

1. Ciod a' phris a tha air an iasg ?   2. Fhuair Iain an da iasg air
tasdain   3. Ciod thainig eadar duibh, a Sheumais ?   4. Bha mise
agus an ciobair air a' mhonadh ach bha an abhainn eadarainn.   5.
C'ait' an robh thu anns a' mhaduinn ?   6. Bha mi ag iasgach.   7.
Co bha leat ?   8. Bha Calum, mac an t-saoir leam.   9. Bu choir
dhuibh a bhi anns an achadh.   10. Bu choir, ach gheall mi breac no
dha do mhathair Chaluim.   11. Thug am balach beag an cat dubh
bho 'n bhord.   12. Fhuair mi an sgian eadar a' chraobh agus an tigh.
13. Chaidh sinn troimh 'n bhaile mu fheasgar agus rainig sinn ar
dachaidh roimh mhaduinn.   14. Bhuail an duine sin mi le cloich
air a' ghruaidh.   15. Bithidh mi aig an dorus le maide aig coig
uairean.   16. Chaidh an duine seachad air an dorus an trath so.
17. Thilg mi a' chlach thar na sraide.* 18. Chaidh an luch troimh
'n toll nuair a bha an cat 'na deidh.   19. Tha an duine sin gun
churam.

612. Translate into Gaelic :—

1. Where were you this morning ?   2. I was fishing.   3. Who was
with you ?   4. John, the fisherman's son, was with me.   5. Was
that man not with them ?   6. The house is between the river and the
sea.   7. The boys go home during the summer.   8. We like fishing
on the river in the evening.   9. I went round the house about five
o'clock.   10. I found a man at the window.   11. Which of them do
you prefer to come with you this time ?   12. I must go to the town
now.   13. You ought not to go alone.   14. I will come with you
to-day.   15. I am going to the town alone.   16. You can go now
and you can be there before me.   17. I was before you at the bridge
to-day but he was there before me.   18. You were before me at the
town last night.   19. This wall is high, but I am going over it (*m*).
20. The rain is heavy but it is going past us.   21. That man is going
over the river in a boat.   22. Do not stand between me and the fire.
23. It is cold and the wind is going through me.   24. John was
between us this morning, but James is between you and me now.
25. This is too big for me now.   26. The wind will go through it.   27.
He was without money or sense.   28. You speak of him as being
senseless.   29. He is a man of the greatest sense.   30. He must be
an educated man.   31. He has come in place of his father.   32. I
fell into a hole and almost broke my leg.   33. We have come through
a land without trees.

*__thar chun thun, re__ and **trid**, are followed by the genitive of nouns.

LESSON LII.

613. THE COMPOUND PREPOSITION.

a chum to, unto.
thun for the purpose.
a dhith (*yee*) without.
a dheasbhuidh (*yesvi*) for want of.
a los, for the purpose of.
a reir (*ŭ rār*) according to.
a thaobh (*ŭ hŏv*) as to, regarding.
air feadh (*ār fyŏgh*) among.
air ghaol (*ghŏll*) ⎫ for the sake
air sgath (*skâh*) ⎭ of.
air muin, on the back of, top of.
air son (*ār-son*) for, because.
air culaobh (*koolŭv*) behind (at the back of).
air beulaobh (*bālŭv*) in front, before.
an cois (*kosh*) ⎫ near to,
am fagus (*fakŭs*) ⎭ beside.
an lathair (*llâ ŭr*) in presence of, before.

am measg (*ŭm mesk*) among.
an aghaidh (*ŭn ŏghy*) against.
an aite (*ŭn âh tchŭ*) in place of.
an coinneamh (*konnyŭv*) to meet.
an deidh (*ŭn tchāy*) after, behind.
as eugmhais (*ākvās*) for want of.
comhla ri (*kolla ree*) ⎫ along
cuide ri (*koo tchŭ ree*) ⎭ with.
dhionnsaidh (*yoonsy*) to, unto, towards.
fa chomhair (*cho-ŭr*) opposite.
mu choinneamh, opposite.
mu 'n cuairt, round about.
mu thimchioll(*himichŭl*),
mu dheighinn (*yā ynn*), concerning, about.
os ceann (*os kyaunn*) ⎫ above.
as cionn (*os kyoonn*) ⎭ overhead.

614. Compound prepositions are mostly formed of a noun and simple preposition and are generally followed by the genitive case of the qualifying noun. That it should do so is according to rule, as will be seen when the sentence is transposed into Gaelic idiom (par. 290). " For the girl " we transpose to " for the sake of the girl " **air son na caileige**. Whose sake ? The girl's sake. **Caileige** here is the genitive of **caileag**, qualifying the noun **son**.

Further examples :—

An lathair an t-sluaigh, *before the people—in presence of the people.*
An aghaidh naduir, *against nature—in the face of nature.*

615. The pronouns governed by these prepositions :—

(1) are placed between the simple preposition and the noun and
(2) are rendered in the genitive case.

Ann ar measg, *in the midst of us* (lit. : *in our midst*).
Os bhur cionn, *above you* (,, *over your head*).
Air do chulaobh, *behind you* (,, *at your back*).
Air mo shon, *for me* (,, *for my sake*).

616. That these prepositions should in this way govern the pronouns is quite natural, as is plain from their meaning.

In English the words " in our midst " is the same as " in the midst of us "; the possessive pronoun " our " holds the same place as the genitive personal pronoun " of us "; its corresponding term in Gaelic is **ar**, " of us " = " our "; it is compounded with the preposition **ann** thus :—'**nar measg** " in our midst " (pars. 422-4).

617. Read in Gaelic and translate into English :—

1. Tha an cu donn air do chulaobh. 2. Chunnaic mi an duine air beulaobh an tighe. 3. Bha e 'na sheasamh ri h-aghaidh. 4. An uair a bha sinn 'nar seasamh aig an dorus thilg am balach beag clachan 'nar measg. 5. Cheannaich an duine na leabhraichean 'nam lathair. 6. Bha mise air feadh na coille anns a' mhaduinn agus fhuair mi uan beag aig ceann an rathaid. 7. Chaidh mi mu 'n cuairt air a' gharradh agus fhuair mi clachan mora ann an aite nan craobhan. 8. Chaidh e a steach do 'n tigh. 9. Chuir e a lamh air mo cheann agus shuidh mise air a bheulaobh. 10. Thainig mi a dh'ionnsaidh na h-aibhne agus chunnaic mi caora comhla ris an uan. 11. Dh'fhag mi an cu comhla ris na h-eich. 12. Am bheil an cu dubh comhla riutha? 13. Cha'n eil. 14. Chaidh sinn mu 'n cuairt air a' phairc.

618. Translate into Gaelic :—

1. I saw a man in front of the house. 2. My faithful dog ran in front of me towards him. 3. We were standing at the door and a big boy threw stones amongst us. 4. There is a black cat behind you. 5. Strike it with a stick for me. 6. We will go round about the house now. 7. Have you heard concerning that man yet ? 8. I have come for the purpose of speaking about that. 9. Will you come along with me into the house ? 10. What is that above us ? 11. The wind is against us ; will we take shelter*behind this wall ? 12. That house opposite is mine. 13. I have it in place of one I lost by fire. 14. He came amongst us. 15. We went for the sake of the girl. 16. I put my hand on her head and she sat in front of me. 17. When we were sitting at the window a bad boy threw stones amongst us. 18. We sent the dog after him and he ran in front of a man. 19. The minister was standing there in the presence of the people. 20. We were at sea and we lost the oars during the night.

* fasgadh ——————

LESSON LIII.

THE ADVERB.

619. Adverbs are not so called because they are added to verbs, for they are joined to other words, including verbs, for the purpose of modifying references to time, place, manner, and quality.

620. Most adjectives can be converted into adverbs by placing **gu** before them. **Gu** expresses the same as the English suffix " ly " does ; **gu** prefixes **h-** before vowels. Thus **math** " good " an adjective becomes adverbial when **gu** is placed before it, **gu math** "well"; **olc** "bad"; **gu h-olc** " badly, worse." **Gu** used thus before an adjective has of itself no definite meaning ; an adjective used with **gu** to limit a verb suffers no change ; no addition is made to it ; an adjective used with **gu** is subject to limitation by another adjective.

Thuit clach gu luath,	*a stone fell quickly.*
Thuit clach gu math luath,	*a stone fell very quickly.*
Tha e gu math dheth,	*he is well off (off it.)*

621. The prefixed particles—**glé, fior, ro***—denote a higher degree of quality ; they also aspirate their adjectives.

gle mhath, very well.   **ro dhileas**, exceedingly faithful.

622. Compound adverbs or adverbial phrases are generally made up of the article and prepositions combined with nouns and adjectives. Some of these adverbial phrases, in certain circumstances, are regarded as prepositions.

623.   ADVERBS OF TIME.

roimhe (*royü*) before.
cian, ages ago, far distant.
cheana (*chenü*) already.
a chlisgeadh, quickly.
a chaoidh, for ever (future).
a nis, nise, now.
a ris, rithist, again.
ainmig (*animik*) seldom.
am feadh, whilst.
am feasd (*fāst*) for ever.
am maireach, to-morrow.
an ceart uair, presently.
an comhnuidh (*üng kony*), habitually, continually.
an de, yesterday.
an diugh, to-day.
an earar (**ear-thrath**), the day after to-morrow.
an nochd, to-night.
an raoir (*rōyrr*) last night.
an uraidh (*oor-y* last year.

am bliadhna, this year.
an trath so } just now.
an drasda }
an toiseach, first. front,
an uair (**'nuair**) (*nooür*) when.
cuin ? c'uin ? (*koon*) when ?
a la, by day, daily.
a dh'oidhche (*ghoy chü*) by night.
a ghnath }
do ghnath } always.
fadheoidh (*fa y o y*) at last.
fathast (*fah-üst*) yet.
gu brath, for ever.
gu minig } often, frequently.
gu tric }
gu siorruidh, (*shyorry*) for ever.
idir (*y tchür*) at all.
mu dheireadh (*y ārügh*) at last.
re seal } for a time.
re tamuill }
riamh (*ree-üv*) ever (past).

* **ro** is an old particle (identical with Latin **pro**) surviving in disguise as a particle however in only two verbal forms, **robh** and **rinn**, although it is in common use as a particle intensifying the signification of an adjective : thus **mor** " great " ; **ro mhor**, " very great."

624. ADVERBS OF PLACE.

an ear (*ün er*) east.
an iar (*ün eeür*) west.
a bhos, bhos, on this side (rest).
a leth taobh, to one side.
a mach ⎰ out, without,
a muigh ⎱ outside.
a bhan, downwards (motion).
an aird, upwards (motion).
a nall, nall, to this side.
a null, nunn, to the other side.
a nuas, from above, down.
a nios, from below, up.
an sin, there.
an so, here.
an sud, yonder.

tuath (*tooü*) north.
deas (*tchäss*) south.
a thaobh, aside.
a steach ⎰ within, inside,
a stigh ⎱ into.
far (before am, an, nach), where
seachad, past.
sios (*shyüs*) downwards (motion)
suas (*sooüs*) upwards (motion).
shios (*hhyüs*) below, down (rest).
shuas (*hhooüs*) above (rest).
thall, on the other side (rest).
an sud 's an so ⎰ here and there
thall's a bhos ⎱
c'aite? (*kätchü*) where? (inter.)

625. ADVERBS OF MANNER, ETC.

anabarrach, exceedingly.
air eiginn scarcely, with difficulty
air leth, apart, separately.
air seacharan, astray.
a mhain, only.
amhuil, like as.
am bitheantas, usually.
comhla, together.
da rireadh, really.
fa leth, individually.
gle, ro, fior, very truly.
gu buileach, thoroughly.
uidh air n-uidh, gradually.

gu dearbh, ⎰ truly.
gu cinnteach, ⎱ certainly.
gu leir, altogether.
gu leoir, enough, plenty.
le cheile, together.
mar an ceudna, likewise.
maraon (araon), together.
mar sin, as that.
mar so, as this.
mar sud, as yon.
mu seach, alternately.
theagamh, perhaps.

626. A number of adverbs denote a state of rest, motion to, and from. Note carefully the rendering of some of these, and principally the rendering of the English words "up" and "down."

A **suas** and a **sios** are used when there is motion "up" or "down" from where we stand; **shuas** and **shios** are used for "rest" at some distance "above" or "below" us; a **nuas** and a **nios** are used when there is motion "towards" us from "above" or "below." A **bhos** is used when there is a question of "rest" near us; and **thall** when there is "rest" some distance away. Verbs of "rest" are used with adverbs of "rest"; and verbs of "motion" with adverbs of "motion."

" A chaidh sios (*went down*) gu h-ifrinn; a dh' eirich an treas la o mharbhaibh, a chaidh suas (*went up*) air neamh "—A' Chreud.

"*He descended into Hell; the third day He rose again from the dead; and ascended into Heaven*"—The Creed.

Tha e shuas ann an neamh,   *He is up in heaven.*

627. Deas and **tuath** also mean " right " and " left " hand. As regards the points of the compass, the observer, like the ancient Druids and sun-worshippers of old, is supposed to face the rising sun. Thus " the east " is called **an ear**, meaning " before," " in front of," the land or country immediately in front of the observer ; the country to the " right hand " is thus the " south," hence **an deas** ; for the same reason the " north " was called **an tuath**, the country to the " left hand " ; and the " west " **an iar**, the country at the " back," " after," " behind," i.e., the " hinterland," because in this way it was to them the land to which the " back " was turned. From these we have :—

o'n deas,	from the south.	**taobh an iar,**	the western side.
gaoth o'n deas,	the south wind.	**tuath-air,**	northerly exposure.
o 'n tuath,	from the north.	**Uibhist-a-Tuath,**	North Uist.
gaoth o'n tuath	the north wind.	**deas-ail,**	southward.

628. *Vocabulary.*

sloc nm. or nf., a pit, a hole.   **daonnan** (*dtönnün*) *adv.* always.
Gaidhlig (*gàlik*) nf. Gaelic   **tarsainn,** *adv.*, cross

629. Read in Gaelic and translate into English :—

1. Bha na coin a' ruith thall 's a bhos. 2. Chaidh iad a mach le cheile. 3. Am bheil an duine aig obair ? 4. Tha e shios anns an t-sloc. 5. Chaidh e a sios an raoir. 6. Thig e a nios am maireach. 7. Chaidh an ciobair a suas an de. 8. Chaidh na gillean thar a' cheile. 9. Cha robh mise riamh ann am bàta. 10. Bha mise ann am bàta an de agus bithidh mi ann am bàta eile am maireach. 11. C'aite am bheil am bàta ? 12. Tha i shios aig a' chladach. 13. Co tha shuas aig an tigh ? 14. Is e an duine sin. 15. Tha e gle mhath gu dearbh. 16. Chuala mise gu'n robh Iain tinn. 17. Cuin a thainig e ? 18. Am bheil e a stigh ? 19. Cha'n eil, chaidh e a mach air eiginn. 20. Co tha comhla ris ? 21. Is e Seumas a tha ann. 22. Tha Gaidhlig gu leoir aige. 23. Suas leis a' Ghaidhlig. 24. Thainig e a nall chun an doruis an drasda. 25. Tha e a nis a bhos aig ceann an tighe. 26. Bha mi deas is tuath, s-iar is s-ear, ach tha mi a nis ann an Albainn. 27. Cha'n fhag i gu brath e gus an traigh an cuan s-iar. 28. Chaidh mo dheadh chu air thoiseach orm is rinn e oirre.

630. Translate into Gaelic :—

1. The shepherd went up the hill in the morning but he came down in the afternoon. 2. He went out of town. 3. Was he ever from home before ? 4. He was from home last year. 5. When will he come home ? 6. Where is your son ? 7. He is in the house at the side of the river. 8. Will he cross the river ? 9. He will not cross to the other side to-day. 10. The river rose gradually. 11. His dog is running here and there. 12. He has been in my house but he will never (say " not ever ") be in it again. 13. Have you any Gaelic ?

14. I have plenty Gaelic.   15. We always speak Gaelic in this place.
16. Where is your other son to-night ?   17. They went out together.
18. I came up from Glasgow this morning and I go down again the
day after to-morrow.   19. According to John I should go oftener.
20. It is better to go oftener certainly.   21. I cannot go at present.
22. I saw him on the other side of the river among the trees.   23.
He comes often but seldom stays long.   24. When will he be back
again ?   25. Let us say individually " Up with the Gaelic."   26.
I am going over the ocean to the great west land and it is not likely
I will come eastwards again.   27. I may go to the south next year.

LESSON LIV.

631.   CONJUNCTIONS.

Simple Conjunctions.

ach,	but.	**na,**	than.
agus, 's, is,	and.	**ma,**	if.
bho'n, o'n,	since.	**mu'n,**	before, lest.
a chionn,	because.	**mur,**	if not.
coma,	however.	**mar,**	like, as.
eadhon,	even.	**no,**	or.
ged,	though.	**oir,**	for, because.
gidheadh,	yet, nevertheless.	**co, cho,**	as, so.
gu,	that.	**ri,**	as.

632. NOTE.—The word " only " is usually put in Gaelic
by using the negative verb and the conjunction **ach,** " but ";
e.g., **cha robh aige ach da each** (He had not but two horses).
He had only two horses.

633. The conjunction couples like cases of nouns, tenses
of verbs, etc.

Thuit agus bhris clach,	*a stone fell and broke.*
Fion agus bainne,	*wine and milk.*
Cha mheal e sith no solas,	*he shall not enjoy peace nor comfort.*
Thig no cha tig e,	*he shall come or shall not.*
Bagair ach na buail,	*threaten but don't strike.*

634. Some conjunctions are used in pairs and are said
to be co-relative.

Cho or **co** expressing a comparison requires **ri** or **ris**.

Tha e cho geal ris an t-sneachd,	*it is as white as snow.*
Tha Iain cho ard ri Seumas,	*John is as tall as James.*
Tha ise cho glic riut-sa,	*she is as wise as you.*

635. When **cho** signifies " so " ; when a certain condition is pointed out ; when it is followed by a verb ; **agus** is the co-relative of **cho**.

Tha e cho math agus is feumail dha,	*he is as good as is necessary.*
Bi cho math agus an dorus fhosgladh.	*be so good as to open the door.*
Cha robh mi cho bronach agus dall,	*I was not so mournful and blind.*
Bha e cho trom agus nach do thog mi e.	*it was so heavy that I did not lift it.*
Tha e cho laidir agus a bhitheas e,	*he is as strong as he will be.*
Bha e cho cinnteach agus gu'n do chuir e geall,	*he was so certain that he laid (put) a wager.*

636. **Cho** signifies " as " when followed by **ri, le**, etc.

Tha e cho caoin ri uan,	*he is as mild as a lamb (as=that he can be compared with a lamb).*

637.   INTERJECTIONS.

ma seadh!	verily !	**seadh!**	ay !
ob ob!	alas !	**gu deimhinn!**	verily !
ochon a righ!	alas !	**mo thruaighe!**	alas !
mata!	well !	**da rireadh!**	verily !
mo chreach!	alas !	**och, och!**	dear, dear !

An interjection requires the vocative case of nouns (aspirated).

Vocabulary.

Meal, *v.*, enjoy   **Solas** *nm.*, comfort pleasure.

638. Read in Gaelic and translate into English :—

1. Tha tigh agus garradh agam. 2. Is e fear no bean. 3. Cha tusa ach Seumas. 4. Mairi agus a brathair. 5. Cho mor ri creig. 6. Bha coin a' chiobair a' sealg nam fiadh an raoir. 7. Mheal mi sith agus solas. 8. Is gile a' ghrian na a'ghealach. 9. Bha e cho cinnteach sin cuin a'thainig e dhachaidh, A Sheumais. 10. Tha mi cho laidir agus a bhitheas mi. 11. Is e sin **na laghan** reir barail Iain. 12. Mata, mata. 13. Slan leibh.

dleasnas dleasanas (*dlăss(ŭ)nŭs*) *m.* duty, filial duty.

639. Translate into Gaelic :—

1. Is it man or woman ? 2. My house and garden. 3. Mary and her sister are here. 4. Her sister is as tall as ever she will be. 5. She was so certain that she was coming here. 6. I will have no peace nor comfort now. 7. Be so good as to shut the door and open the window. 8. John is as wise as Mary. 9. Is that according to John. 10. I shall go or shall not go according to time. 11. Nevertheless it is your duty to go. 12. Good-night. 13. Good-bye.

THE GAELIC LANGUAGE.

640. As an organ of intellectual expression and as a means of producing an aesthetical effect, what sort of language have we got ? As an organ of intellectual expression, the Gaelic, in common with Greek, German, Sanskrit, and all self-evolved languages, has the advantage of being able on all occasions to fling out new branches from the native stem and to grow to exuberant enlargement as occasion may require. What a patch-work has been our old Saxon, by the bitter frost that nipped its early budding, and the constant habit of borrowing thence resulting, the learned among us, as well as the unlearned though in very different ways, are constantly made to feel. The English language, as we have it now, is not so much a coherent growth as a disturbed organism. Our words accordingly are not coins with an intelligible sign and superscription, but mere counters. How different is Gaelic, where every word tells the story of its own composition to the unlettered peasant as vividly as to the most learned etymologist. A whale, for instance, is **muc-mhara**, literally " a sow of the sea ; " " an adopted son " is **uchd-mhac**, literally " a son of the bosom," as contrasted with the womb ; a swallow is **gobhlan-gaoithe**, i.e. " a bird that oars the breeze with its forky tail " ; while the word **cruthachadh**, " to create " used in the first verse of the first chapter of Genesis, to a Highland laddie under a competent teacher will at once suggest the fundamental notion of the Platonic philosophy is that **cruth** or " form " is the necessary and legitimate product of the action of Divine reason upon matter. Now every one knows that the English language, without a long process of root-digging in Greek and Roman soil, cannot be made to yield such significant results ; and therefore the Gaelic language for the education of the Highland peasantry has an advantage which English to the English peasant has not, and can never be made to have. But from this great advantage the poor Highlander has got little benefit, partly from the neglect of his language by schoolmasters and people of the middle and upper classes ; partly from the fact that beyond the sphere of the Scriptures and popular theology the language has received very scanty culture, and so instead of developing its own native powers it has fallen into a general habit of pilfering from the English.

The consequence is that though the Gaelic dictionary contains Celtic equivalents for such modern scientific terms as " chemistry," **feallsanachd-brighe**, yet as they have obtained no currency among the people, who in ninety-nine cases out of a hundred cannot spell the tongue which they speak, they are not to be regarded as forming part of the language ; and even in talking of objects which move in the familiar sphere of common life, for every Highlander that asks for his **biadh-maidne** nine hundred and ninety-nine would ask for his " breakfast."—*Prof. J. S. Blackie.*

How to Learn to Read Gaelic.

It was when well up in years that Professor John Stuart Blackie, in his rambling flights through the Highlands, began to take an interest in Gaelic. He says, " I began to gather a small collection of Gaelic words from the mere names of the places through which I travelled, aided by accidental incidents. The very name of the broad sloping ben, which I saw every morning, had its meaning and suggested cognate words to me. I am setting down these small personal experiences of mine, principally because I have found a notion generally prevalent that it is an extremely difficult language to learn and not to be overcome by any ordinary resolution. For the sake of those who may be disposed to follow in my track through these unfrequented ways I will jot down here the remaining steps of my procedure in the acquaintance of that venerable old tongue. I took the Gaelic Bible which, from my previous acquaintance with the English, I soon learnt to read. A Gaelic Grammar helped me over the difficulties of flexion. Southey, I remember, somewhere in his diary says, ' that it was his fashion always to commence the study of a new language with a version of the New Testament,' and there can be no doubt that to those who know their Bibles there can be no better method proposed. The language of both Gaelic and English versions is classic, and about the best to be had. Let the student read the Gaelic Bible daily, along with the English, and translate the one back into the other alternatively, and this will be a hundred times more efficient than any other method, and will work the language into his head.

" Various entertaining scraps of biography, history, and fictitious narrative furnished me, by degrees, with a large vocabulary, but gave no help in the ready use of those colloquial terms which are most necessary for intercourse with the people. To remedy this, my studies turned to the ' West Highland Tales ' and the dialogues in ' Caraid nan Gaidheal.' After this I kept steadily reading for an hour or two a day, till by frequent repetition the dictionary became superfluous. This, of course, is merely a matter of resolution and determination."

There have been published recently several volumes of Gaelic Tales, accompanied by English translations, legends and translations being printed on opposite pages, page for page. This has been done to help students of the language and enable them to arrive at the meaning of every sentence with ease and at once. The Gaelic and the English translations are so arranged into short paragraphs that there will be no difficulty in following the grammar. These are well calculated to help and encourage the student and sure to make him take pleasure in Gaelic.

A New Gaelic Numeration.

We have in Gaelic Self Taught kept to the present standards of the language. There is no doubt that a few improvements on standard Gaelic could be made—there is no living language perfect (and least of all is English). The following suggested improvement in the method of Gaelic numeration is put forward for consideration by the Gaelic Academy and Gaelic writers generally for gradual adoption.*

The " vigintal " system of numeration, as we may term the present Gaelic system, is a departure from the old decimal system of counting which still survives in the language of our cousins in Ireland. Our signs, both Roman and Arabic, are based on " tens," but in order to write or say mixed figures in words, we have at present to subject our minds to an acrobatic feat, e.g. take the figure " seventy-nine," this, after our mental struggle, becomes

---

* See an article by E. M. D. in " Alba," No. 10, new series.

" three-twenties-and-nineteen " **trì fichead 's naoi deug**. Arithmetic can never be successfully taught in Gaelic unless we change from this method.

The decimal system only requires a beginning. After **naoi ar fhichead** " twenty-nine " will come **trichead** " thirty " ; then **trichead 's a h-aon** "thirty-one " ; etc ; **ceithreachad** " forty " ; **caogad** " fifty " ; **siathad** " sixty " ; **seachdad** " seventy " ; **ochdad** " eighty " ; **naochad** " ninety " ; and so on with the higher numerals. Compare the effect of using such decimals in the following example :

" If Cain shall be avenged sevenfold, truly Lamech seventy and sevenfold." Gen. iv. 24.

" Ma dhiolar Cain a sheachd uiread, gu deimhin diolar Lamech a sheachd deug agus a thri fichead uiread."

This is the Gaelic of our familiar version, observe that we lose the pungency and the play on the figure words " seven " and " seventy-and-seven," the effect of which is to be considered. In using these decimal tens, we preserve and realise to some extent this play on the words " seventy-and-seven " in **seachdad 's a seachd.** Compare also the same as it is to be found in Bedel's Irish Bible.

Used in columns for addition, subtraction, etc., thus :—

35	thirty-five	**trichead 's a coig**
21	twenty-one	**fichead 's a h-aon**
43	forty-three	**ceithreachad 's a tri**
99	ninety-nine	**naochad 's a naoi**

Synopsis of Aspiration.

The following examples give the position and circumstances in which the initial letters are aspirated, if aspirable, for the exceptions see pars. 21 and 38. Some of the causes of aspiration can only be learned as they arise.

Nouns are aspirated after the possessive pronouns :—**mo** my ; **do** thy ; **a** his :—**mo bhrog, do chu, a cheann.**

Nouns commencing with a vowel are aspirated by the feminine possessive pronoun **a** her :—**a h-athair** her father.

Nouns are aspirated after the prepositions :—**do** to ; **mar** like ; **de** of ; etc. (see pars, 595-6-7) :—**do bhaile, mar chloich, bho dhuine, mu thom.**

The initial consonant of a noun is aspirated when preceded by certain adjectives, and when the first noun of a compound term qualifies the second noun :—**droch dhuine, cìs-mhaor, cas-cheum.**

The vocative of nouns in both genders, singular and plural, is aspirated: —**A ghille! A ghillean!**

Names of places, titles, and proper names of men are aspirated :— **Cuil-fhodair, Muilt Bharasdail, Failte Shir Seumas, cas Dhomhnuill.**

Nouns are aspirated after the numerals **aon, da, a' cheud** :—**aon fhear, da ghille, a' cheud mhac.**

The definite article **an** " the " becomes **a'** and causes aspiration ; after a preposition ending in a vowel becomes **'n** and causes aspiration, of all aspirable nouns in genitive and dative singular masculine, and nominative and dative singular feminine :—**aig a' ghille, do'n bhaile, a' chlach, aig a' chloich.**

The definite article **na** aspirates nouns commencing with a vowel in the genitive singular feminine, and the nominative and dative plurals of both genders :—**na h-aibhne, na h-aithrichean.**

An adjective immediately following and qualifying a genitive singular masculine noun is aspirated. An adjective following a definite dative masculine noun is aspirated. An adjective following a nominative or dative singular feminine noun is aspirated :— **an eich dhuinn, aig an each dhonn, bean mhor, leis a' chaileig bhig.**

An adjective qualifying a nominative plural noun which is formed like the genitive singular is aspirated (par. 336) :—**na h-eich dhonna.**

Compound nouns have the first consonant of the second word of the compound aspirated whether noun or adjective in agreement as an adjective with the gender of the first element. If the second element is a noun in the genitive plural it is aspirated in all cases— ***balla-chlach, coileach-dubh, ceann a' choilich-dhuibh.** (par. 295)

Adjectives are aspirated after the intensive prefixes **fior, ro, gle, sar** (par. 621) :—**gle ghlan**, very clean. **Gu** before vowels (par. 620) :—**gu h-olc** very badly.

Compound adjectives have the second element always aspirated : —**fairge thonn-gheal** (f), **cuan tonn-gheal** (m).

The verb is aspirated by the particles **ma, cha** (except **d** and **t**, par. 494) ; by the relative **a** (par. 440) ; the conjunction **ged** (page 123) ; the infinitive after **do** or **a** (par. 538). The past dependent and subjunctive are aspirated (Lessons xli., xlii.)

The verb **bu** aspirates words immediately following except initial **d** or **t** (par. 156) :—**bu cheart dhuit.**

Some words are always aspirated when naturally they should not be : **their** will say, **thoir** give, **thig** come, **gheibh** will get, **bho** from, **bhur** your, etc.

Some words are found aspirated and unaspirated without regard to rule, **fein fhein** self, **ta tha** is, **domh dhomh** to me, **diom dhiom** of me, etc.

---

* The Gaelic in this instance is more logical than English, **balla-chlach** is literally " a wall of stones." This qualifying noun is in the genitive plural for after all " a stone wall " is " a wall made of stones " and Gaelic construes accordingly, " of stones " being translated in the genitive plural, not genitive singular—**chloiche.**

GAELIC-ENGLISH VOCABULARY

The usual grammatical abbreviations are used.

The words in parenthesis are, in the case of nouns, peculiar forms of the genitive ; of verbs, forms of the verbal noun ; of adjectives, forms of the comparative. The numbers refer to pars. in Gaelic Self Taught.

A, *rel. pron.*, who, which, that.
A, *poss. pron.*, his, her, its.
A', *art.*, the.
Abair, *irr. v.*, say (ag radh).
Abhag, *nf.*, a terrier.
Abhainn (aibhne), *nf.*, a river.
Ach, *conj.*, but.
Achadh, *nm.*, a field.
Acras, *nm.*, hunger.
Ad (aide), *nf.*, a hat.
Adharc, *nf.*, a horn.
Agam, agad, etc. (see par. 114).
Aghaidh, an aghaidh, *prep.*, in the face of, against.
Agus, *conj.*, and.
Aig, ag, *prep.*, at.
Aige, aice, etc. (see par. 114).
Air, *prep.*, on (*pp.* on him, etc.) par. 138.
Air ball, *adv.*, immediately.
Airgiod (airgid), *nm.*, money.
Air-son, *prep.*, for, because.
Aithne, *nf.*, knowledge, acquaintance.
Aite, *nm.*, a place.
Aite (an aite), *prep.*, in place of.
Alba (Alba and **Albainn),** *nf.*, Scotland.
Allt (uillt), *nm.*, a brook.
An, am, *art.*, the.
An, am, *poss. pron.*, their.
An, am, *interr. particle.*
An, am, *relative pron.*, whom.
Anmoch, *adj.* and *adv.*, late.
An drasda, *adv.*, now. presently,
Ann, anns, *prep.*, in, into.
Ann, *adv.*, there, here.

Annam annad, etc. (*p.p.* 404).
Aon, h-aon, *nu. adj.*, one.
Aodach, *nm.*, a cloth, clothes.
Aonar, *nu. n.*, one person, alone.
Ar, *poss. pron.*, our.
Aran, *nm.*, bread.
Arbhar, *nm.*, corn in sheaf or growing.
Ard (airde), *adj.*, high.
Arsa (ars'), *defect. v.*, said.
As, *prep.*, out of.
As (*rel. form of verb***,** is). [etc.
Asam, asad, etc., out of us, you,
Athair (athar), *nm.*, a father.
Ba, *nf.*, cows; *pl.*, of bó.
Bad *nm.*, a tuft.
Baile, *nm.*, a town, village.
Bainne, *nm.*, milk.
Balach, *nm.*, a boy.
Balla, *nm.*, a wall.
Ban (baine), *adj.*, white, fair.
Ban, bhan, *gen. pl.* of **bean**.
Barail (baraile or **baralach),** *nf.*, an opinion.
Bard, *nm.*, a poet.
Barr (barra), *nm.*, a crop, top.
Bata, *nm.*, staff.
Bàta, *nm.*, a boat.
Beag (bige or **lugha),** *adj.*, small, little.
Bean (mnatha), *nf.*, a woman.
Beanntan, *pl.*, of **beinn**.
Beartach (beartaiche), *adj.*, rich.
Beinn, *nf.*, a mountain, hill.
Beir, *irr. v.*, bear, bring forth (**breith** and **beirsinn**).
Beir (air), catch, seize.

Beulaobh (air), *prep.*, in front of.
Bha, *v. past*, was, were.
Bheil, *dept. v.*, am, is, are.
Bheir, *v.*, will give.
Bhitheas, bhios, *rel. v.*, will be.
Bho, o, *prep.*, from.
Bhos (a bhos), *adv.*, down, below.
Bhur, ur, *poss. pron.*, your.
Bhuam, bhuat (see par. 122).
Bi, *v.*, be.
Biadh (bidhe), *nm.*, food.
Bithinn, *subj. v.*, would be.
Bith, *vn.*, **air bith**, being.
Binn (binne), *adj.*, sweet, melodious.
Blath, *adj.*, warm.
Bliadhna (bliadhna), *nf.*, a year ;
  pl., **bliadhnachan**.
Bo (ba), *nf.*, a cow.
Bochd (bochda), *adj.*, poor.
Boidheach (boidhche), *adj.*, pretty beautiful.
Borb (buirbe), *adj.*, fierce.
Bord (buird), *nm.*, a table, board.
Bradan, *nm.*, a salmon.
Brath, gu brath, *adv.*, for ever.
Brathair (brathar), *nm.*, a brother
Breab, *v.*, kick.
Breac (bric), *nm.*, a trout.
Breac (brice), *adj.*, spotted,
  speckled.
Breug (breige), *nm.*, a lie.
Bris, *v.*, break (**briseadh**).
Briste, *v. adj.*, broken.
Brog, *nf.*, a shoe.
Bronach, *adj.*, sad.
Bruach, *nf.*, a bank, brink.
Buachaill (buachaille), *nm.*, a shepherd.
Buidhe, *adj.*, yellow.
Buth (butha), *nf.*, a shop, *pls.*,
  buthan (buthannan, buithean).
Cabhag, *nf.*, a hurry, haste.
Cach, *indef. pron.*, the rest, the others.
Cach-a-cheile, one another.
Caidil, *v.*, sleep (**cadal**).
Caileag (caileige), *nf.*, a little girl.
Caillte, *v. adj.*, lost.
C'aite ? *inter.*, where ?

Calum, *nm.*, Malcolm.
Caol (caoile), *adj.*, thin, slender, small. narrow.
Caora (caorach), *nf.*, a sheep.
Caoraich, *pl.*, of **caora**.
Caraid, *nm.*, a friend.
  (*pl.*, **cairdean**).
C'arson ? *inter.* why? wherefore?
Cas (coise), *nf.*, a foot, a shaft, or haft.
Cat, *nm.*, a cat.
Cathair (cathrach), *nf.*, a chair ;
  pl., **cathraichean**.
Ceangail, *v.*, tie, bind (**ceangal**).
Ceann (cinn), *nm.*, a head.
Ceannaich, *v.*, buy, bought,
  (**ceannach**).
Cearc (circe), *nf.*, a hen.
Cearr, *adj.*, wrong.
Ceathramh, *nu. adj.*, the fourth.
Ceithir, *nu. adj.*, four.
Ceo (ceo and ceotha), *nm. or f.*, mist.
Ceol (ciuil), *nm.*, music.
Ceud (an ceud, a' cheud), *nu. adj.*, the first.
Ceud, *nu. adj.*, a hundred.
Cha, *neg. part.*, not.
Chaidh, *v.* went, *past tense* of **rach**.
Cheile (le cheile), *adv.*, together.
Chi, *v.*, *fut. of v.* **faic**, see.
Cho, *conj.*, as.
Chuala, *v.*, did hear.
Chugam, chugad, etc. (*p.p.* 404).
Chuireas, *v.*, *rel. fut. of v.* **cuir**; put
Chunnaic, *v.*, did see.
Cia mar ? *inter.*, how ?
Cia meud ? cia mheud ? *inter.*, how many.
Ciad, *nu. adj.*, a hundred.
Ciall (ceille), *nf.*, sense, understanding.
Cinnteach (cinntiche), *adj.*, sure, certain.
Ciobair, *nm.*, a shepherd.
Ciod ? *inter.*, what ?
  (= **Gu de ? de ?**).
Clach (cloiche), *nf.*, a stone.
Cladach, *nm.*, a shore.

Clachair, *nm.*, a mason.
Cliabh, *nm.*, a creel ; also breast, chest.
Cluas, *nf.*, an ear.
Cluinn, *irr. v.*, hear (**cluinntinn**).
Cnoc (**cnuic**), *nm.*, a hill.
Co ? *inter. pron.*, who ?
Co leis ? *inter. pron.*, whose ?
Coig, *nu. adj.*, five.
Coigreach, *nm.*, a stranger.
Coignear, *nu. n.*, five persons.
Coille, *nf.*, a wood ; *pl.* **coilltean.**
Coir (**corach, coire**), right, justice ;
Comhla (**comhla ris**), *prep.*, along with; together.
Con, chon, *gen. pl.*, of **cu,** a dog,
Corrach, *adj.*, steep
Craobh, *nf.*, a tree.
Creag (**creige**), *nf.*, a rock.
Crubach (**crubaiche**), *adj.*, lame.
Cu (**coin**), *nm.*, a dog.
Cuan, *nm.*, ocean.
Cuid, *indef. pron.*, some, certain (ones).
Cuid-eiginn, *indef. pron.*, some person or persons.
Cuide (**ri, ris,** etc.), along with.
C'uin ? cuin ? *inter. adv.*, when ?
Cuir, *v.*, put, set, sow, (**cur**).
Cuis, *nf.*, a matter
Cul (**cuil**), *nm.*, the back part of anything.
Culaobh, *nm.*, the back, the back parts.
Cupan, *nm.*, a cup.
Da, *nu. adj.*, two.
Da, dha, *pp.*, to him.
Dachaidh, *nf.*, a home.
Dad, *nm.*, anything,
Dall (**doille**), *adj.*, blind.
Damh, *nm.*, an ox, a stag.
Dan (**dain**), *nm.*, poem.
Daoine, *pl.*, of **duine.**
Daonnan, *adv.*, always.
Dara, darna, *nu. adj.*, the second.
De, an de, *adv.*, yesterday.
De, *inter. pron.*, what ?
De, *prep.*, of.
Dean, *irr. v.*, do, make (**deanamh**)
Dearbh (**gu dearbh**) *adv.* certainly.

Dearg (**deirge**), *adj.*, red.
Deas, *nf.*, the south (for, **an airde deas** = south airt), the right hand.
Deich, *nu. adj.*, ten.
Deicheamh, *nu. adj.*, tenth.
Deidh (**an deidh**), *prep.* and *adv.*, after.
Deoch (**dibhe**), *nf.*, a drink ; *pl.*, **deochan** or **deochannan.**
Deug, *nu. particle,* teen.
Dhachaidh (**dachaidh**), homewards ; *adv.*, *is generally aspirated.*
Dhiom, dhiot, etc. (*p.p.* **de,** 404).
Dhomh, dhuit, etc. (*p.p.* **do,** 404).
Diubh, *pp.*, of them.
Diugh (**an diugh**), *adv.*, to-day.
Do, *poss. pron.*, thy.
Do, *prep.*, to. into.
Dol, a' dol, *vn.*, going.
Donn (**duinne**), *adj.*, brown.
Dorus, *nm.*, a door.
Dorcha, *adj.*, dark.
Drasda (**an drasda**), *adv.*, just now.
Droch, adj., bad—precedes the noun always.
Druid, *v.*, shut, close (**druideadh**).
Druidte, *v. adj.*, closed.
Dubh (**duibhe**), *adj.*, black.
Duibh, *gen. masc.*, of **dubh.**
Duibh, *pp.*, to you ; *pl.*
Duneideann, Edinburgh.
Duin, *v.*, close, shut (**dunadh**).
Duine, *nm.*, a man.
Duit, *pp.*, to thee (see **dhomh**).
Dun, *nm.*, a hill, a heap.
Duthaich (**duthcha**), *nf.*, a country ; *pl.* **duthchannan.**
E, *pron.*, he ; him.
Each (**eich**), *nm.*, a horse.
Eadar, *prep.*, between.
Eadarainn (*p.p.* 404).
Eadh, seadh, that's it, it is.
Eagal, *nm.*, fear.
Eallach, *nm.*, a load, a burden.
Ear, the east (for, **an airde 'n ear**)
Earar, day after to-morrow.
Earb, f. a roe.

Eiginn (or **eigin**), *indef. pron.*, some, see **cuid eiginn**.
Eile, *indef. pron.*, other, another.
Eilid (**eilid, eilde**), *nf.*, a hind.
Eirich, *v.*, rise (eirigh).
Eisg. *nm* (see **Iasg** a fish)·
Eolach (**eolaiche**), *adj.*, acquainted, skilled.
Eun (**eoin**), *nm.*, a bird ; *pl.*, **eoin**.
Facal, *nm.*, a word.
Fada, *adj.*, long.
Fag, *v.*, leave (**fagail**).
Fagus (**faisge**), *adj.*, near.
Faic, *irr. v.*, see, behold (**faicinn**).
Faigh, *irr. v.*, get (see *irr. verbs*).
Falbh, *v.*, go (**falbh**).
Fan, *v.*, wait (**fantainn**).
Fang (**fainge**), *nf.*, a sheep-pen.
Faod, *v.* depend, form of **faodaidh**
Faodaidh mi, etc., I, thou, etc., may.
Faotainn (see **faigh**).
Far, *adv.*, where.
Fas, *v.* grow.
Feadan, *nm.*, pipe, a chanter.
Feadh. air feadh, *prep.*, among,
Feadhainn some people.
Feairrd, *adv.*, better, best.
Fear (**fir**), *nm.*, a man.
Fear-ciuil, *nm.*, a musician.
Fearr (see **math**).
Feasgar, *nm.*, evening.
Fein, *emph. part.*, self.
Feoraich *v.* asking, inquire,
Feum (**feuma**), *nm.* and *f.*, need,
Feumaidh mi, thu, etc., I, thou, etc., must.
Fiacail (**fiacla**), *nf.*, a tooth.
Fiadh (**feidh**), *nm.*, a deer.
Fiabhras, *nm.*, a fever.
Fichead, *nu. adj.*, twenty.
Fion, *nm.*, wine.
Fios, *nm.*, knowledge, information.
Fhathast, fathast, *adv.*, yet.
Fhuair, *v.*, *past tense* of **faigh**
Fliuch (**fliuiche** or **fliche**), *adj.*, wet.
Fo, *prep.*, under.

Fodham, fodhad (see *p.p.* 404).
Fosgail. *v.* open (fosgladh).
Fosgailte, *v. adj.*, opened.
Fraoch, *nm.*, heather.
Fras (**froise**), *nf.*, a shower.
Fuar (**fuaire**), *adj.*, cold.
Fuireach *vn.* staying.
Gabh, *v.* take.
Gach, *indef. pron.*, each, every
Gaidhlig, *nf.*, Gaelic (language).
Gann, *adj.*, scarce.
Gaol, *nm.*, love.
Garradh, *nm.*, a garden, a wall.
Geal (**gile**). *adj.*, white.
Gealach, *nf.*, moon.
Gearr, *v.*, cut (**gearradh**).
Ged, *conj.*, though.
Geug (**geige**), *nf.*, a branch.
Geur (**geire, geoire**), *adj.*, sharp.
Gheibh, *irr. v.*, will get.
Gille, *nm.*, a lad, youth.
Gin, *indef. pron.*, any.
Glas., *v.*, lock (**glasadh**).
Glas (**glaise**), *adj.*, grey.
Glas (**glaise**), *nf.*, a lock.
Glascho, Glasgow.
Gle, *an intensive particle*, very.
Gloine, *nf.*, a glass, a pane.
Gorm (**guirme**), *adj.*, blue.
Gradh, *nm.*, love.
Grian (**greine**), *nf.*, sun.
Gu, gus, *prep.*, to.
Gu, *conj.* that ; **gu'n**, that which
Gu, *prefixed to adjectives to form adverbs.*
Gual, *nm.*, coal.
Gun, *prep.*, without.
Gur, *v. part*, that it is.
Gus, *prep.*, to (the).
Guth (**gutha**), *nm.*, a voice.
I, ise, *pers. pron.*, she, her, it.
Iad, iadsan, *pers. pron.*, they.
Iain, *nm.*, John.
Iar, west (an airde 'n-iar).
Iarr, *v.* ask, seek (**iarraidh**).
Iarunn, *nm.*, iron.
Iasg (**eisg**), *nm.*, a fish.
Iasgach, *vn.*, a fishing.
Idir *adv.*, at all.
Im (**ime**), *nm.*, butter.

Iongantas, astonishment.
Innis, *v.*, tell, relate (**innseadh**).
Innte, in her (see *p.p.* **ann**).
Is, *v. emph.*, is.
Is, *a conj.*, and.
Ith, *v.* eat (**itheadh**).
Iuchair, *nf.*, a key.
La, latha, *nm.*, a day ; *plur.*, **laithean**.
Labhair, *v.*, speak (**labhairt**).
Lagh (**lagha**), *nm.*, law.
Laidir (**laidire** or **treasa**), *adj.*, strong.
Lair (**laire, larach**), *nf.*, a mare ; *plur.*, **laraichean**.
Lamh, *nf.*, a hand.
Laighe, *vn.*, lying down.
Laigse, *n.* faint.
Lar, *nm.*, the ground, floor.
Lathair, *prep.*, **ann an lathair**, in the presence of.
Le, leis, *prep.*, with.
Leabhar, *nm.*, a book. *pl.*, **leabhraichean**.
Leam, leat, etc. (see par. 185).
Lean, *v.*, follow, pursue (**leantuinn**).
Leir, gu leir, *adv.*, altogether, wholly.
Leisg, *adj.*, lazy.
Leoir, gu leoir, enough. plenty.
Leotha with them, theirs.
Leth, *nm.*, a half.
Leughadh, *n.* and *vn.*, a reading,
Linne, *nf.*, a pool, firth. *pl.*, **linneachan**.
Lion (**lin**), *nm.*, a net ; *pl.*, **lin, liontan**.
Lionn or **leann**, *nm.*, *gen.*, **leanna**, beer.
Loch (**locha**), *nm.*, a loch, lake.
Long (**luinge**), *nf.*, a ship.
Luath (**luaithe**), *adj.*, swift.
Luch (**lucha, luchainn**), *nf.*, a mouse.
Lugha, less (see **beag**).
Ma, *conj.*, if, **ma ta**, if so.
Mac (**mic**), *nm.*, a son.
Mach, *adv.*, out.
Machair *nf.*, a field, plain.

Maduinn (**maidne**), *nf.*, morning.
Maide, *nm.*, a stick.
Maireach, am maireach, *adv.*, to-morrow.
Mairi, *nf.*, Mary.
Maith, *adj.*, good (see **math**).
Mall (**maille**), *adj.*, slow, easy going.
Mar, *adv.*, as, like as, **mar sin**, in the same manner.
Math (**fearr**), *adj.*, good.
Mathair (**mathar**), *nf.*, a mother.
Meadhon-la, *nm.*, mid-day.
Measg (**am measg**), *prep.*, among.
Meud ? cia mheud ? how much ?
Mi, mise, *pers. pron.*, I.
Mi-fhein, *emph. pron.*, myself.
Mile *nm.*, a thousand.
Milis (**milse**) *adj.* sweet.
Min (**mine**), *adj.*, smooth.
Ministeir, *nm.*, a minister.
Mionaidean, *nm.* minutes.
Miosa, *adj.*, worse; see **olc** and **dona**.
Misd, misde, *comp.* of **olc**, worse.
Mna, mnatha, *gen.* of **bean**.
Mnathan, *pl.* of **bean**, a woman.
Mo, *poss. pron.*, my.
Modh, *nm.*, style.
Monadh, *nm.*, a mountain ; a moor.
Mor (**mo, motha**), *adj.*, great, large.
Mor, *nf.*, Sally, Sarah.
Moran, *adj.* and *n.*, many, much.
Mu, *prep.*, about, around.
Muir, a' mhuir, *nf.*, a sea, the sea generally.
Muir, am muir, *nm.*, a sea, the sea, a wave.
Mullach, *nm.*, the top, summit.
Mur, *conj. part.*, if not.
Na, *conj.*, than.
Na, *pl. art.*, the.
Na, *neg. imper. particle*, do not ; let not.
Na, *the rel. pron.*, what, that, which.
'Na (*cont.* for **ann a**), in his, her.

Nach, *the rel. neg. pron.*, what not, who not, that not, etc.
Nach ? *inter. neg. part.*, is not ?
Nach, *irr. v.*, that it is not.
Nall, *adv.*, **a nall**, to this side.
'N am, **'n an** (*cont*, for **ann am, ann an**), in their.
Na 'm, na 'n, *conj.*, if.
Nan, nam, *gen. pl. art.*, of the.
Naoi, *nu. adj.*, nine.
Neul (neoil), *nm.* a cloud.
Ni, *nm.*, a thing.
Nis. *adv.*, now.
No, *conj.*, or.
Nochd, an nochd, *adv.*, to-night.
'Nuair (an uair), *adv.*, when.
Nuas, a nuas, *adv.*, down—from above.
Nunn, a null, to the other side.
O, *prep.*, from.
Obair (oibre, oibreach), *nf.*, work; *pl.*, **oibrichean, obraichean**.
Ochd, *nu. adj.*, eight.
Og (oige), *adj.*, young.
Oglach, *nm.*, a youth.
Oidhche, *nf.*, night.
Oirre, *pp.*, on her.
Ol, *v.*, drink (**ag ol**).
Olc (miosa), *adj.*, bad, wicked.
Or (oir), *nm.*, gold ; *pl.*, **oir**.
Oran, *nm*, a song.
Ord (uird), a hammer ; *pl.*, **uird**.
Orm, ort, orra, etc. (see par. 138).
Pairc, *nf.*, a park.
Peann (pinn, peanna), *nm.*, a pen ; *pl.*, **pinn, peannan**.
Piob (pioba), *nf.*, (1) a tobacco pipe ; (2) the bag-pipe.
Piuthar (peathar), *nf.*, a sister ; *pl.*, **peathraichean**.
Poit (poite), *nf.*, a pot.
Port (puirt), *nm.*, a port, a harbour, a tune.
Preas, *nm.*, a bush.
Pris (prise), *nf.*, a price.
Punnd, *nm.*, pound.
Rach, *irr. v.*, go (**a'dol**).
Radh, ag radh, *vn.*, saying.
Rainig, *irr. v.*, reached.
Ramh, *nm.*, an oar ; *pl.*, **raimh**.

Raoir, an raoir, *adv.*, last night.
Rathad, *nm.*, a way, a road.
Re, *prep.*, during.
Reic, *v.* and *n.*, sell, selling.
Ri, ris, *prep.*, to.
Riamh (a riamh), *adv.*, ever, *at any time before*—used of past time only.
Rinn, *v.*, did make, did.
Righ, *mn.*, a king.
Ris, *pp.*, to him.
Ris, a ris, or **rithisd**, *adv.*, again.
Rium, riut, etc. (*p.p.* 404).
Robh, *dept. v.* was.
Roimh, *prep.*, before.
Ruadh (ruaidhe), *adj.*, red, reddish.
Rug, *irr. v.*, *past of* **beir**, caught ; bore ; gave birth.
Ruig, *irr. v.*, reach (**ruigsinn, ruigheachd**).
Ruith, *v.* and *n.*, run, running.
Saighdear (saighdeir), *nm.*, a soldier.
Salach (salaiche), *adj.*, dirty.
Saillte. *adj.*, salt, salted.
Salm *nf* a psalm.
Samhach (samhaiche), *adj.*, quiet calm.
Sam-bith, ever, along with **co, fear**, etc. ; **co sam-bith**, whoever ; **fear sam-bith**, anyone.
Saor, *nm.*, wright, joiner ; also *adj.*, free ; cheap.
Seach, seachad air, *prep.*, past,
Seachd, *nu.*, *adj.*, seven.
Seachduin (seachduine), *nf.*, a week.
Sean(n), (sine), *adj.*, old.
Seas, *v.*, stand (**seasamh**).
Seasmhach, steadfast.
Seinn. *v.* and *n.*, sing, singing.
Seol, *nm.*, a sail. (**siuil.**)
Seoladair, *nm.*, a sailor.
Seumas (Sheumais), *nm.*, James.
Sgeul (sgeoil), *nm.* a story.
Sgian, *nf.*, a knife (*irreg dec.*)
Sgillinn (sgillinne), *nf.*, a penny ; **sgillinn Shasunnach**, an English penny, *i.e.*, a shilling.

H

Sgine, *gen.* of **sgian**.
Sgith (sgithe), *adj.*, tired, fatigued
Sgoil, *nf.*, a school.
Sibh, sibhse, *pro.*, you.
Sin, *dem. pron.*, that, those.
Sine, *com. adj.*, older.
Sinn, *pro.*, we, us.
Sios, *adv.*, down—resting.
Sios, a sios, *adv.*, down, down-
    wards ;   motion to.
Siuil, *nm.*, see **Seol**
Slan leibh, leat, farewell.
Slat (slaite), *nf.*, a rod ;   *pl.*,
    slatan
Sliabh, *nm*, a moor.
Sluagh, *nm*, people.
Sloc, (sluic), *nm.*, or *nf.*, a pit,
    a hole.
Snamh, *v.* and *n.*, swim, swim-
    ming.
So, *dem. pron.*, this, those.
Sobhrach, *nf.*, a primrose ;   *pl.*,
    sobhraichean.
Sporan, *nm.*, purse.
Spag, spog (spaige, spoige).
    nf., a paw.
Sraid (sraide), *nf.*, a street.
Sruth, *nm.*, a stream.
Stabull, *nm.*, a stable.
Steach, *adv.*, in, inwards—ex-
    pressing motion.
Stigh, a stigh, *adv.*, in, inside—
    rest in.
Suas, *adv.*, up, upwards.
Sud (siod), yon, that.
Suidhe, *n.* and *vn.*, sitting.
Suil (sula), *nf.*, an eye.
Taillear (tailleir), *nm.*, a tailor.
Taobh, *nm.*, a side.
Tapaidh, *adj.*, clever.
Tarbh, *nm.*, a bull.
Tasdan, *nf.*, a shilling.
Teich, *v.*, flee, escape **(teich,
    teicheadh)**.
Teine, *nm.*, a fire ;   *pl.*, **teintean,
    teineachan**.
Thachras, *v.*, will happen, *from*
    tachair.
Tha, *v.*, is, am, art, are.
Thainig, *v.*, came, *past of* **thig**.

Thairis, thairis air, *prep.*, over,
    across.
Thall, *adv.*, over, beyond—rest in.
Thar, *prep.*, across, over.
Theab, *defect. v.*, had almost, had
    nearly.
Theid, *v.*, will go, *fut. of* **rach**.
Thig, *irr. v.*, come **(tighinn,
    teachd)**.
Thu, thusa, *pers. pron.*, thou, thee
Thubhairt, *v.*, said, *past of* **abair**.
Thu-fhein, *pers. pron.*, thyself.
Thug, *v.*, gave, *past of* **thoir**.
Tig (see **thig**).
Tigh, *nm.*, a house, a home.
Tighinn, *vn.*, coming.
Tilg, *v.*, throw **(tilgeil)**.
Till, *v.*, return, turn **(tilleadh)**.
Tinn (tinne), *adj.*, sick.
Tir (tire), *nf.*, land.
Tog, *v.*, lift, raise **(togail)**.
Togail (togalach), *nf.*, a building ;
    pl., **togalaichean**.
Tollichte, *adj.*, pleased, satisfied.
Toir, *irr. v.*, give (page 139).
Toll (tuill), *nm.*, a hole.
Traigh (traghad), *nf.*, a sea-shore,
    a sandy beach
Trath (traithe), *adj.* and *adv.*,
    early, just now.
Treas, *nu. adj.*, third.
Treasa, treise, *compar.* of **laidir**.
Treig, *v.* forsake **(treigsinn)**.
Tri, *nu. adj.*, three.
Treun, *adj.*, brave, strong.
Trom (truime), *adj.*, heavy.
Tromham, tromhad, etc.   (see
    p.p.—**troimh**).
Truas, *nm.*, pity.
Trus, *v.*, gather, collect **(trusadh)**.
Tu, tusa, *pers. pron.*, thou, thee.
Tuath, north **(an airde tuath**, the
    north).
Tuathanach, *nm.*, a farmer.
Tuig, *v.*, understand **(tuigsinn)**.
Tuit, *v.*, fall.
Uair, *nf.*, an hour, time.
Uairean, *pl.* of **uair**.
Uaireadair, *nm.*, a timepiece, a
    watch.

Uam, uat, etc. (see par. 122).
Uan, *nm.*, a lamb.
Ud. *dem. pron.*, yon, yonder.
Uile, *indef. pron.*, all, every.
Uillt, see allt.
Uinneag, *nf.*, a window.
Uird, *gen.* and *pl.* of ord

Ulridh, an uiridh, *adv.*, last year.
Uisge, *nm.*, water, rain; *pl.*, uisgeachan.
Ur, *poss. pron.*, your.
Ur (uire), *adj.*, new, fresh.
Urrainn, *v.*, can; is urrainn domh, I can.

ENGLISH-GAELIC VOCABULARY.

About, *prep.*, mu, mu thimchioll.
Across, *prep.*, thar, thairis air.
Acquainted, *adj.*, eolach.
Afraid, fear, *n.* eagal (par. 136).
After, *prep.*, an déidh.
Afternoon, an deidh mheadhon la'
Again, *adv.*, a ris (rithisd).
Against, *prep.*, an aghaidh.
All, *indef. pron.*, na h-uile, iad uile.
Alone, *n. m.*, aonar (par. 383).
Already, *adv.*, cheana; mar tha (literally, as it is).
Always *adv.*, daonnan
Also, *adv.*, cuideachd, mar an ceudna.
Among, *prop.*, am measg.
Anger, *nm.*, fearg.
And, *conj.*, agus.
Another, eile, fear eile; one another, càch-a-chéile.
Any, sam-bith, air-bith; any money, airgiod sam-bith.
Are, *v.*, tha, bheil, is.
Arrive (at), *v.*, ruig (see irreg. verbs).
Ask, *v.*, iarr (ag iarraidh).
Asleep (sleeping), a' cadal; he is asleep, tha e 'na chadal.
Astonishment, *nm.*, iongantas.
At, *prep.*, aig.
Axe, *nf.*, tuagh (tuaighe).
Bad, *adj.*, olc, dona.
Bag, *nf.*, maileid.
Bagpipe, *nm.*, a' phìob (mhór).
Bank, *nf.*, bruach.

Bè, *v.*, bi, being (bhi).
Bed, *nf.*, leabaidh (*gen.*, leapa).
Beer, *nm.*, lionn.
Before, *adv.*, roimhe.
Behind, *adv.* and *prep.*, an deidh, air cùlaobh.
Belong (see idiom, par. 413).
Better, *adj.*, fearr, na's fearr.
Between, *prep.*, eadar.
Big, *adj.*, mór (mo).
Bird, *nm.*, eun, *pl.*, eòin.
Black, *adj.*, dubh.
Blue, *adj.*, gorm.
Boat, *nm.*, bàta.
Book, *nm.*, leabhar.
Boy, *nm.*, balach, gille.
Branch, *nf.*, geug.
Brave, *adj.*, treun.
Bread, *nm.*, aran.
Break, *v.*, brist.
Briar, *nf.*, dreas.
Bridge, *nf.*, drochaid.
Bright, *adj.*, soilleir.
Broken, *v. adj.*, briste.
Brother, *nm.*, bràthair.
Brought, *v.*, thug.
Brown, *adj.*, donn.
Build, *v.*, tog.
Bull, *nm.*, tarbh.
But, *conj.*, ach.
Butter, *nm.*, ìm.
Buy, bought, *v.*, ceannaich.

Calf, *nm.*, laogh.
Calved, *v.*, the cow calved, rug a' bhó (laogh).

Came, *v.,* thàinig.

Can, *defect. v.,* is urrainn (domh, etc.)

Cannot, *defect. v.,* cha'n urrainn (domh, etc.).

Cap, *nm.,* or *f.,* boineid.

Carriage, *nf.,* carbad.

Cat, *nm.,* cat.

Catch, *v.,* glac, beir air.

Caught, *v.,* rug (e, i, etc.), àir.

Certain, certainly, cinnteach.

Chair, *nf.,* cathair (cathrach).

Clever, *adj.,* tapaidh.

Clock, *nm.,* uaireadair ; **o'clock,** uairean ; *e.g.,* **eight o'clock,** ochd uairean.

Cloud, *nm.,* neul (neoil).

Coal, *nm.,* gual.

Coat, *nm.,* còta.

Cold, *adj.,* fuar.

Collie, *nm.,* cu-chaorach.

Come, *v.,* thig ; **coming,** *vn.,* a' tighinn).

Corn, *nm.,* arbhar.

Country, *nf.,* duthaich, tìr ; **in the country,** air an duthaich.

Cross, tarsainn

Dark, *adj.·,* dorcha

Day, *nm.,* là, latha.

Death, bàs.

Deer, *nm.,* fiadh ; *pl.,* féidh.

Dirk, *nf.,* biodag.

Dirty, *adj.,* salach.

Do, *v. irreg.,* dean (*past,* rinn).

Dog, *nm.,* cù ; *pl.,* coin.

Door, *nm.,* dorus.

Down, *adv.,* sìos, a sios.

Drink, *v.,* òl.

Drink, *nf.,* deoch (*gen.* dibhe).

During, *prep.,* ré, troimh.

Ear, *nf.,* cluas ; *pl.,* cluasan.

Eat, *v.,* ith (itheadh).

Early, *adv.,* moch.

Edinburgh, Duneideann.

Enough, *adv.,* gu leòir.

Evening, *nm.,* feasgar.

Ever, *adv.,* **in the past**—riamh ; **in the future**—chaoidh.

Every, *adj.,* a h-uile, gach.

Everyone (*collectively*), na h-uile ; (*distributively*), a h-uile neach, gach neach, a h-uile duine, etc.

Eye, *nf.,* sùil ; *pl.* sùilean.

Face, *nf.,* aghaidh, aodann (*nm.*); **in face of,** an aghaidh.

Faithful, *adj.,* dìleas.

Fall, *v.,* tuit.

Family, *nm.,* teaghlach.

Farmer, *nm.,* tuathanach.

Father, *nm.,* athair.

Fear, *nm.,* eagal (par. 136).

Fever, *nm.,* fiabhras.

Field, *nm.,* achadh.

Fierce, *adj.,* borb.

Find, *v. irr.,* faigh.

Fine, *adj.,* maith (math), gasda.

Fire, *nm.,* teine.

Fish, *nm.,* iasg ; *gen.,* éisg.

Fish, *v.,* iasgaich.

Fisherman, *nm.,* iasgair.

Fishing, *n.* and *vn.,* iasgach ; **going a-fishing,** a' dol a dh'iasgach.

Five, *nu. adj.,* cóig.

Floor, *nm.,* làr, urlar.

Follow, *v.,* lean (a' leantuinn).

Foot, *nf.,* cas (coise).

For, *prep.,* air son, air sgath

Found, *v. irr.,* fhuair.

Friend, *nm.,* caraid ; *pl.,* càirdean.

From, *prep.,* bho, o.

Front (in front of), *prep.* and *adv.,* roimhe, air beulaobh.

Full, *adj.,* làn.

Gaelic, *nf.* Gaidhlig.

Garden, *nm.,* gàrradh.

Gathering, *vn.,* a' trusadh.

Gave, *v.,* thug.

Get, *v. irr.,* faigh.

Girl, *nf.,* caileag (caileige) ; *pl.,* caileagan.

Give, *v. irr.,* tabhair, thoir (*fut.* bheir).

Glasgow, Glascho.

Glass, *nf.,* gloine.

Glen, *nm.,* gleann (*gen.,* glinne).

Go, *v.,* rach, imich.

Going, *vn.,* a' dol.
Gold, *nm.,* òr.
Good, *adj.,* maith (math).
Good-bye, beannachd leibh (leat)
Good-night, oidhche mhath leibh (leat).
Got, *v.,* fhuair.
Grey, *adj.,* glas.
Great, *adj.,* mor (mo).
Grow, *v.* fas.
Hammer, *nm.,* òrd.
Hand, *nf.,* làmh ; *pl.,* làmhan.
Happy, *adj.,* sona.
Harbour, *nm.,* port.
Hair, *nm.,* falt (fuilt).
Hat, *nf.,* ad (*gen.,* aide).
Have, *v.,* tha—aig ; tha cu aig an duine, **the man has a dog** (par. 111-3).
He, *pers. pron.,* e ; *emph.,* **esan.**
Head, *nm.,* ceann.
Hear, *v. irr..* cluinn (a' cluinntinn)
Heard, *v. irr.,* chuala.
Heavy, *adj.,* trom.
Hen, *nf.,* cearc (*gen.,* circe).
Her, *pron.* i ; *emph,* ise; *poss.* a.
Here, *adv.,* an so.
Hero, *nm.,* laoch. curaidh. gaisgeach,
High, *adj.,* àrd ; **highest,** as airde.
Hill, *nm.,* cnoc, monadh ; *pl.,* cnuic.
Himself, *pers. pron.,* e-fhéin.
His, *poss. pron.,* a.—aspirates its noun.
Hit, *v.,* buail.
Hole, *nm.,* toll ; *pl.,* tuill.
Home, *nf.,* dachaidh ; **at home,** aig an tigh.
Horn, *nf.,* adharc.
Horse, *nm.,* each ; *pl.,* eich.
Hour, *nf.,* uair ; *pl.,* uairean.
House, *nm.,* tigh, taigh.
How ? *inter. adv.,* ciamar ?
How many ? cia meud ? cia lion ?
Hunger, *nm.,* acras (par. 136).
I, *pers. pron.,* mi ; *emph.,* mise.
If, *conj.,* ma.

If not, mur.
Immediately, *adv.,* air ball.
In, into, *prep.,* ann an, anns.
In. *adv.,* a stigh. (rest).
Into, *adv.,* a steach (motion).
Is ? Am bheil ? An e ? etc.
Is, tha, bheil, is.
James, *nm.,* Seumas.
John, *nm.,* Iain.
Joiner, *nm.,* saor.
Just now, *adv.,* an trath so.

Kick, *v.,* breab (a' breabadh).
King, *nm.,* rìgh ; *pl.,* rìghrean.
Knife, *nf.,* sgian.
Know, *v.,* **I know,** tha fhios (fios) agam; **I do not know,** cha'n eil fhios agam, aithne, etc. (par. 127-30).

Lad, *nm.,* gille ; *pl.,* gillean.
Lamb, *nm.,* uan ; *pl.,* uain.
Lame, *adj.,* crùbach.
Land, *nf.,* tìr.
Large, *adj.,* mór.
Last (night), *adv.,* an raoir.
Last (year), *adv.,* an uiridh.
Late, *adv.,* an-moch.
Lazy, *adj.,* leisg.
Leave, *v.,* fàg.
Lift, *v.,* tog.
Little, *adj.,* beag.
Little, *adj. nm.,* beagan.
Loch, *nm.,* loch.
Long, *adj.,* fada.
Lost, *v. adj.,* caillte.
Love, *nm.,* gradh.

Make, *v. irr.,* dean.
Malcolm, *nm.,* Calum.
Man, *nm.,* fear, duine ; *pl.,* fir, daoine.
Many, *adj.,* (*many a*), iomadh.
Many, *adj. n.,* móran.
May, *v.* faod.
Mary, *nf.,* Màiri.
Mason, *nm.,* clachair.
Meal, *nf.,* min.
Middle, *nm.,* meadhon ; **in the middle,** anns a' mheadhon.
Midnight, meadhon-oidhche.

Milk, *nm.,* bainne.
Minute, *nf.,* mionaid.
Mine (see *poss. prons.,* par. 413).
Mist, *nm.,* ceò.
Month, *nm.,* mìos.
Moon, *nf.,* gealach.
Moor, *nm.,* raon, monadh, sliabh.
More, na's mò.
Morning, *nf.,* maduinn (maidne).
Mother, *nf.,* màthair.
Mountain, *nf.,* beinn ; *pl.,* beann-tan.
Mouse, *nf.,* luch (*gen.,* luchainn)
Must, feumaidh, is eudar ; **I must** feumaidh mi, is eudar dhomh.
My, *poss. pron.,* mo.
Myself, *pers. pron.,* mi-fhéin.

Near, *adj.,* fagus, faisg.
Nearly (see defective verbs).
Neat, *adj.,* grinn, sgiobalta ; **she is neater than,** tha i na's grinne na, etc.
Need, *nm.,* feum ; tha feum agam air bainne, **I need milk,** *lit.,* **there is need at me on (with) milk.**
Nest, *nm.,* and *f.,* nead.
Net, *nm.,* lìon (lìn).
New, *adj.,* ùr.
Never, *adv.* (say " not ever "), **I never saw him,** cha'n fhaca mi riamh e.
Nice, *adj.,* gasda, laghach.
Night, *nf.,* oidhche ; **at night,** am beul na h-oidhche (**at dusk**).
Nine, *adj.,* naoi.
No, *adv.,* cha'n eil, cha'n e, cha.
None (say **not one**), par. 476.
Noise, *nm.* and *f.,* fuaim.
Now, *adv.,* a nis, an dràsda.
Nut, *nf.,* cnò ; *pl.,* cnothan.

Oar, *nm.,* ràmh ; *pl.,* ràimh.
O'clock (**hour**), uair, uairean.
Off (**away**), *adv.,* air falbh.
Off (e.g., **put off you**), dhiot (see *p.p.*).
Old, *adj.,* aosda, sean.
Older, eldest, sine.

On, *prep.,* air.
One, *nu. adj.,* aon.
One (**any one**), *indef. pron.;* fear-sam-bith.
One (**one of**) aon de, etc.
Open, *v.,* fosgail (fosgladh).
Open, *v., adj.,* fosgailte.
Other, *adj.,* eile ; **other friends,** càirdean eile.
Ought, *v.,* is coir.
Our, *poss. pron.,* ar.
Out, *adv.* (**rest in**), a muigh.
Out, *adv.* (**motion towards**), a mach.
Out of (see *prep. pron.* par. 404).
Over (**towards one**), *adv.,* a nall. (away from), a null.
Over (**me**), *prep.,* thairis orm == tharam.
Over *prep.,* thar, thairis air.
Own, fein, fhein.
Ox, *nm.,* damh (daimh).
Park, *nf.,* pàirc.
Past, *prep.,* seachad air
Pay, *v.,* pàigh or pàidh (paidh-eadh).
Pen, *nm.,* peann (*gen.,* pinn or peanna).
Penny, *nf.,* sgillinn, peighinn.
Pen, sheep-pen, fang.
Pity, *nm.,* truas.
Pipe, *nf.,* plòb.
Pit, *nm.* or *f.,* sloc.
Place, *nm.,* àite.
Poet, *nm.,* bàrd.
Poor, *adj.,* bochd.
Pound, *nm.,* punnd.
Present, *adv.,* an lathair.
Presently, *adv.,* an drasd.
Pretty, *adj.,* boidheach (boidhche).
Price, *nf.,* prìs.
Primrose, *nf.,* sobhrach.
Purse, *nm.,* sporan.
Put, *v.,* cuir.
Quick, *adj.,* luath, clis ; (*adv.,* gu luath).
Quiet, *adj.,* samhach, ciùin.
Quietly, *adv.,* gu samhach, gu ciùin.

Rain, *nm.*, uisge.
Reach, *irreg. v.*, ruig.
Read, *v.* leugh.
Ready, *adj.*, deas.
Reap, *v.*, buain.
Reaping, *n.* and *vn.*, buain.
Rich, *adj.*, beartach.
Rise, *v.*, éirich.
River, *nf.*, abhainn (aibhne).
Rod, *nf.*, slat ; *pl.*, slatan.
Run, *ran*, *v.* ruith.

Sad, *adj.*, bronach.
Said, *irr. v.*, thubhairt.
Sailor, *nm.*, seoladair.
Salt, salted, *adj.*, saillte.
Say, *irr. v.*, abair.
Saying, ag radh.
Saw, *v.*, chunnaic.
Scotland, Alba, Albainn.
Scotsman, *nm.*, Albannach.
School, *nf.*, sgoil.
Score, *nu. adj.*, fichead.
Sea, *nm.* or *f.*, muir.
Second, *nu. adj.*, dara.
See, *v. irr.*, faic.
Sell, *v.*, reic (a' reic).
Seed, *nm.*, siol (sil).
Sharp, *adj.*, geur.
Sheep, *nf.*, caora ; *pl.*, caoraich.
Shepherd, *nm.*, ciobair.
Shilling, *nf.*, tasdan.
Ship, *nf.*, long.
Shoe, *nf.*, bròg ; *pl.*, brògan.
Shore, *nm.*, cladach ; *f.*, tràigh (tràghad).
Shower, *nf.*, fras (froise).
Shut, *v.*, druid, dùin.
Shut, *v. adj.*, druidte, dùinte.
Sick, *adj.*, tinn.
Side, *nm.*, taobh.
Sing, *v.*, seinn (a' seinn).
Sister, *nf.*, piuthar.
Sit, *v.*, suidh (suidhe).
Sleep, *nm.*, cadal.
Sleep, *v.*, caidil (a' cadal).
Slow, *adj.*, mall.
Small, *adj.*, beag, caol.
Snow, *nm.*, sneachd.
Soldier, *nm.*, saighdear.

Someone, *indf. pron.*, cuid-eiginn.
Some, cuid.
Song, *nm.*, òran.
Son, *nm.*, mac ; *pl.*, mic.
Soon, *adv.*, luath.
Sound, *nm.* and *f.*, fuaim.
Sowing (seed), *v.*, a' cur (sìl).
Speak, *v.*, labhair, bruidhinn.
Stable, *nm.*, stàbull.
Stand, *v.*, seas (seasamh).
Still, *adj.*, samhach.
Stick, *nm.*, maide.
Stone, *nf.*. clach (cloiche)
Story, *nm.*, sgeul
Stream, *nm.*, sruth.
Strike, *v.*, buail.
Strong, *adj.*, laidir.
Sun, *nf.*, grian (*gen.*, gréine).
Sure, *adj.*, cinnteach.
Sweet (in taste), *adj.*, milis.
Sweet (music), *adj.*, binn, ceòlmhor.
Sweetness, *nf.*, mìlsead, mìlseachd.
Swift, *adj.*, luath.
Table, *nm.*, bòrd.
Take, *v. irr.*, Thoir (page 142).
Tailor, *nm.*, taillear.
Tall, *adj.*, àrd.
Tell, *v.*, innis (ag innseadh).
Tell (say to), *v.*, abair ri *or* ris.
Ten, *nu. adj.*, deich.
Terrier, *nf.*, abhag.
Than, *conj.*, na.
Thank you, gu'n robh math agaibh (agad).
That, those, *dem. pron.*, sin.
That, *rel. pron.*, a,
That, *conj.*, gu'n (m).
Their, *poss pron.*, an (am).
Then, *adv.*, an sin.
There, *adv.*, ann, an sud (pars. 61-144).
This, *dem. pron.*, so.
Though, *conj.*, ged (a).
Throw, *v.*, tilg.
Tied, *adj.*, ceangailte.
Tired, *adj.*, sgìth.
To, *prep.*, do, ri, ris.
To-day, *adv.*, an diugh.

Told, *v.*, dh'innis mi (**I told**).
To-morrow, *adv.*, am màireach ; **the day after to-morrow**, an earar.
To-night, *adv.*, an nochd.
Too, *adv.* (*of deg.*), ro.
Too (**also**), cuideachd, mar an ceudna.
Took, *v.*, thug.
Tooth, *nf.*, fiacail (fiacla).
Top, *nm.*, barr, mullach.
Towards, *prep.*, gu, thun, a dh' ionnsuidh. a' tarraing
Town, *nm.*, baile.
Train, carbad-iaruinn.
Tree, *nf.*, craobh.
Trout, *nm.*, breac (*gen.*, bric).
Truthful (**true**), fior, fìrinneach.
Twig, *nf.*, geug ; *nm.*, meangan *or* meanglan.

Under, *prep.*, fo.
Until, *adv.* and *prep.*, gus ; gus a' chrioch, **until the end**.
Up, *adv.* (**motion towards**), suas, a suas.
Up, *adv.* (**rest in**), shuas.
Us, sinn, sinne.

Very, *adv.*, glé ; very big, glé mhór
Voice, *nm.*, guth (gutha).

Wait, *v.*, fan (a' fantuinn).
Waken, *v.*, dùisg (a' dùsgadh).
Wall, *nm.*, balla ; *pl.*, ballachan.
Want (idiom, par. 121-3).
Warm, *adj.*, blàth.
Was, **were**, *v.*, bha, robh.
Watch, *nm.*, uaireadair.
Water, *nm.*, uisge.
Wealthy, *adj.*, beartach.
Week, *nf.*, seachduin.
Welcome, *nf.*, failte, faoilte.

Well, *adv.*, gu math.
Went, *v.*, chaidh.
Wet, *adj.*, fliuch.
What ? *inter.*, ciod ? dé ?
What, *rel. pron.*, na.
When ? *inter.*, cuin, c'uin ?
When, *adv.*, nuair, an uair.
Where ? *inter.*, c'àite ?
Where, *adv.*, far.
Which, *rel.*, a.
Which (**of them**) **?** có aca ?
White, *adj.*, geal, bàn.
Who ? *inter.*, có ?
Whoever, *indef. pron.*, co-air-bith.
Whose ? *inter.*, có leis ?
Why ? *inter.*, c'arson ?
Wife, *nf.*, bean (see *irreg. nouns*).
Wind, *nf.*, gaoth.
Window, *nf.*, uinneag ; *pl.*, uinneagan.
Wine, fion.
Wise, *adj.*, glic.
Wish, **desire**, *n.* miann, iarrtas.
With, *prep.*, le, leis.
Woman, *nf.*, bean ; *pl.*, mnathan (see *irreg. nouns*).
Wood, *nf.*, coille, fiodh.
Work, *nf.*, obair (*gen.*, oibre, oibreach).
Wrong, *adj.*, ceàrr, mìcheart.
Worse, misd (e), miosa, *comp.* of olc.

Year, *nf.*, bliadhna ; *pl.*, bliadh-nachan.
Yesterday, *adv.*, an dé.
Yet, *adv.*, fathast.
Yonder, *adv.*, an sud.
Young, *adj.*, òg.
Your, *poss. pron.*, bhur, ur, do.
Yourself, *poss. pron.*, thu-fhéin.
Youth, *nm.*, oglach, *pl.*, òigridh.

KEY TO EXERCISES

AND

ANSWERS TO EXAMINATION QUESTIONS

IN

MACLAREN'S
GAELIC SELF-TAUGHT

FOURTH EDITION

ALSO ADAPTED AS

A GAELIC EXERCISE BOOK.

THE KEY TO GAELIC SELF-TAUGHT.

WHILE this is prepared as a key to "Gaelic Self-Taught,"
the idea has been borne in mind throughout to adapt it
for use as an independent exercise book for an additional
course of Gaelic exercises after the student has gone
through all the exercises in "Gaelic Self-Taught." The
key to this book would therefore be the exercises as they
appear in the original, and the reference numbers coincide
with the paragraph numbers in that volume.

J. M'L.

The words in parenthesis ( ) are alternative renderings.

THE KEY TO GAELIC SELF-TAUGHT.

---

46. Translate into Gaelic :—

1. The day is cold. 2. The man is wet. 3. He is there now.
4. The boy is here. 5. I am tired. 6. We are ready. 7. The
day is warm. 8. It is wet now. 9. They are yonder. 10. You
are ready. 11. The man is swift. 12. The boy is yonder. 13.
I am cold. 14. The man is ready now. 15. The boy is wet.
16. We are cold. 17. They are tired.

47. Read in Gaelic and translate into English :—

1. Tha an duine fliuch. 2. Tha mi deas. 3. Tha e sgith. 4.
Tha sinn blath a nis. 5. Tha iad fliuch. 6. Tha thu sgith. 7.
Tha i an so. 8. Tha an gille luath. 9. Tha e an so a nis. 10.
Tha e deas. 11. Tha an la fliuch. 12. Tha an duine an so. 13.
Tha an gille sgith. 14. Tha iad an sin a nis. 15. Tha iad fuar.
16. Tha e deas a nis. 17. Tha thu luath. 18. Tha sinn fuar a nis.
19. Tha an la blath.

LESSON III.

57. Translate into Gaelic :—

1. Is the day cold ? 2 The day is not cold, it is warm. 3 Though
it is warm it is wet. 4. The horse is lame if it is slow. 5. Is not
the man there now ? 6. No, he is here now. 7. If the boy is not
cold he is wet. 8. The boy is here to-day. 9. The boy is tired, but
he is not cold. 10. He says that he is young, but I say that he is
not. 11. Are you going home now ? 12. No, I am going to the
town. 13. Are they going to the town ? Yes. 14. She is coming
home now. 15. Is the day not warm ? . It is = yes.

58. Read in Gaelic and translate into English :—

1. Tha thu a' dol do'n bhaile an diugh. 2. Nach eil thu deas
fathast ? 3. Cha'n eil, tha e deas ach cha'n eil mise. 4. Tha an
t-each crubach an diugh. 5. Cha'n eil e an so fathast. 6. Tha
an gille og. 7. Mur eil an duine fliuch tha e fuar. 8. Tha an la
blath. 9. Tha an t-each luath ach tha an cu mall. 10. Nach eil
an duine a' tighinn dachaidh ? 11. Cha'n eil, tha e a' dol do'n
bhaile. 12. Cha'n eil thu a' tighinn do'n bhaile an diugh. 13.
Tha an gille fuar agus fliuch. 14. Mur eil an duine an sin tha an
gille an so. 15. Ged nach eil an gille og. 16. Mur eil an t-each
sgith tha e crubach. 17. Tha i ag radh gu'm bheil an duine a'
tighinn an so ach tha iad ag radh nach eil. 18. Nach eil thu a' dol
dachaidh a nis ?

4

LESSON IV.

63. Translate into Gaelic :—

1. Who was going there? 2. I am not going now. 3. I was there last night. 4. Who was at the door? 5. The men were there. 6. The boys were coming home. 7. The horse was slow but it was lame 8. The dogs were going home. 9. When you were there I was tired. 10. We were there yesterday. 11. Who was at the town? 12. They were at the town. 13. The dog was at the door (or There was the dog at the door). 14. The dogs were here last night. 15. They were there yesterday. 16. Is she here now? 17. She was here when you were here. 18. She was cold. 19. Who was here yesterday? 20. He was at home.

64. Read in Gaelic and translate into English :—

1. Bha an t-each a' dol do'n bhaile. 2. Bha na gillean aig an dorus an raoir. 3. Tha duine a' tighinn do'n bhaile. 4. Bha e a' tighinn an de. 5. Bha mi an sin an raoir. 6. Bha na coin a' dol dachaidh. 7. Bha cu aig an dorus. 8. Bha e aig an dorus an diugh. 9. Nuair a bha e an so bha e fliuch. 10. Bha iad sgith an raoir. 11. Bha e a' dol dachaidh an de. 12. Bha mi a' tighinn dachaidh nuair a bha mi sgith. 13. Bha an t-each crubach. 14. Bha na coin an so an de. 15. Bha cu an so ach bha na coin aig an tigh an raoir. 16. Co bha an so an de? 17. Bha duine aig an dorus. 18. Bha e deas.

LESSON V.

71. Translate into Gaelic :—

1. Was the man at the door? 2. He was not at the door. 3. Was the horse in the park? 4. It was not 5. I was tired. 6. Were the boys in the town? 7. They were not in the town. 8. The dogs were slow. 9. The dogs were swift, but they were lame. 10. Were they not in the park? 11. They were in the wood. 12. When they were here last night I was tired. 13. Were they not tired? 14. No, but they were wet. 15. The dogs were lost in the wood yesterday. 16. He said that he was lost in the town last night. 17. If they were not yonder to-day I was there yesterday. 18. If I had been slow I was tired. 19. We are coming now. 20. Were we not there? 21. No. 22. He said that he was going home.

72. Read in Gaelic and translate into English :—

1. An robh an t-each anns a' phairc? 2. Cha robh, bha an t-each anns a' choille. 3. An robh na daoine aig an dorus? 4. Cha robh iad aig an dorus. 5. Bha duine aig an dorus an raoir. 6. An robh e fliuch? 7. Thubhairt e nach robh e fliuch. 8. Bha iad anns a' choille an raoir. 9. Bha an t-each an sin an diugh. 10. Ma bha e an sin an diugh cha robh e an sin an raoir. 11. Bha na coin luath ged a bha iad crubach. 12. Bha an la fliuch. 13. Bha sinn sgith an raoir. 14. Thubhairt e na'n robh sinn a' dol dachaidh

gu'n robh e a' dol do'n bhaile.   15. Nach robh e mall ?   16. Cha
robh, bha e luath.   17. Bha an cu caillte anns a' choille an raoir.
18. Tha e ag radh gu'n robh an cu caillte anns a' bhaile an de.
19. Ma bha mise leisg bha esan mall.   20. Bha sinn fuar anns a'
phairc an diugh.   21. Co bha anns a' phairc an de ?   22. Cha
robh mise an sin.

LESSON VI.

76. Translate into Gaelic :—

1. Thou would'st be tired.   2. You would be late last night.   3.
We would be coming home now.   4. They would be slow.   5. I
would be there now but I was late.   6. The men would be going
to the town.   7. The horse would be lame.   8. The dogs would
be lost.   9. They would be wet.   10. It would be wet in the wood.
11. The knife would be lost.   12. The window would be broken.
13. It would be lost in the house.   14. He would be late going to
the town to-day.   15. I would be there if you were.

77. Read in Gaelic and translate into English :—

1. Bhithinn (b'abhaist dhomh a bhi) luath ach tha mi sgith a nis.
2. Bhitheadh tu an-moch a' tighinn dachaidh an raoir.   3. Bhitheadh na daoine aig an tigh an de.   4. Bhitheadh na coin crubach.
5. Bhitheadh an t-each a' tighinn dachaidh mall.   6. Bhitheadh
iad sgith.   7. Bhithinn aig an tigh an de ach bha mi aig a' bhaile
an raoir.   8. Bhitheadh an sgian briste.   9. Bhitheadh i caillte
anns an tigh.   10. Bhitheadh an uinneag fliuch.   11. Bhitheadh i
briste.   12. Bhitheadh na gillean anns a' choille an diugh.   13.
Bhitheadh iad fliuch.   14. Bhithinn an sin na'n robh thusa ann.
15. Bhitheadh e anns a' phairc anns an fheasgar

LESSON VII.

81. Translate into Gaelic :—

1. We would not be tired if she would be going.   2. If she would
be ready I would be.   3. The knife would not be broken.   4. The
knife was broken but it is lost now.   5. The man would be at home
in the evening.   6. They would be in the wood yesterday.   7.
When they were young they would be at school.   8. Would he not
be in town to-morrow ?   9. He said that he would not be there
to-morrow but that he would be the day after (two days hence).
10. Would I be warm in the town ?   11. You would be warm in
the town.   12. Would I not be cold in the park ?   13. You would
not be cold in the park.   14. Would he not be tired in the wood ?
15. He would be tired in the wood.   16. If I would not be cold
I would be warm.   17. The window would be broken.   18. If I
had been there it would not be broken.

82. Read in Gaelic and translate into English.

1. Ged a bhitheadh na coin an sin bhitheadh iad sgith.   2. Bhitheadh e fuar.   3. Bhitheamaid a'dol ann ged a bhitheadh na
daoine an-moch.   4. Cha bhithinn sgith na'm bitheadh i an sin.

B

5. Na'n robh mi an sin bhithinn blath.   6. Thubhairt e gu'm
bitheadh e an-moch am maireach.   7. Bhitheadh an uinneag briste.
8. Cha bhitheadh i briste na'm bitheadh tu an sin.   9. Thubhairt
e gu'm bitheadh iad a' dol do'n bhaile am maireach.   10. Am
bitheadh iad a' dol do'n bhaile anns an fheasgar ?   11. Am bitheadh
e blath anns a' bhaile ?   12. Bhitheadh an duine sin aig an tigh
an raoir.   13. Nuair a bha iad og bhitheadh iad anns an sgoil.
14. Nach bitheadh an sgian briste ?   15. Bhitheadh i caillte anns
a' choille.   16. Bhitheadh iad anns a' choille an raoir.   17. Nach
bithinn fuar anns a' phairc ?   18. Cha bhitheadh tu fuar anns a'
phairc.   19. Nach bitheadh e fliuch anns a' choille ?   20. Bhitheadh e fliuch anns a' choille.   21. Thubhairt e gu'm bitheadh e
deas is gu'm bitheadh e anns a' bhàta.   22. Thubhairt iad gu'm
bitheadh iad aig an tigh am maireach.

LESSON VIII.

87. Translate into Gaelic :—

1. The farmer was not here last night (2) but he will be here to-day.
3. These horses will be tired.   4. The shepherd will be there.
5. The boat will be here immediately.   6. It will be dark immediately.   7. Those horses were not there yesterday.   8. The boys
will be lazy.   9. I will be going home now.   10. He will be going
to the town.   11. You will be tired now.   12. I will be cold to-day.
13. These horses will be young.   14. He will be in the boat in the
evening.   15. We will be going to the house to-morrow.   16. They
will be there to-day.

88. Read in Gaelic and translate into English .—

1. Bithidh an ciobair an so air ball.   2. Bha an tuathanach an so
an de agus bithidh e an so an diugh.   3. Bithidh na h-eich so sgith.
4. Bithidh iad a' tighinn dachaidh an-moch.   5. Bithidh iad an
sin a nis.   6. Bithidh sinn a' tighinn do'n bhaile anns an fheasgar.
7. Bithidh thu a' dol do'n bhaile.   8. Bithidh e dorcha air
ball.   9. Bha am bàta an so an raoir agus bithidh e a' tighinn
an diugh.   10. Bithidh e an so fathast.   11. Bithidh na h-eich
so a' dol dachaidh a nis.   12. Bithidh na gillean leisg.   13. Bithidh
e fuar an diugh.   14. Bithidh an tuathanach a' tighinn dachaidh
air ball.   15. Tha e an so a nis.   16. Bithidh sinn a' dol do'n tigh
am maireach.   17. Bithidh thu a' dol an sin an nochd.

LESSON IX.

93. Translate into Gaelic :—

1. Though he will be at the town to-day he will be in the boat in
the evening.   2. The man who will be late.   3. Will you be in
the town ?   4. Will he be very tired ?   5. He will be very tired and
he will be very lazy.   6. Will I be in the town to-night ?   7. I will
be in the town this evening.   8. Will he not be in the wood ?
9. He will not be in the wood.   10. I said that he will be here to-
morrow.   11. You say that he will not be here.   12. That farmer

will be there to-morrow, but the shepherd will be there the day after to-morrow (two days hence). 13. If he will be there to-morrow I will not be here. 14. The night will be very dark. 15. It will not be. 16. The man who will be going with him is here. 17. This boy will be there. 18. Will the boys not be in the boat this evening ? 19. They said that they would be there to-night. 20. If they will not be ready immediately we will be late.

94. Read in Gaelic and translate into English :—

1. Thubhairt mi gu'm bi e an-moch. 2. Am bi e an so an nochd ? 3. Cha bhi e an so an deidh mheadhon la ach bithidh e an so am feasgar so. 4. Cha bhi mi leis. 5. Nach bi e anns a' bhaile an diugh? 6. An duine a bhitheas anns a' bhaile am maireach. 7. Bithidh mi a' tighinn leis. 8. Cha bhi mi an sin am maireach. 9. Ma bhitheas an gille a' dol leis bithidh iad gle an-moch. 10. Cha bhi an gille gle luath. 11. Bithidh e anns a' choille air ball. 12. Co a bhitheas leis ? 13. Bithidh an duine deas air ball. 14. An duine a bhitheas deas cha bhi e leisg. 15. Bithidh e gle sgith nuair a thig e dachaidh. 16. Cha bhi na gillean so a' tighinn dachaidh an diugh. 17. Thubhairt iad gu'm bi iad anns a' bhaile am maireach. 18. Ged a bhitheas iad anns a' bhàta an diugh cha bhi mise an sin. 19. Ma bhitheas e fliuch anns an fheasgar cha bhi sinn a' dol do'n bhaile. 20. Bithidh mi deas am maireach. 21. Am bi thu a' dol do'n bhaile an earar ? 22. Bithidh.

LESSON X.
102. Translate into Gaelic :—

1. Be not faint-hearted. 2. Let us be in the wood to-night. 3. Let the man be brave. 4. Let the door be shut. 5. Let the window not be opened. 6. Let us be ready. 7. Let them not be in the town to-day. 8. Let us be in the town to-night. 9. Let him not be lazy. 10. Let the window be shut. 11. Let him be going home now. 12. Let him not be late now. 13. Let the window not be broken. 14. Let not the knife be lost. 15. Let me be going now. 16. Let not the boys be in the wood this evening. 17. Let them be brave. 18. Let us be with him the day after to-morrow.

103. Read in Gaelic and translate into English :—

1. Bitheamaid anns a' choille an nochd. 2. Bitheadh an duine treun. 3. Na bitheadh e lag-chridheach. 4. Bi treun. 5. Bitheadh iad leis anns a' choille am maireach. 6. Na bitheadh na gillean samhach. 7. Bi thusa samhach. 8. Bitheamaid treun. 9. Na bitheadh e an-moch an nochd. 10. Bitheamaid anns a' bhaile an nochd. 11. Na bitheadh an uinneag briste. 12. Bitheadh an uinneag fosgailte air ball. 13. Na bitheadh an dorus duinte. 14. Bitheamaid deas am feasgar so. 15. Bitheadh an dorus duinte a nis. 16. Na bitheadh an sgian caillte. 17. Na bi lag-chridheach. 18. Bitheamaid treun an nochd. 19. Bitheam leis am maireach. 20. Na bitheamaid fuar. 21. Bi samhach.

LESSON XI.

105. Translate into Gaelic :—

1. The sheep are in the pen.   2. Were they on the hill last night ?
3. No, but they are in.the pen just now.   4. The cows were lost yesterday.   5. The deer were on the hill this evening.   6. When he came
into the boat he was tired.   7. When they were young they would
be in the town.   8. The boys are here to-day but they were not here
yesterday.   9. We would be coming home last night.   10. The
window would be broken.   11. The door is shut.   12. They would
be late last night.   13. Let us be brave.   14. These horses are here
now.   15. Is the dog at the door ?   16. It is at the boat.   17. The
cows are in the pen but they were on the hill yonder yesterday.
18. Let us be in the town to-morrow morning.   19. If he will be
at home to-night I will be there presently.

106. Read in Gaelic and translate into English :—

1. Nuair a bha mi anns a' choille an de cha robh an gille an lathair.
2. Bithidh e an so an nochd no am maireach.   3. Bha an tuathanach
anns a' bhaile anns a' mhaduinn nuair a bha mise an sin.   4. Nach
eil an uinneag briste ?   Cha'n eil.   5. Cha'n eil an cu anns an
achadh so, tha e air a' mhonadh.   6. Tha feidh air a' mhonadh.
7. Nach robh na daoine an so an raoir ?   8. Cha robh, bha iad
anns a' bhàta.   9. Ged nach bi thu deas bithidh mise   10. Cha
robh na feidh anns an achadh so, bha iad air a' mhonadh.   11. Cha
robh na gillean so anns a' bhàta.   12. Nuair a bha*sinne an sin
cha robh iad an lathair.   13. Bithidh iad an sin am maireach.
14. Mur eil na caoraich anns an fhang bithidh iad anns an achadh.
15. Bha an ciobair air a' mhonadh.   16. Na bitheadh am maide
sin caillte.   17. Am bi an uinneag fosgailte anns a' mhaduinn ?   18.
Nuair a bha an ciobair an sin bha an tuathanach anns a' bhaile.

* The emphatic forms should be used here.

LESSON XII.

119. Translate into Gaelic :—

1. Will I have a cow ?   2. I will have a cow and you will not have
a cow.   3. Though you have not a cow.   4. If she will have a cow.
5. He has a pen.   6. You have a house.   7. Have I not a knife ?
8. I have not a knife.   9. The boy has the knife.   10. He has the
boat.   11. You have these horses.   12. You have the knife.   13
They have the dogs but we have a cow.   14. I have the horse but
you have the dog.   15. I have the book and the girl has a book.
16. We had those horses last night.

120. Read in Gaelic and translate into English :—

1. Tha each agam.   2. Tha tigh aige   3. Nach eil tigh aige ?
4. Tha each agus cu againn.   5. Bha cu aige ach cha'n eil e aige
a nis.   6. Tha bo againn.   7. Am bheil ad agad ?   8. Tha ad aice
9. Cha'n eil ad agam a nis.   10. Tha truas agam ris.   11. Nach
eil an leabhar aige ?   12. Bha an leabhar aige an de.   13. Cha'n
eil sgian aige an diugh.   14. Bha an sgian agad an raoir.   15. Bha

na coin againn air a' mhonadh ach bha a' bho anns an fhang an sin.
16. Tha i an sin a nis. 17. Bithidh bo agad am maireach. 18.
Am bi bo aig an tuathanach an diugh ? 19. Am bi an leabhar
sin aig a' chaileig a nis ? 20. Tha an leabhar agam an diugh, bithidh
e aig a' ghille am maireach, agus bithidh e aig a' chaileig an earar.
21. Bha e aig an duine an raoir.

LESSON XIII.

125. Translate into Gaelic :—

1. You want a book. 2. They want the boat. 3. They had the
boat last night but they want it now. 4. What does she want ?
5. They want*to be there. 6. What do I want ? 7. I want the
book to-night. 8. Do you want a book ? 9. The girl does not
want the book. 10. She wanted a pen. 11. The fisherman wants
(seeks) the ocean. 12. The fisherman will have the boat just now.

126. Read in Gaelic and translate into English :—

1. Tilg uait an leabhar sin. 2. Tha an ad o Sheumas an diugh.
3. Am bheil an t-airgiod uait ? 4. Tha an t-airgiod sin uam a
nis. 5. Tha uait a bhi ann am maireach. 6. De tha uaipe ?
7. Tha ad uaipe. 8. Ciod tha uaithe ? 9. Bha leabhar uaithe
ach cha bhi e aige a nis. 10. Nach robh leabhar aige an de ? 11.
Bha leabhar aige an de ach tha e uaithe an diugh. 12. Uaithe no
aige e tha e agam-sa a nis. 13. Bithidh an leabhar so uaithe
an earar.

*It beholds them to be there or It is up to them to be there.

LESSON XIV.

132. Translate into Gaelic :—

1. Do you know James ? 2. I have no knowledge of him (= I do
not know him). 3. The farmer has the horse. 4. Who has the
money ? 5. The man has it. 6. Who had the boat ? 7. The
fisherman had it. 8. James had the boat but he has not it now.
9. If the girl will have the money the boy will have the house.
10. The shepherd has a dog. 11. Have you no book ? 12. I
have not (= no) 13. The boy will have a knife. 14. The girl
had five shillings. 15. The fisherman had a knife yesterday but
he has not got it to-day. 16. If the man had got a knife he would
be very pleased. 17. I did not know you were there. 18. If the
farmer does not know that the boy was there he will know now.
19. He has a house in the town. 20. I do not know it. 21. When
did you get the information. 22. I had information of (I knew)
where his house was.

133. Read in Gaelic and translate into English :—

1. An aithne dhuit an leabhar so ? 2. Cha'n eil aithne agam air.
3. Cha'n eil an leabhar sin agam. 4. Nach eil an leabhar so agad ?
Cha'n eil. 5. Co aig an robh e ? 6. Bha an leabhar aig Seumas
an de. 7. Tha an leabhar so uam. 8. Cha'n eil am bàta aig an

iasgair a nis ach bithidh e aige am maireach. 9. Cha robh coig
tasdain agam. 10. Cha'n eil an sgian aig a' ghille. 11. Co aig am
bheil i ? 12. Am bheil fios agad co aig an robh i ? 13. Tha fios
agam gu'n robh i aig a' chaileig an raoir. 14. Am bheil fios agad
ma tha an t-airgiod aig an tuathanach a nis ? 15. Tha fios agam
nach bi e aige. 16. Am bi e aige am maireach ? 17. Bithidh gu
cinnteach. 18. Am bheil fios agad ma tha each uaithe ? 19. Am
bheil fios agad ma tha cu aig an duine sin ? 20. Cha'n eil fios
agam am bheil cu aige a nis ach bha cu aige an uiridh. 21. Am
bheil thu fada eolach air a' chiobair ? 22. Tha mi fada eolach air.
23. Tha e 'na dhuine eolach. 24. Bha e aig an tigh an de. 25. An
robh e an sin a' mhaduinn so ?

LESSON XV.

140. Translate into Gaelic :—

1. The man was hungry. 2. The stag had horns. 3. There are
no horns on the hinds. 4. The girl has a pound. 5. The cat has
an ear. 6. If the farmer does not know that the sheep are in the
corn he will know soon. 7. Where were you yesterday ? 8. I will
be in the town soon. 9. You were very sorrowful. 10. What ails
him ? 11. They are afraid. 12. Were you fishing in the loch
yesterday ? Yes. 13. Did you get a trout ? 14. The man had
great sorrow. 15. Do you know what time it is ? 16. I have not
a watch.

141. Read in Gaelic and translate into English :—

1. Tha an t-each crubach. 2. Nach robh fios aig an duine gu'n robh
an t-each aige crubach. 3. Cha robh fios aige. 4. Tha sporan aig
Seumas. 5. Bha slat agus lion againn nuair a bha sinn ag iasgach.
6. Cha robh fios agam gu'n robh na caoraich anns an arbhar. 7.
Nach robh e gle bhlath nuair a bha thu anns a' bhaile ? 8. Bha.
9. Am bheil thu a' dol a dh' iasgach (pars. 539, 575) an diugh ? 10.
Tha. 11. Cha'n eil fios agam ma tha an t-uaireadair aige. 12. Am
bheil uaireadair agad ? 13. Tha uaireadair aig Seumas a nis. 14.
Nach robh an t-acras air a' ghille ? 15. Cha robh an t-acras air ach
bha e gle sgith. 16. Bha iongantas mor air an duine. 17. Bha
eagal air. 18. Bha iongantas orm. 19. Cha'n eil adhaircean air
na h-eildean ach tha adhaircean air an damh. 20. Bha an t-acras
air an duine. 21. Fhuair mi punnd (Sasunnach) bho'n chaileig.
22. Bithidh i aig an tigh gu trath. 23. Ciod a tha oirre ? 24. Tha
am fiabhras oirre. 25. Tha gradh aige dhi 26. Bha an t-acras
orra an raoir. 27. An d'fhuair iad dachaidh an raoir ?

LESSON XVI.

149. Translate into Gaelic :—

1. Is there bread ? 2. There is rain now. 3. Are you there ?
4. There is rain to-day. 5. The trout is in the sea. 6. There is a
river. 7. Put the fish in the river. 8. The boy is in the town.
9. He went to the town. 10. I am in the boat. 11. Is it not rain
that we will have ? 12. There will be rain. 13. It is a good day.
14. It is a wet night. 15. He was there.

150. Read in Gaelic and translate into English :—

1. Tha bàta air an abhainn.   2. Tha duine anns a' bhàta.   3. Bha aran agus im aig an duine air a' bhord.   4. Tha aran air a' bhord, ach cha'n eil im ann.   5. Tha iasg anns an abhainn.   6. Bha uisge ann an raoir.   7. Bha e fuar agus fliuch an de.   8. Bha na frasan trom an raoir.   9. Tha uisge ann a nis.   10. Na'm bitheadh aran againn cha bhitheadh an t-acras oirnn.   11. Am bheil thu ann (an sin) ?   12. An tu a tha ann ?   13. Bithidh an t-uisge ann am maireach.   14. Tha e fliuch an nochd.   15. Tha an t-uisge ann a nis.

LESSON XVII.

166. Translate into Gaelic :—

1. Is this a dog ?   2. This is a dog.   3. That is a cat.   4. That is coal.   5. Isn't coal (very) black ?   6. It is coal.   7. Where is the coal ?   8. You are Malcolm.   9. Is this John ?   10. It is = he is = yes.   11. Is he a man ?   Yes.   12. Am I the boy ?   13. I was the boy.   14. Malcolm is the farmer.   15. Isn't he a shepherd ?   16. Is he a joiner ?   17. Yes.   18. Is a boy a man ?   19. She is my mother and he is my father   20. This is the hen.   21. Is a hen a bird ?   22. It is = yes.   23. This day is COLD.   24. You were not the joiner.   25. Was it not a hen ?   26. Though it is not a hen it is a bird.   27. This is the king.   28. I am the king.

167. Read in Gaelic and translate into English :—

1. Ged is cu e tha e luath.   2. An iasg breac ?   3. Cha'n iasg eun. 4. Is eun cearc.   5. Is e so cearc.   6. Is e sin cat.   7. Is e sud cu. 8. Bu e an gille a bha ann.   9. An e so an gille ?   10. Is e sin Iain. 11. Nach e Calum ?   12. Ma's e sud an gille a bha an so an raoir cha'n eil e crubach.   13. Is mise an duine.   14. Cha tu an duine. 15. B'e an gille.   16. Nach b' i a' chearc a bha aige ?   17. Cha b'e an gille a bha an so.   18. Is fear Iain.   19. Is iasg breac.   20. Is e sin an righ.   21. Is e so an duine.   22. Is iad so na h-eich.   23. Is e Iain an righ.   24. An e so gual?   25. Nach ann dubh a tha gual ?

176.

LESSON XVIII.

1. Tha e 'na fhear.   He is a man.   Is fear e.   He is a MAN.   2. Tha an la fuar.   The day is cold.   Is fuar an la.   The day is COLD. 3. Tha mi 'nam shaor.   I am a joiner.   Is saor mi.   I am a JOINER. 4. Tha thu bronach.   You are sad.   Is bronach thu.   Sad are you. 5. An robh an la fuar ?   Was the day cold ?   Am bu fhuar an la ? Was the day COLD ?   Cha'n eil an la fuar.   The day is not cold. Cha'n fhuar an la.   The day is not COLD.   7. Am bheil thu bronach? Are you sad ?   Am bronach thu ?   Are you SAD ?   8. Tha am fear fliuch.   The man is wet.   Is fliuch am fear.   The man is WET. 9. Tha mi sgith.   I am tired.   Is ann sgith a tha mi (or Is sgith mi) I am TIRED.   10. Tha an gille ard ach cha'n eil e laidir.   The boy is tall but he is not strong.   Is ard (a tha) an gille ach cha laidir e. The boy is TALL but he is not STRONG.   11. Bha na h-eich so sgith.

12

These horses were tired.   Bu sgith na h-eich so.   TIRED were these
horses.   12. Nach eil mi crubach ?   Am I not lame ?   Nach ann
crubach a tha mi ?   It is not lame that I am ?   13 Ged nach robh
thu leisg.   Though you were not lazy.   Ged nach ann leisg a bha
thu.   Though it is not LAZY you were.   14. Mur an robh mi samhach.
If I was not quiet.   Mur bu shamhach mi.   If I was not QUIET.
15. Nach robh thu treun ?   Were you not brave ?   Nach bu treun
thu ?   Were you not BRAVE ?

LESSON XIX.

182. Translate into Gaelic :—

1. What is that ?   2. That is coal.   3. Where is the coal ?   4. The
coal is in (on) the fire.   5. Is there a boat on the loch ?   Yes 6. Where
is the boy ?   7. The boy was on the hill with the dogs.   8. This is
a boat.   9. What is in the boat ?   10. Sheep are in the boat.
11. This is milk isn't it ?   It is.   12. Is it ?   13. It is not it at all.
14. It is heavy rain to-day and it was heavy yesterday.   15. John
is a mason—isn't he so ?   16. Yes, but James is a joiner (—it is a
joiner that is in James).   17. This is the man.   18. Is he the man ?
19. I am the man.   20. Am I the boy ?   21. Was I the boy ?
22. You were the man.   23. He was the boy.

183. Read in Gaelic and translate into English :—

1. An e an duine ?   2. Cha'n e an duine idir.   3. Is mise an gille.
4. Nach bu mhise an gille ?   5 B'esan an duine.   6. Is tusa an
duine.   7. Nach uisge sin ?   8. Cha'n eadh, is bainne e.   9. Bha e
fliuch an raoir agus tha e fliuch a nis.   10. Cha'n eil na frasan trom.
11. Tha e fliuch an diugh.   12. Tha an t-acras orm agus cha'n eil
mir arain anns an tigh.   13. An robh am fiabhras air an raoir ?
Bha.   14. Nach eil Iain a' dol dachaidh ?   Tha.   15. Am bheil
thu a' dol ?   Cha'n eil.   16. An robh thu sgith an de ?   17. Cha robh
mi sgith.   18. Bhithinn air bhi sgith.   19. Am bu tusa am fear ?
Cha bu mhi.   20. An e am fear so ?   21. Seadh.   22. B'e Iain an
gille.   23. Cha b'e.   24. An e so an t-aran ?   25. Cha'n eadh idir.
26 Tha aran air a' bhord.   27. So !   28. Seadh.

LESSON XX.

190. Translate into Gaelic :—

1. He was a good man   2 Was he the man ?   3 He is the man.
4. Who is this ?   5. This is James.   6. What is that ?   7. That
is a dog   8. This is the horse.   9. Where is the dog ?   10. The
dog is at the door.   11. Is the butter fresh ?   12. It is not.   13.
What is this ?   14. This is a net.   15. Who is that ?   16. He was
a soldier.   17. Is it the dog ?   18. It is not.   19. This is the
terrier.   20. James was a young man.   21. I know.   22. Whose
is this book ?   23. I am your son and you are my father.   24. Are
these the king and my father?   25. Are you the man of the house ?
(i.e., the husband).   26. I am he.   27. I am sick (It is I who am
sick).   28. The day is cold.   29. It is lazy the man is.   30. It is

heavy the stone is. 31. Whose is the place ? 32. You are the best man, James. 33. Where was he ? 34. He was in the town last night. 35. Did you know that ? 36. Who are you ? 37. I am not hungry. 38. Have you salt butter ?

191. Read in Gaelic and translate into English :—

1. Am bheil leabhar agad ? 2. Tha. 3. An e so e ? 4. Cha'n e, tha an leabhar so leis a' chaileig ; tha am fear sin leamsa. 5. Co leis am bàta sin ? 6.An leis an iasgair e ? 7. Cha'n eadh. Bha e leis an uiridh ach reic e i, agus is leis a' chiobair a nis e. 8. Nach eil bàta aig an iasgair ? 9. Cha'n eil e aige a nis ach bithidh i aige am maireach. 10. Nach eil an leabhar so le Iain ? 11. Cha'n eil, Is le Seumas e. 12. Ciamar a tha fios agad ? 13. Cha'n eil mi cinnteach. 14. A Sheumais, an leat an leabhar so ? 15. Is eadh. 16. An leat an cu so ? 17. Cha'n eadh, tha abhag dhubh agam. 18. Cha'n eil am fear sin leam-sa. 19. C'aite am bheil t-fhear-sa ? 20. Tha e aig an tigh. 21. An cu mor e ? Cha'n eadh. 22. C'aite an d'fhuair thu e ? 23. Cheannaich mi e an uiridh. 24. Am bheil e agad a nis ? 25. Tha. 26. An e so im ur ? 27. Cha'n e, is e sin im saillte. 28. Am bheil aran sam-bith ann ? 29. Tha aran air a' bhord. 30. Am bheil an t-airgiod agad ? 31. Tha. Tha e an so. 32. Gu'n robh math agad.

LESSON XXI.

205. Translate into Gaelic :—

1. He is after going home (He has gone home). 2. The window was broken by the boy. 3. Is he going there ? 4. No. 5. He is coming here. 6. Are you going now ? 7. The boy is kicking the horse. 8. The man was striking the dog. 9. Is the train going to go ? 10. I do not know. 11. Was it not away last night ? 12. I am buying that sheep. 13. Have you sold the dog ? 14. I am after singing (I have sung) a song. 15. He will be singing a song this evening. 16. He is lying down now. 17. I lifted my hand to strike him. 18. He was striking me. 19. The farmer had struck him.

206. Read in Gaelic and translate into English :—

1. Tha mi air ceannach nan caorach so am feasgar so. 2. Am bheil thu air an cu a cheannach an diugh cuideachd ? 3. Cha'n eil, Cheannaich mi e an raoir. 4. Am bheil thu a' dol dachaidh a nis ? 5. Tha mi a' dol do'n charbad-iaruinn air ball. 6. Cuin a tha thu a' dol dachaidh ? 7. Tha mi a' reic nan caorach so an duigh agus bithidh mi aig an tigh an nochd. 8. Nach eil a' charbad-iaruinn air falbh a nis ? 9. Cha'n eil, ach tha e a' dol am maireach. 10. Am bheil an gille air briseadh na h-uinneig sin ? 11. Cha'n eil fios agam. 12. Bha an uinneag air a briseadh an raoir. 13. Bha an gille air bualadh an eich a' mhaduinn so. 14. Bha e air breabadh a' choin an de. 15. Bha mi a' togail na cloiche 16. Bha a' chlach 'ga togail leis a' ghille.

C

223. Answers to the Questions on the Article :—

1. **Abhainn** is a fem. noun and fem. nouns beginning with a vowel do not require a **t**- prefixed to them. The absence of the **t**- is a guide to the gender of a noun beginning with a vowel.

2. Try to say **an bard** and then **am bard**, the **an** is much harder to say than the **am** ; the **m** sound merges more naturally into the sound of any of the four consonants **b, f, m** or **p**, and facilitates pronunciation. The glossing over of sounds is the keynote throughout Gaelic pronunciation.

3. For the same reason **an duine** is preferred to **a' dhuine**, because **n** of the article and the **d** of the noun being lingual and dental represent a more musical union.

4. **Clach** is a fem. noun and has an aspirable consonant initial, the **n** of the article therefore drops out before the aspiration.

5. **An saoghal** is a nom. sing. masc. noun and is definite, and a prefixed **t**- is not allowed to these masculine nouns, only to feminine, being again an indication of gender to a Gaelic speaker who hears the word used. In the dative sing., however, both masc. and fem. nouns in this **a** group prefix the **t**-.

6. **An spog** is correct because the **s** of **spog** is not immediately followed by a vowel or a lingual.

7. "An " or " a " in English is the *indefinite article* and the Gaelic noun when *indefinite* requires no *article.*

8. **Athair ; d' athair ; air n-athair.**

It will be observed that a knowledge of the varying forms of the article is a sure help to trace the gender of the noun, and that without a knowledge of such gender it is impossible to write Gaelic correctly. A few helps to trace gender are given in introducing the noun (page 59, G.S.T.).

LESSON XXII.

224. Examples of the article applied to nouns :—

anns a' bhàta, in the boat
am bàta, m. the boat.
a' bhean f. the wife
am bord m. the table
a' bhuird, of the table
an long f. the ship
na luinge, of the ship
an t-ord m. the hammer
an uird, of the hammer
an lorg f. the track
na luirge, of the track
am mac m. the son
a' mhic, of the son
am fear m. the man
an fhir, of the man
air a' chreig f. on the rock
an t-slat f. the rod
na slaite, of the rod
leis an t-slait, with the rod

an t-saoir, of the joiner
an leabhar m. the book
na bruachan f. the banks
an t-each m. the horse
am fiadh m. the deer
na h-eich m. the horses
an fheidh, of the deer (*sing.*)
a' chas f. the foot
air a' chois, on the foot
do'n righ, to the king
air an luing, on the ship
air na craobhan, on the trees
na muice f. of the pig
an t-iasg m. the fish
an lamh f. the hand
na laimhe, of the hand
an sgian f. the knife
an sruth m. the stream
an t-srutha, of the stream

an cu m. the dog
air a' chat m. on the cat
am facal m. the word
an taobh m. the side
lamh na caileige, the girl's hand
ceann an eich, the horse's head

ceann na circe, the hen's head

air an t-sruth, on the stream
leis an laimh, with the hand
an t-eun m. the bird
na h-eoin, the birds
casan a' ghille, the boy's feet
casan nam fiadh, the feet of the deer
bun na craoibhe, the root of the tree

226 (corrected). Read in Gaelic and translate into English :—

1. Bha lamh na caileige dubh.   2. Cha robh an gille laidir.   3. Bha an gille fliuch.   4. Cha'n eil am bàta air a' chuan ; tha i air an t-sruth. 5. Cha'n eil an gille an so fathast, ach tha a' chaileag.   6. Tha ceann an eich dubh.   7. Tha ord an fhir sin trom.   8. Tha ceann an uird trom.   9. Cha'n eil na gillean anns a' bhaile.

226 (translated). Translate into Gaelic :—

1. The girl's hand was black, *or* The hand of the girl was black. 2. The boy was not strong.   3. The boy was wet.   4. The boat is not at sea ; it is in the stream.   5. The boy is not here yet, but the girl is.   6. The horse's head *or* The head of the horse is black.   7. That man's hammer is heavy.   8. The hammer head is heavy *or* The head of the hammer is heavy.   9. The boys are not in the town.

227. Read in Gaelic and translate into English :—

1. Tha mac an t-saoir gle thapaidh.   2. Am bheil na slatan agad ? 3. Cha'n eil ; tha iad aig a' chiobair.   4. Tha leabhar a' ghille air a' bhord.   5. Tha athair na caileige aig a' bhaile.   6. Bha e aig tigh an iasgair.   7. Am bheil thu air bhi aig tigh a' chiobair ?   8. Am bheil fios agad c'aite am bheil sgian a' ghille ?   9. Mur eil i aig an tigh tha i caillte. 10. Tha na raimh aig na fir, anns a' bhàta. 11. Am bheil fios agad c'aite am bheil iad ?   12. Bha iad aig na fir an raoir. 13. An robh iad a' seinn air an abhainn an raoir ?   14. Bha na h-eoin a' seinn anns na craobhan air bruachan na h-aibhne.   15. Co a b'e Righ na h-Alba ?   16. Is geur sgian a' ghille.   17. Bha bàta aig an fhear aig taobh na h-aibhne an diugh.   18. Bha mi aig taobh srutha an raoir.

LESSON XXIII

258. Declension of definite nouns :—

N	a' chluas	an t-àl	an dàn	an lòn	an laogh
G.	na cluaise	an àil	an dàin	an lòin	an laoigh
D.	a' chluais	an àl	an dàn	an lòn	an laogh
N.	na cluasan	na h-àil	na dàin	na lòin	na laoigh
G.	nan cluas	nan àl	nan dàn	nan lòn	nan laogh
D.	na cluasan	na h-àil	na dàin	na lòin	na laoigh

N.	a' bhruach	am maor	an tuadh	an t-slat	an ospag
G.	na bruaiche	a' mhaoir	na tuaidhe	na slaite	na h-ospaig
D.	a' bhruaich	a' mhaor	an tuaidh	an t-slait	an ospaig.
N.	na bruachan	na maoir	na tuadhan	na slatan	na h-ospagan
G.	nam bruach	nam maor	nan tuadh	nan slat	nan ospag
D	na bruachan	na maoir	na tuadhaibh	na slatan	na h-ospagan

Declension of indefinite nouns :—

N.	cat	cuan	gradh	dos	sguab	clar	salm
G.	cait	cuain	graidh	dois*	sguaibe	clair	sailm
D.	cat	cuan	gradh	dos·	sguaib	clar	salm
N.	cait	cuain	graidh	dois†	sguaban	clair	sailm
G.	chat	chuan	ghradh	dhos	sguab	chlar	shalm
D.	cait	cuain	graidh	dois	sguaban	clair	sailm

* Has a gen. also in *duis*.　† Also nom pl. in *dosan*.

259. Translate into Gaelic :—·

1. A Scotsman is on the hill.　2 The joiner's axe is broken.　3. A tassel is on the officer's pipes.　4. There are trees in the meadow. 5. The people had sung the song.　6. The boat is at sea.　7. The lock is not on the door.　8. The lock of the door was broken last night.　9. The shoes of the boy are dirty.　10. There were five bulls on the heath.　11. The boy is hungry.　12. The lad is singing a song about the banks.

260. Read in Gaelic and translate into English :—

1. Tha craobh air a' mhonadh　2. Is laoch an t-Albannach (Tha an t-Albannach 'na ghaisgeach).　3. Tha raimh a' bhàta an so. 4. Tha tarbh anns an achadh.　5 Tha biodag ann an laimh a' mhaoir. 6. Cluasan cait.　7. Tha glas air an dorus.　8. Tha glas an doruis briste.　9. Tha run an t-sluaigh an so.　10. Bha mi aig an tur air a' mhonadh.　11. Sheinn am balach dan seann duine.　12. Tha dorus an tuir fosgailte.　13. Tha tuadh an t-saoir geur.　14. Bha cluas an oglaich aig an dorus.　15. Tha cul an t-seann duine salach.

LESSON XXIV

270. Examples of nouns declined definitely :—

N.	an calg (m)	an tromp (f)	am balg (m)	an tom (m)
G.	a' chuilg	na truimpe	a' bhuilg	an tuim
D.	a' chalg	an truimp	a' bhalg	an tom
N.	na cuilg	na trompan	na builg	na tuim
G.	nan calg	nan tromp	nam balg	nan tom
D.	na cuilg	na trompan	na builg	na tuim
	the prickle	*the trumpet*	*the wallet*	*the knoll*

N.	an ceann (m)	an lion (m)	am mac (m)	an gleann
G.	a' chinn	an lin	a' mhic	a' ghlinn*
D.	a' cheann	an lion	a' mhac	a' ghleann
N.	na cinn	na lin	na mic	na glinn*
G.	nan ceann	nan lion	nam mac	nan gleann
D.	na cinn	na lin	na mic	na glinn
	the head	*the net*	*the son*	*the glen*

* The gen. sg. sometimes adds -*e* ; and the plurals are varied :
glinn, gleanna, gleanntan ; dat. pl. gleanntaibh.

N.	am mir (m)		am bord (m)
G	a' mhir		a' bhuird
D.	a' mhir		a' bhord
N.	na mirean		na bordan[1]
G.	nam mir		nam bord
D.	na mirean		na bordan[2]
	the piece.		*the table*

[1] *Also* na buird.   [2] *Also* na bordaibh *or* na buird.

271. Examples of indefinite nouns declined :—

N.	calg (m)	clann (f)	ord (m)	crodh (m̀)	long (f)
G.	cuilg	cloinne	uird	cruidh	luinge
D.	calg	cloinn	ord	crodh	luing
N.	cuilg	clanna(n)	uird	——	longan
G.	chalg	chlann	ord	——	long
D.	cuilg	clanna(n)	uird	——	longan
	a prickle	*children*	*a hammer*	*cattle*	*a ship*
N.	cnoc (m)	caileag (f)	im (m)	cir (f)	sraid (f)
G.	cnuic	caileige	ime	cire	sraide
D.	cnoc	caileig	im	cir	sraid
N.	cnuic*	caileagan	imeannan †	cirean	sraidean
G.	chnoc	chaileag	imeannan	chir	shraid
D	cnuic	caileagan	imeannan	cirean	sraidean
	a hill	*a girl*	*butter*	*a comb*	*a street*

* *or* cnocan.   † im has virtually no plural in common use.

272. Translate into Gaelic :—

1. The man was in the street.   2. Five trout were in the net of yon
man.   3. The hammer is on the table.   4. The badger was in the
hole on the hill   5. A big ship is in the harbour.   6. The stranger
is hunting deer on the moor.   7. The horse is lame.   8. Is there
not fish in the basket ?   9. There are stones in the basket now.
10. I know a blind man.   11. There is no wine in the house.   12.
I was at the head of the loch yesterday.   13. The stream is at the
head of the loch.   14. The land question is the question of questions.
15. I have no knowledge (on) of the law.   16. The little girl with
a big voice.   17. The boy is at the end of the street.

273. Read in Gaelic and translate into English :—

1. Tha long mhor anns a' phort.   2. Tha am broc ann an toll air
an t-sliabh.   3. Tha an t-ord air a' bhord.   4. Tha coig bric aig an
duine anns an lion.   5 Tha ceann a' chuird aig an lic.   6. Tha
cliabh sil air a' bhord.   7. Am bheil iasg anns a' chliabh ?   8. Bha
an coigreach a' sealg fhiadh air a' chnoc.   9. Tha cas an eich crubach.
10. Tha lorgan casan each air an t-sliabh.   11. A' chaileag leis a'
ghuth.   12. Cha robh eolas agam air an lagh.   13. Tha tigh a'
choigrich sin anns an t-sraid so.   14. Tha aran agus im anns an
tigh.   15. Is i ceist na tire (an fhearainn) ceist nan ceistean.   16.

Thug faidh beannachd air an tigh.   17. Tha an duine aig ceann
na sraide.   18. Tha coig bric ann an lion an duine (*or* an fhir).

LESSON XXV.

283.   Translate into Gaelic :—

1. Whose are these books ?   2. Are they not yours ?   3. The
branches of the trees are high.   4. The head of a hen.   5. The
heads of hens.   6. They were at the side of the brook.   7. Do you
know where the smith's son is ?   8. The shepherd's dogs were
hunting the deer on that hill.   9. Is that a deer ?   10. It is = yes.
11. Are there birds on the branches ?   12. The hammer of the
carpenter   13. The lock of the door.   14. Horses' heads.   15.
The horses' heads.   16 The legs of the tables.   17. The lambs are
on the top of the hill.   18. The mare was at the door of the stable.
19. The dog's foot is broken.   20. The feet of the dogs are broken.
21. The boy's dog was on the hill.   22. It is now at home.   23.
The carpenter's house is at the side of the loch.   24. The cat's eye
is on the hole.   25. The top of the teeth is broken.   26. The boy
went in the morning with a load on his back.   27. I opened the
law book.   28. The laws are good.

284.   Read in Gaelic and translate into English :—

1. Bha ciobair air an t-sliabh a mhaduinn so.   2. Bha mi aig tigh
a' phiobair an raoir.   3. Tha bàta an iasgair anns a' phort.   4.
Chi mi brathair a' mhorair aig an abhainn.   5. Tha iuchair an
doruis an so.   6. Tha cathair air taobh deas an doruis.   7. Tha canna
uisge aig a' chaileig bhig,   8. Bha gloine fiona aig an duine sin.
9. Bha leaba itean agam an raoir. 10. Bha teine anns a' bhaile am
feasgar so.   11. Bha feill bainnse an so an de.   12. Tha coilltean
anns an duthaich sin.   13. Tha e air gloine a bhriseadh.   14.
Bha eisg anns na liontan a' mhaduinn so.   15. Fhuair mi brog a'
bhalaich am feasgar so.   16. Tha ord an t-saoir briste.   17. Sheinn
na cailleagan oran.   18. Fhuair sinn leabhraichean a' bhalaich air
bruachan na h-aibhne.   19. Bha leabhraichean a' bhalaich sin fliuch.
20. Tha tigh do sheanar aig ceann-ard an rathaid.   21. Tha daoine
ag obair aig ceann an tighe.   22. Tha tarbh air a' mhachair.

285.   Answers to Examination Questions.

1. The gen. sing. masc. is generally formed by the insertion of
an **i** after the final broad vowel of the nom. ; if the last vowel is **i**
no change takes place.   The insertion of the **i** may displace a diphthong or alter the qualities of the vowels forming it.

2. The gen. sing. fem. is chiefly distinguished by the presence of
a final **e** in addition to the insertion of an **i** as described for the
gen. masc.

3. Fem. nouns never aspirate the gen. sing. and aspirable masc.
nouns only aspirate when used definite.   When indefinite no aspiration takes place.

4. A def. gen. and dat. masc. noun resists aspiration if its initial
consonant is a **d, t ; l, n, r ; sb, sg, sm, st,** or **sp.**

5. Any noun with the definite article, whose initial consonant is either **d, t ; l, n, r ;** or **s,** always resists aspiration.

6. The nom. and dat. plur. of masc. nouns usually takes the same construction as the gen. sing. ; the gen. plur. is the same as the nom. sing. A few masc. nouns of more than one syllable and those ending in **chd** add **-an -ean** and sometimes **-ichean -tean,** chiefly to distinguish these from diminutive forms.

7. The gen. plur. of both masc. and fem. nouns is simply the same as the nom. sing.—indefinite nouns are aspirated if the initial consonant is aspirable.

8. The old dative plur. was formed in (a)**ibh** and this form is still found when the language used is impressive, and especially in proverbs and poetry.

9. Aig dan, dain, do dhan, gutha, do ghuth, ghuthan.

10. The definite article when governing a gen. sing. masc. noun causes the noun to be aspirated if it commences with one of the aspirable consonants b, f, m, p ; c, g. The aspirable consonants **d, t** and **s** do not require aspiration following the **n** of the article, initial **s** when followed by **l, r, n,** or a vowel is however eclipsed by a **t-.**

11 Aspiration is a softening of an initial consonant as an easy approach from a preceding sound. When a gen. fem. noun is not governed by the article the sound is easily produced without requiring this softening influence. Note, however, that an indefinite gen. fem. noun is aspirated when it is used as a qualifying term to another noun, when it follows that noun, ascribing a quality to it as if it were an adj. **(ceann tigh-cheare** top of a hen-house).

LESSON XXVII.

338. Translate into Gaelic :—

1. There are heavy stones in that field. 2. Money is scarce now. 3. The boy is fair. 4. The little girls were fair. 5. A little dog is here. 6. There are not little dogs there. 7. With a sharp rod. 8. In a big town. 9. The feet of a black cat. 10. Heads of black cats. 11. The feet of a black hen. 12. The sheep has black feet. 13. The horns of fierce deer. 14. The head of a fierce deer. 15. In the little ship. 16. The white sails of a big ship. 17. In big towns. 18. White hens are there. 19. This is a big lad's book.

339. Read in Gaelic and translate into English :—

1. Bha an duine beartach crubach. 2. Bha cu beag aige. 3. Is e cu beag dubh a bha ann. 4. An i abhag dhubh a bha ann ? Cha'n e. 5. An abhag cu ? 6. Is cu beag abhag. 7. Nach e cu ban a bha ann ? 8. Bha cu donn aig an dorus. 9. Bhuail caileag olc bheag* cu beag donn an de. 10. Bha i 'na caileig bhoidheich. 11. Bha balach olc a' breabadh eich mhoir. 12. Bha each mor 'ga bhreabadh le balach olc beag*. 13. Is e tigh lom a tha ann. 14. An e tigh lom le dorus caol a bha ann ? 15. Bha e 'na dhuine beartach. 16. Ceann circe duibhe. 17. Cas eich dhuinn. 18. Bo bhorb (or fhiadhaich) ann an achadh mor. 19. Tha caora le casan dubha agus ceann dubh an sin a nis.

* *Better* beag olc.

LESSON XXVIII.

343. Translate into Gaelic :—

1. The day is COLD. 2. Are they the big horses ? 3. They are = yes. 4. Big stones are in this field. 5. Money is scarce now. 6. The black horse is heavy. 7. The spotted cat is lazy. 8. The white dogs are big. 9. Is a hen on the little rock ? 10. The young man had broken the big window. 11. The little white-cow is coming home. 12. The blue hen is blind. 13. Had the young man broken the narrow door ? 14. It's black the small door is. 15. A grey cloud is on the top of the blue firth. 16. The primrose has a beautiful colour (beautiful is the colour that is on the primrose).

344. Read in Gaelic and translate into English :—

1. An robh na gillean olca dhachaidh fathast ? Cha robh. 2. Bha a' chaileag bhoidheach anns an achadh sin am feasgar so. 3. Tha an sgian cheart geur. 4. Bha am maide crom aig an duine sin. 5. Cait' an robh e leis a' mhaide chrom ? 6. Bu mhor an duine e. 7. Tha an tigh leis an dorus bheag chaol an sud. 8. Cha'n e sin an tigh leis an dorus mhor. 9. Bha an t-each dall aig a bhualadh leis na gillean olca. 10. Bha am balach og aig an tigh mhor dhubh an raoir. 11. Tha na craobhan loma air a' mhonadh. 12. Tha na craobhan lom a nis. 13. Cait' am bheil an cu beag donn ? 14. Tha an cu mor dubh leis an duine leis a' mhaide chrom (aig am bheil am maide crom).

345. Correction and Translation :—

a' bhean mhor *the big woman* ; an tigh beag *the little house* ; laimh gile *of a white hand* ; mac an duine bhig *son of the little man* ; ceann an locha *head of the loch* ; beagan de'n aran *a little of the bread* ; lamh-an an droch dhuine *the hands of the bad man* ; lamhan a' ghille shalaich *the hands of the dirty boy* ; mac an tailleir bhig *the son of the little tailor* ; an duine math *the good man* ; bean ghlic *a wise woman* ; na clachan beaga *the little stones* ; seann dana *old songs.*

346. Answers to Examination Questions :—

1. As a general rule a Gaelic adj. follows its noun—there are many exceptions however.

2. The adj. in English has no inflection for gender, but the Gaelic adj. agrees with the gender of its noun when it follows the noun as a qualifying term.

3. Adjs. of one syllable form their plural by adding an **a** or an **e** according to the correspondent vowel. Adjs. of more than one syllable have the plural like the nom. sing.

4. The nom. sing. masc. is the primary form of the adj. To form the gen. masc. the nom. is aspirated and an **i** is generally in-troduced or the vowel suffers a change in the same manner as the noun having similar vowels and diphthongs

5. The nom. sing. fem. of the adj. is the primary (nom masc) form aspirated ; while the gen. fem. introduces an **i** or makes a vowel

charge, and also adds a final **e**, all after the same manner as nouns having similar vowel combinations.

6. It is chiefly adjs. of one syllable which precede their nouns. These suffer no change in termination but they are aspirated by the article and themselves cause aspiration of the noun, if its initial letter is one of the aspirable consonants.

7. All adjs. aspirate the noun when the adj. is first word of the compound, except when some linguals and dentals meet in close contact.

8. Some adjs. preceding nouns do not aspirate these nouns because it is found that when some words end in a certain sound it is easy to approach the following word without aspiration. Aspiration is a softening of a consonant to avoid two harsh sounds in close contact. In some cases the words are mutually accommodating.

9. Aspiration of an adj. when nom. indicates a fem.; asp. in a gen. indicates a masc. Aspiration will be found a key to gender in most instances.

10. When the adj. is used attributively and follows its noun it agrees with the noun in gender, number and case. **bean mhor, an fhir mhoir, na fir mhora.**

LESSON XXIX.

351. Exercise on **tha** and **is** + adj.

1. Tha na coin tapaidh. 2. Is tapaidh na coin. 3. Bha an laoch treun. 4. Bu treun an laoch. 5. Bha an drochaid duinte. 6. Bu duinte an drochaid. 7. Tha an t-each luath. 8. Is luath an t-each. 9. Tha an t-sobhrach buidhe. 10. Is buidhe an t-sobhrach. 11. Tha na neoil dubh. 12. Is dubh na neoil. 13. Tha a' ghaoth laidir. 14. Is laidir a' ghaoth. 15. Tha an t-uan og. 16. Is og an t-uan. 17. Tha an cu dileas. 18. Is dileas an cu. 19. Tha mi sona. 20. Is sona mise. 21. Tha an cu donn borb. 22. Is borb an cu donn.

LESSON XXX.

368. Translate into Gaelic :—

1. John was the tallest of the family. 2. This tree is the biggest in the wood. 3. James is taller than John. 4. Sarah was smaller than James. 5. Sarah is the eldest of the family. 6. The heaviest stone in the field. 7. The richest man in Scotland. 8. A sheep is smaller than a cow. 9. Sarah is worse than James. 10. James was stronger than John. 11. Is the dog worse than a cat? 12. This tree is nearer than that tree. 13. Whiter is your hand than my hand. 14. Are you going farther? 15. I would be the better of that. 16. Is John the eldest in the company? 17. Edinburgh is prettier than Glasgow. 18. It is not the worse of that. 19. James is old but Sarah is older. 20. The horse is tired but the dog is more tired. 21. The farmer came and he broke (bruised) the feet of the dogs.

369. Read in Gaelic and translate into English :—

1. Tha Iain na's airde na Seumas. 2. Is e as sine de'n teaghlach. 3. Cha'n e as sine de'n teaghlach. 4. Is sine Mor na e. 5. Is i Mor as sine a bhitheas de'n teaghlach. 6. Nach eil Iain na's sine na

Seumas ? 7. Tha Iain na's oige na Seumas. 8. Is lugha a' chaora na a' bho. 9. Am boidhche Duneideann na Glascho ? 10. Is bige Duneideann na Glascho. 11. Is e Glascho as mo na Duneideann ach is e Duneideann as boidhche. 12. Is truime na clachan anns an achadh so na iad sud anns an achadh sin. 13. Cha mhisde iad sin. 14. Tha na craobhan as airde air a' mhonadh sin. 15. An abhainn as mo an Albainn. 16. A' bheinn as airde an Albainn. 17. Cha'n eil a ghealach cho soillear ris a' ghrein. 18. Ciod as fearr na or ? 19. An gille as miosa anns an sgoil. 20. An la as giorra anns a' bhliadhna. 21. Is e sin an tigh as mo anns a' bhaile.

370. Answers to Examination Questions.

1. A comparative may express an equality or an inequality. There is only one form of the comparative adj. in Gaelic. What we term the comparative is not used in Gaelic when we compare an equality.

2. A comparative of equality is expressed by using the conjunction **cho** preceding the positive or primary form of the adj. with the prep. **ri** following the adj.

3. When **de** is used with a comparative adj. we are most likely to have a superlative in the English translation.

4. The positive adj. is the simple, primary or root form, as we might term it, as used with the nom. sing. masc. noun.

5. The English superlative adj. ending in -est is translated by transposing it into a relative phrase, using the relative verbal form of **is** or **as** which may be translated in English " who is " or " which is."

6. The three most common comparative adjs. are—

beag little, small	**lugha** less
math good	**fearr** better, best
mor great, big	**mo** greater

Others will be found in par. 366 *Gaelic Self Taught.*

LESSON XXXI.

386. Translate into Gaelic :—

1. Four men and five women were on that boat. 2. Two hundred lambs and a hundred and (a half) fifty sheep were in the sheepfold. 3. The fourth boy and three dogs are on the hill. 4. One of the dogs is lame. 5. Seven lambs were in the sheepfold yesterday. 6. Two sheep were there this evening. 7. Sixty sheep and forty lambs are in the park. 8. Two little rods and one net are in the boat. 9. How many fish were in the net ? 10. Eighteen hundred and five fish. 11. The boy's two shoes are in the house. 12. Seven days are in each week. 13. What time is it ? 14. It is ten minutes to two o'clock. 15. When will the train leave ? 16. It goes away at nine thirty-five o'clock (before mid-day = a.m) 17. I have ten books, but the tenth one is my father's. 18. The third man is tired. 19. How many men are in the town ? 20. Yonder is the twenty-first man (or one). 21. How many lambs are in the sheepfold ? 22. Seventy. 23. Were the dogs on the hill yesterday ? 24. How many were there ? 25. Three. 26. The three dogs were with the shepherd.

* How many a lamb.

387. Read in Gaelic and translate into English :—

1. Tha naoi caoraich dheug anns an achadh sin agus tha aon chaora dheug anns an achadh so.   2. Cia meud caora tha anns an da achadh so ?   3. Tha deich caoraich fhichead anns an da achadh so.   4. Tha deich ba agus da tharbh anns a' phairc sin.   5. Tha tri fir agus da bhalach anns a' bhàta sin an sin.   6. Tha ceithir slatan agus da lion aca leotha.   7. Cia meud iasg tha aca ?   8. Tha an ciobair agus a thri coin air a' mhonadh.   9. Tha ceithir fichead caora agus a coig aige air a' mhonadh sin agus ceithir fichead caora agus a deich air a' mhonadh sin.   10. Tha an ceathramh cu aige crubach an diugh.   11. Cuin a dh' fhalbhas an carbad-iaruinn as an so ?   12. Falbhaidh a' cheud charbad iaruinn aig deich mionaidean ar fhichead an deidh naoi uairean roimh meadhon la.   13. Nach eil aon aig aon uair deug ?   14. Falbhaidh an dara carbad-iaruinn aig da uair dheug air a' mheadhon la.   15. Cha'n eil e ach naoi uairean an drasda.   16. Tha m' uaireadair coig mionaidean deug air deireadh.   17. Tha fichead tasdan anns a' phunnd (Shasunnach) agus da sgillinn dheug anns an tasdan.   18. Cia meud sgillinn tha anns a' phunnd ?   19. Bha coig tasdain deug aige agus bha deich tasdain agam-sa.   20. Cia meud a bha againn ?   21. Tha da chois agus da laimh aig a' bhalach bheag so.   22. Tha da bhroig aige air a chasan.   23. Tha se balaich aig an treasa duine.

388.   Correction and Translation :—

Aon bho *one cow* ; aon bhuth *one shop* ; aon duine *one man* ; da chois *two feet* ; da dhuine *two men* ; da fhichead *forty,—two score* ; da mhile *two thousand* ; da bhroig *two shoes* ; tri casan *three feet* ; tri tasdain *three shillings* ; aon fhear deug *eleven men* ; naoi earbaichean deug *nineteen roes* ; mile caora *a thousand sheep* , tri mile fear *three thousand men* ; a' cheud fhear *the first man* ; a' cheud chlach *the first stone* ; an ceud duine *the first man* ; seachd caoraich dheug *seventeen sheep.*

389.   Answers to Examination Questions :—

1. We always say **aon duine** and never **aon dhuine** because a final **n** never aspirates an initial d in a following word, the hiatus between the two letters is not conflicting and the **d** is not requiring the smoothing breathing sound which aspiration provides.

2. **da dhuine** is correct; we would never say **da dhaoine,** because as already stated, the numeral **da** governs an old dual form which is similar to the dat. sing. in form.

3. **da shgillin** should read **da sgillinn, sg** is a consonant combination which resists aspiration ;   **da broige** should read **da bhroig, broige** should be aspirated and should omit the final e of the gen. as **da** governs a dual or dative form ;   **da choise** should read **da chois,** the final **e** of the gen. fem. being omitted in this dual or dat. fem.

4. **Ooig tasdain dheug** should read **eoig tasdain deug**—the **deug** here should not be aspirated (see answer to Number 1).

5. In certain circumstances **deug** does not aspirate (see par. 376, G.S.T.).

6. **da** is only aspirated when standing alone as a noun. In this position it has a separated particle **a** in front which causes aspiration, **a dha**.

7. **a dha** is the cardinal number when it is used as a noun ; **an da**— the article **an** is often used before the numeral when it means "the two." Notice that the particle **a** causes **da** to be aspirated but the final **n** of **an** does not require the **da** to be aspirated : **na dha** which is a plural form is sometimes met with, an instance of the dual and the plural form being used indiscriminately.

8. **A' cheud** requires a noun following it to be aspirated. No other ordinal requires aspiration.

LESSON XXXII.

399. Translate into Gaelic :—

1. It was wet yesterday.   2. A man is at the door ; he is tired.   3. The boys are going to the town.   4. They are going there* to-day. 5. I will be in the town to-morrow.   6. He threw a stone and he struck me.   7. You struck him.   8. Did you not strike him ? 9. How are you ?   10. I am very tired.   11. This is the dog.   12. It is not.   13. This is a cat.   14. It is not mine.   15. We were there ourselves last night.   16. I saw him and the girl in the door.   17. Were they not in the house ?   18. Are they at the door ?   19. They are at the door.   20. Are they not at the door ?   21. No.   22. Will they be in the town.   23. No.

* *or* into it.

400. Read in Gaelic and translate into English :—

1. Bithidh mi anns a' bhaile am maireach.   2. Tha e fliuch a nis. 3. Bha an gille aig an dorus.   4. Bhuail thu e an raoir.   5. Bha e an sin an de.   6. An do bhuail thu e ?   7. Thilg mi clach agus bhuail si e.   8. Bhuail a' chlach a' chaileag.   9. Bha i aig an dorus.   10. Chaidh iad do'n bhaile an nochd.   11. Tha iad a' dol am maireach. 12. Bithidh sinn an sin an earar.   13. An robh thu aig an tigh an raoir ?   14. Bha.   15. Bithidh thu aig an tigh am maireach.   16. Thubhairt mi nach bi i an sin.   17. Bha mise mi-féin ann an raoir. 18. Cha robh mi an sin an diugh.   19. Thubhairt thu gu'm bitheadh thu a' dol am feasgar so.   20. Tha an leabhar so leam-sa agus am fear sin leis a' ghille.   21. Bha e an sin an de

LESSON XXXIII.

406. Translate into Gaelic :—

1. We have books.   2 I am afraid (fear is on me).   3. I gave bread to him.   4. Put from you the book and tell us a story or sing a song. 5. Put your coat under her.   6. They were greatly afraid.   7. I said to her.   8. Go with him to the town.   9. Put off your wet coat. 10. There is rain.   11. I will go with you in the morning.   12. I came with them last night.   13. Give me your hand.   14. Farewell. 15. That book is James's (belongs to James).   16. James has a book 17. They took from you these books.   18. She put on her coat and she came with my son to the hill.

407. Read in Gaelic and translate into English :—

1. Na biodh eagal ort. 2. Cha robh eagal orm agus cha bhi eagal orm. 3. Bha fearg air an duine an diugh. 4. Bha fearg ort an raoir. 5. Cha'n eil aithne agam air agus cha'n eil aithne aige orm. 6. Is leam-sa an tigh so. 7. Tha tigh aige. 8. Tha tigh agam ach cha'n e mo thigh fein e. 9. Nan robh aran againn cha bhitheadh acras oirnn. 10. Nach eil an t-acras ort ? 11. Tha an t-acras orm. 12. Am bheil an t-uisge ann ? 13. An robh an t-uisge ann an de ? 14. Bithidh an t-uisge an so am maireach, bha an t-uisge an sin an diugh. 15. Tha an t-uisge ann. 16. Tha na leabhraichean aca. 17. Innis daibh an sgeul. 18. Na cuir fodham d'ad. 19. Thainig mi romhad an raoir. 20. Thainig thu eadar Iain agus Seumas. 21. Bithidh iad as a' bhaile an diugh. 22. Bithidh mi leo anns a' bhaile an earar. 23. Bithidh sinn a' dol ris a' bhaile a nis.

LESSON XXXIV.

416. Translate into Gaelic :—

1. Our horses are in the stable. 2. Is your horse there ? 3. No. 4. It is in the park. 5. My father is at the door but my mother is in the house. 6. Is your dog here ? 7. Yes. 8. My hair is wet now. 9. This is my dog. 10. The boy is at the town. 11. Her son was there yesterday. 12. He will not be here to-morrow. 13 These shoes are mine. 14. The book is James's (belongs to James) 15. You will go with me. 16. My chair was broken. 17. He threw a stone, it struck my foot and cut it.

417. Read in Gaelic and translate into English :—

1. Tha mo mhathair aig an dorus. 2. Am bheil do chu an sin ? 3. Cha'n eil, tha mo chu anns an tigh. 4. Tha m' athair an so a nis. 5. Cha'n eil a mhac an so. 6. Bithidh a mac anns a' bhaile am maireach. 7. Cha'n eil e an sin a nis. 8. Bhuail am bàta creag. 9. Bha aca ri tighinn aiste. 10. Chaidh iad g'am marbhadh. 11. Tha an ad sin leat-sa. 12. Is leo-san an tigh so. 13. Is e sin a cota 14 Theid mi leat. 15. Is le Seumas an leabhar. 16. Thilg mi clach agus bhuail i a chas.

418. Correction of errors and translation.

m' fhalt *my hair* ; m' athair *my father* ; do chu *your dog* ; do chas *thy foot* ; am fear *their man, one* ; an cu *their dog* ; bhur tigh *your house* ; mo bhrog-sa *my shoe* ; do shuil-sa *thine eye* ; ar bàta-ne *our boat* ; an athair *their father* ; am mac *their son* ; bhur n-athair *your father*.

419. Answers to Examination Questions :—

1. The possessive adj. precedes the noun to which it is a defining term

2. The possessive adj. does not change for gender in any circumstances.

3. Mo chathair, do chathair, a chathair, a cathair.

4. m' fhalt, t' fhalt, ' fhalt, a falt.

5. The emphatic increase with the possessive adj. is placed after the noun, or if one or more adjs. qualify the noun the emphatic increase is attached to the last adj. These emphatic increases are always the same according to the person of the pronoun and do not follow the rule " **caol ri caol.**"

6. The English possessives " mine," " thine," " hers," etc., are translated by the verb **is** with the prepositional pronoun formed from **le**, thus : **is leamsa**. mine ; **is leatsa** thine ; **is leibh** yours ; **is leatha** hers.

7. We use **a** when " his " is used in the English sentence as an adj. qualifying a noun. We use **leis** when " his " is a pronoun and when it means " ownership " or " belonging to him."

LESSON XXXV.

435. Translate into Gaelic :—

1. He is a youth. 2. He is in haste. 3 I am in my garden. 4. I am in my house. 5. They are in their boat. 6. We are asleep. 7. I am lying (abed). 8. He was sensible. 9. He is a minister. 10. He is being struck. 11. She is being struck. 12. Was a horse kicking you ? 13. No, it was kicking him (*bhreabadh-san*). 14. You are a good man. 15. You are a liar. 16. He was a bad man.

436. Read in Gaelic and translate into English :—

1. Tha m' each anns an achadh ach tha fhear-san 'na gharradh. 2. Tha a braithrean ann an tigh t'athar. 3. Bha iad air an long. 4. Bha Seumas 'na sheoladair. 5. Tha iad ag radh gu bheil Iain 'na shaor. 6. Bha i 'ga bhualadh agus bha e 'ga bualadh. 7. Bha mi 'nam choigreach. 8. Tha e 'na bhàta. 9. Tha mi 'nam sheasamh. 10. Bha e 'na chadal 'na thigh. 11. Tha thu 'nad chabhaig. 12. Tha mi 'nam shlainte. 13. Bha i 'na ban-chealgair. 14. Bha an gille 'na amadan. 15. Bha e 'na ghealtair 16. Bha an duine sin 'na dhuine uasal.

LESSON XXXVI.

454. Translate into Gaelic :—

1. He is the man who ate the bread. 2. He is the boy who was cold. 3. The man from whom you took his boat. 4. How are you ? 5. He is the boy who struck me. 6. The work at which you were. 7. He said that I was sick. 8. The cup out of which you will drink. 9. The table on which he will not be. 10. I heard all that they said. 11. Did they say that they were cold ? 12. Where is the boy who found the knife ? 13. Is he not in the stable? 14. Who was in (at) the door ? 15. It is the man who will not take the woman. 16. The man who did not hear me. 17. The house in which he was. 18. Who was with the boys in the field ? 19. The men were with the boys.

455. Read in Gaelic and translate into English :—

1. Phaidh an duine sin na fhuair e. 2. Co e ? 3. Ciod e ? 4. Is e an duine aig am bheil an t-each. 5. Chaidil mi anns an tigh 'san robh e. 6. Co aige a tha an t-each ud anns an achadh ? 7. Co chaill an sgian anns an tigh ? 8. Co e a chaill an sgian so 'nam thigh ? 9. Chunnaic sinn an gille a bha anns a' bhàta. 10. Bha mi an sin. 11. Is e mo mhiann-sa gu'm fàic thu slan mi. 12. Is esan am fear as fearr a bhitheas (ann). 13. A' bheinn as airde an Albainn. 14. Ciod is crioch araid do'n duine ? 15. Cha'n e sin an tigh far (*or* anns) an robh sinn. 16. Is e sin an duine a dh' fhosgail an dorus.

LESSON XXXVII.

460. Translate into Gaelic :—

1. Whose is this ? 2. Do you not know who he is ? 3. The boat on which we were was broken. 4. That is the field in which there is no tree. 5. Who has the money ? 6. Whose is the money ? 7. The man from whom we got the boat was a sailor. 8. What is it about which you are speaking ? 9. I bought the horse which you did not buy. 10. I gave this book to a man who had no money. 11. Who did this ? 12. What is this ? 13. This is a dog. 14. What is that ? 15. It is that bag which the girl had. 16. Whoever (=who in the world) gave it to the girl ? 17. Who were with the boys in the field ? 18. The men were with the boys. 19. Who broke the window ? 20. Which of them did that ? 21. It is Malcolm or John who broke it ?

461. Read in Gaelic and translate into English :—

1. Co e ? 2. Cha'n eil fios agam co e. 3. Am bheil fios agad co a tha aig an dorus ? 4. Co e ? 5. Tha an gille a bhris an uinneag an so a nis. 6. Theich a' chaileag a chunnaic thu. 7. Co rinn e ? 8. Co aca rinn e ? 9. Ciod e ? 10. Thug Seumas dhomh e ach bhris duine e. 11. Chaidh e a steach do'n tigh anns an robh a mhic. 12. Cheannaich e am bàta bho sheoladair aig nach robh airgiod. 13. Bha am fear o'n d' fhuair mi an sgeul 'na shaighdear nach robh og. 14. Theich am fear a bhuail mi. 15. Co a b'e ? 16. Cha robh aithne agam air. 17. Tha am bàta mu'n robh thu a' labhairt air a' chladach. 18. Co leis an robh e ? 19. Is e bàta an iasgair a bhiodh ann. 20. Co aca a thubhairt sin ? 21. Co sam bith a thubhairt e theich e. 22. Ciod e so ? 23. Is e maileid a thug iad dhomh. 24. Co aca a thug dhuit sin ? 25. Co leis a tha so ? 26. Nach leat-sa e ? 27. Cha'n eadh.

LESSON XXXVIII

469. Translate into Gaelic :—

1. This cow is black. 2. It is black this cow is. 3. It is a black cow that is here. 4. What is this, Mary ? 5 This is a big stick. 6. Where was yon woman ? 7. She was in that house. 8. This man is wet. 9. That man is in his boat. 10. What is that ? 11. That is a dog. 12. What is yon ? 13 Yon is a boat. 14. Yon is not

a boat.   15. That is to say that I am a liar ?   16. There you have it.
17. With that I struck him.   18. Lift that.

470.   Read into Gaelic and translate into English :—

1. Tha an cu so dubh.   2. Cha'n eil an cu sin dubh.   3. Is i so bo
bhan.   4. Cha'n eil a' bho ud ban.   5. Ciod e sin ?   6. Co e so ?
7. Is e am fear sin.   8. Tha an gille so fliuch.   9. Tha e ag radh
gu'n robh e an sin.   10. Leis a sin theid mi dachaidh.   11. Ciod e
sin a tha agad ?   12. Cha'n aithne dhomh an cu so.   13. Cha'n e
so an leabhar a fhuair mi an raoir.   14. Sin iad a' tigbinn o'n bhaile.
15. Sin am baile air a' mhonadh an sin.

471.   Answers to Examination, Questions :—

1. The demonstrative in Gaelic changes for neither gender nor case.

2. We may term the demonstrative an adjective when it serves
to point out one noun from another.   Thus :—

3. **An duine so** this man, the man here, close at hand—distinguishing him from any others who may be about.

4. The demonstratives may be termed pronouns when they are
not attached to a noun, but are used in place of a noun.

5. As a pronoun the demonstratives are generally used with the
verb **is** which may, however, be omitted, but if so its influence may
still be felt.   Thus : **sin a' bheinn** that is the mountain.

6. **Sin** for " that " is used when " that " is a demonstrative adj.
or pronoun, but never used before a verb.   Before a verb " that "
is a relative and is translated by **a**, **an**, or **nach**.

7.   (a) As an adj.   an duine so   this man
      (b) As a pronoun   sin an duine   that is the man
      (c) As a relative   an duine a bhuail the man that I
                            mi   struck

8. When the demonstratives are used adverbially they are almost
pronouns.
          so iad a' tighinn   here they are coming
          sin iad a' dol   there they are going

LESSON XXXIX.

474.   Translate into Gaelic :—

1. How many trees are in the garden ?   2. What are you saying ?
3. The boys were in the park yesterday and they threw stones on one
another.   4. Who broke the window ?   5. All were breaking windows.   6. Whoever is here now, I will be there to-night.   7. Some
say that I am poor.   8. We do not know.   9. When did you go ?
10. We are in our own house.   11. Each man went to his own house.
12. Most of the big stones are in that field   13 The whole of the
small stones are in that other field.   14. Whatever you have done
other men will do.   15. I was alone (with myself) on the boat.
16. Nobody was there (not any-one—there was nobody there).
17. Many people will go there now.   18. All the people were in the
park.   19. Each man will go home.   20. Who is that man and
what is his work?   21. Some say that he is a joiner.   22. When
did he go ?   23. Silver or gold have I none, but that which I have I
will give to you

475. Read in Gaelic and translate into English :—

1. Tha cuid de na clachan anns an achadh so mor ach tha cach beag.
2. Tha barrachd de chlachan mora anns an achadh ud eile. 3. Tha chuid*as mo de na clachan so mor. 4. Tha clachan mora agam 'nam achadh fein. 5. Tha na clachan 'nad achadh fein beag uile gu leir.
6. Bithidh mi 'na thigh an nochd ach theid mi do mo thigh fein am maireach. 7. Tha cuid ag radh gu'n robh e 'na aonar. 8. Cha robh a h-aon an sin an raoir. 9. Bha moran sluaigh an sin an de ach bha na h-uile air dol air falbh. 10. Tha iomadh bliadhna air ais o'n bha moran sluaigh an so. 11. De tha sin ? 12. Ge b'e ni a ni thusa ni fir eile cuideachd. 13. Ge b'e aite an teid thu leanaidh cach (thu). 14. Tha chuid as mo de na h-uinneagan sin briste. 15. Tha gach uile uinneag briste a nis. 16. Co de na fir a dh'fhalbhas ? 17. Tha neach sam bith dhiubh deas.
18. Tha cuid ag radh gu'm bheil e 'na shaor. 19 Tha na h-uile ag radh sin a nis 20. Tha iad uile cearr. 21. Cha robh fios agam gu robh mi cearr. 22. Ciod a bheir thu air a' chu so ? 23. Cha leat-sa an cu sin is e mo chu fhein (a tha ann).

* Tha a' chuid

LESSON XLI.

504. Translate into Gaelic :—

1. I struck the door. 2. He told a story. 3. I left the book. 4. I did not read the book. 5. He did not break the window. 6. Did the man not break the window ? 7. No = he did not. 8. It is the boy that broke the door. 9. I saw the man going home.
10. He did not leave the book in the house. 11. The book was left by the boy. 12. They would tell that. 13. Was it not left on the table ? 14. The book fell on the floor. · 15. The boy ate the bread that was left on the table. 16. I would be struck on the head. 17. I struck the door of the house. 18. The big door was broken. 19. The big hammer was lifted. 20. I left the stone. 21. The boy grew big. 22. The horse fell. 23. Did the horse not fall ? 24. No.

LESSON XLI.

505. Read in Gaelic and translate into English :—

1. Dh'innis mi sgeul. 2. Bhuail e an dorus. 3. Dh' fhag mi an leabhar air a' bhord. 4. Cha do leugh mi an leabhar. 5. Cuin a dh' fhag thu e ? 6. Dh' fhag mi e air a' bhord anns an tigh an raoir.
7. Bu e an leabhar mor (a bha ann). 8. Cha do bhris mi an uinneag.
9. Bhriseadh an uinneag le duine mor a dh'fhag an t-ord so an so.
10. Nach b'iad feadhainn de dhroch ghillean a bhris an uinneag ?
11. Nach do bhriseadh i leis an ord sin ? 12. Thuit an dorus agus bhris e. 13. An d'innis mi sgeul ? 14. Dh' innis thu sgeul dhoibh-san. 15. Cha d'innis thu sgeul dhuinne. 16 An do leugh thu an leabhar sin ? 17 An do bhris e an uinneag ? 18 Bhuaileadh an uinneag leis a' chloich. 19 Tha an t-aran air itheadh leis a' ghille sin. 20. Tha an t-oig-fhear air cuid de aran itheadh. 21. Nach d'ith an gille an t-aran ? 22. Thog an gille e o'n bhord. 23. Thuit e air an lar. 24. Nach do bhuaileadh an cu leis a' ghille ? 25.

Bhuail an gille an cu leis a' mhaide. 26. An d' fheoraich * thu dheth?
27. Dh'fheoraich mi de'n ghille bheag sa mhaduinn. 28. Mur do
bhuail an gille e, co a bhuail e ?

> * **feoraich** (*fyaurrych*) *v.* asking, inquire, inquiring.

We have two verbs in Gaelic representing the English verb
"ask," so that we have to observe whether it means "beseech" or
"enquire" before we translate. Thus: **iarraidh** asking (a favour),
and **feoraich** asking (for information).

> **Dh' fheoraich mi dhi**   I enquired of her
> **Iarr airgiod air do charaid**   Ask your, friend for money

506. Three regular verbs declined.

Thuit mi *I fell*	dh' ith mi *I ate*	dh' fhas mi *I grew*
thuit thu	dh' ith thu	dh' fhas thu
thuit e, i	dh' ith e, i	dh' fhas e, i
thuit sinn	dh' ith sinn	dh' fhas sinn
thuit sibh	dh' ith sibh	dh' fhas sibh
thuit iad	dh' ith iad	dh' fhas iad
cha do thuit mi	cha d' ith mi	cha d' fhas mi
I did not fall	*I did not eat*	*I did not grow*
cha do thuit thu	cha d' ith thu	cha d' fhas thu
etc.	etc.	etc.
nach do thuit mi ?	nach d' ith mi ?	nach d'fhas mi ?
did I not fall ?	*did I not eat ?*	*did I not grow ?*
nach do thuit thu?	nach d'ith thu ?	nach d'fhas thu ?
etc.	etc.	etc.
na'n do thuit mi	na'n d'ith mi	na'n d'fhas mi
if I did fall	*if I did eat*	*if I did grow*
na'n do thuit thu	na'n d'ith thu	na'n d'fhas thu
etc.	etc.	etc.
mur do thuit mi	mur d'ith mi	mur d' fhas mi
if I did not fall	*if I did not eat.*	*if I did not grow*
mur do thuit thu	mur d'ith thu	mur d' fhas thu
etc.	etc.	etc.

LESSON XLII

515. Translate into Gaelic :—

1. I will put the bread on the table. 2. I shall not put it there.
3. If it will be placed he will lift it. 4. Did they lift the stones ? 5. If
they will lift the stones they will be tired. 6. The little boy will
strike the door. 7. We will strike the door with a hammer. 8.
The door of the house will be struck. 9. I will strike the horse.
10. Will you not strike that horse ? 11. If I will leave the dog will
you strike it ? 12. The man whom I would lift. 13. He said that
he will strike the table. 14. I will lift this stone. 15. The stones
will be broken. 16. When will you leave the town ? 17. I will leave

the town to-morrow.   18. I will not tell when I will leave here.
19. He is the man who would not drink the milk.   20. Whenever that
happens will you tell me ?   21. Will the bread be eaten ?   22. The
water will not be eaten but will be drunk.   23. Will you drink this
milk ?   24. The window will not be broken.

516.   Read in Gaelic and translate into English :—

1. An cuir mi an t-aran air a' bhord ?   2. Tha aran air a' bhord.
3. Cha chuir mi e far an tog se e.   4. Buailidh iad an dorus le maide.
5. Nach bris iad an dorus ?   6. Cha tog iad na clachan sin.   7.
Mur do thog iad na clachan sin, fagar iad an sin. 8. Cha tog mi na
clachan.   9. Cha bhrisear na clachan.   10. Brisidh Iain an uinneag
sin ma thilgeas e clachan.   11. Brisear an uinneag.   12. Cuiridh
mi na clachan air falbh.   13. Cha bhuail sinn an uinneag.   14.
Is esan am fear nach oladh uisge.   15. An ol e bainne ?   16. Cha'n
ol, mur ol e bainne, co a dh' olas e ?   17. Olaidh an cat e.   18.
Cha'n olar e leis a' chat.   19. Cha bhi am bainne sin math.   20.
Ma chuireas thu air a' bhord e olaidh cuid-eiginn e.

LESSON XLIII.

525.   Translate into Gaelic :—

1. I would strike the door.   2. He would strike the door.   3. We
would strike the door with stones.   4. The big boy would be struck
with a stick.   5. I would break the window with the hammer.
6. I would not lift the hammer.   7. I would tell on the man.   8.
I would not tell on the boy.   9. They would lift the stones and
they would fall on the street.   10. What would I tell to the man in
the morning ?   11 I saw the man reading the book.   12. That man
would not read this book.   13. If you would lift it I would not tell
(to) the man.   14. I would put the book on the table.   15. I would
not leave it on the floor.   16. He said that he would come with me.
17. Would the bread not be eaten on the table.   18. No = it would
not   19. I would drink the milk if she would leave it.   20. Malcolm
would break the stones with the heavy hammer.   21. Would I not
strike the door with a stone ?   22. If I would strike the door would
you strike it ?   23. He said that I would strike the door with those
stones.   24 He is the man who would not strike the boy.

526.   Read in Gaelic and translate into English :—

1. Cha thilginn a' chlach sin.   2. An t-aon a thilgeadh a' chlach sin
bhitheadh e gle laidir.   3. Dh' fhagainn na clachan an sin mur
togadh siad iad.   4. Am fear nach togadh an leabhar.   5. Bhris-
eamaid na clachan na'n leigeadh sibh leinn   6 Na'n tilgeadh tu
clach, bhriseadh tu an uinneag   7. Cha bhristeadh an uinneag.   8.
Am bitheadh na caorach air a' mhonadh a' mhaduinn so ?   9.
Thogadh e a' chlach agus thilgeadh e i air a' ghille.   10. Bhuailteadh
an gille leis a' chloich.   11. Bhuaileadh am fear sin an gille le maide.
12. Thubhairt e nach buaileadh e an gille.   13. Am buaileadh tu
an gille ?   14. Bhuaileadh.

LESSON XLIV.

532. Translate into Gaelic :—

1. Strike the door. 2. Strike the big door with a stick. 3. They would strike the big door.4. Let them be struck with the big stones. 5. Lift a hammer and strike the window. 6. Shut the window. 7. Lift that stone. 8. Do not strike the door. 9. Do not shut the window. 10. Do not leave the rod. 11. Let him not break the window. 12. Let the bread be eaten to-night. 13. Let the bread be left on the floor. 14. Let us leave the hammer in the house. 15. Forsake not the Gaelic. 16 Do not forsake me. 17. Let me put the bread away 18. Do not put the bread away. 19. Let me drink the milk. 20. Let the corn be threshed (struck). 21. Do not put the dog away. 22. Let the cat be lifted and let us put it away. 23. The big house would be built on the rock. 24. Put that man's knife on the table and don't break it.

533. Read in Gaelic and translate into English :—

1. Buail an uinneag mhor le ord. 2. Briseamaid an uinneag le clachan. 3. Buail an dorus le d' mhaide. 4. Tog a' chlach sin agus tilg i air a' chu sin. 5. Leig leis a' chu sin. 6. Na buail e. 7. Cuiream a' chlach sin 'nam phoca. 8. Rachamaid air falbh a nis. 9. Cuir a' chlach so air a' bhord 10. Na cuir i an sin. 11. Na treig mi 12. Na treig a' Ghaidhlig. 13. Ith an t-aran sin ach na ol am bainne. 14. Feoraich de'n fhear sin an sin. 15. Iarramaid aran air. 16. Tog an cu sin. 17. Na tog an cu sin; cha leinn e. 18. Innseam sgeul dhuit. 19. Innis sgeul fhada dhuinn. 20. Cuir an t-aran air falbh a nis. 21. Na ith an t-aran so. 22. Fag an t-aran sin air a' bhord. 23. Tog do thigh air creig.

LESSON XLV.

541. Translate into Gaelic :—

1. Where is the boat ? 2. The boat is broken. 3. The bread is eaten. 4. The window is broken. 5. The knife was broken. 6. The big door is open. 7. The window is shut. 8. That stone is broken. 9. That big stone was heavy. 10. Is the black stone broken ? 11. The door was broken with the hammer. 12. The knife of the boy was good but it is broken now. 13. The dog was tied to the table last night. 14. It was untied (liberated) in the morning. 15. The door will be open. 16. It was shut that the door was = the door was SHUT. 17. Is the door open ? 18. When was the house built (completed) ?

542. Read in Gaelic and translate into English :—

1 Am bheil am bàta so briste ? 2. Cha'n eil, is e sin am bàta briste. 3. Tha an uinneag briste. 4. Bha an dorus mor fosgailte an raoir. 5. Cha bhi e fosgailte an nochd. 6. Fag e duinte a nis. 7. Tha an uinneag duinte. 8. Fosgail an uinneag agus duin an dorus. 9. Bha sgian an duine sin math ach tha i a nis briste. 10. Bithidh an sgian air a fagail air a' bhord an nochd. 11. Ma thogar i an nochd cha'n fhagar i an sin a ris. 12. Am bheil a' chlach mhor briste ?

13. Bithidh na h-uile de na clachan briste.   14. Mur eil a' chlach as mo briste fathast bithidh i briste an diugh.   15. Thogadh i bho'n lar.   16 Am bi a' chlach mhor math ?   17. Am bi thu 'ga cur air a' bhord ?   18. Bithidh sinn 'ga briseadh air an lar.   19. An robh an cu ceangailte ris a' bhord 'sa mhaduinn ?   20. Bha e ceangailte ris a' chathair 'sa mhaduinn.   21. Fuasgailidh mi e a nis.   22. Bithidh e fuasgailte air ball.

LESSON XLVII.

552.   Translate into Gaelic :—

1. He said that I was away.   2. No, but he says that you are going.
3. If he said that he was wrong.   4. Though I would not say anything at all to him he would break the door.   5. Though I would say to him that he was wrong he would say that he himself was right.   6 Catch the man and you will get a knife.   7. I will catch him if I get a penny.   8. Have you caught him ?   9 No, but I will catch him to-morrow.   10. The shepherd said that I would not find a sheep or a lamb.   11 If I will not get my father's house I will leave the country.   12. You will never get that.   13. Who got this fish ?   14. Will I get a fish ?   15. I saw a black man but you never saw a green man.   16. Though we did not see the boat we saw the fishermen.   17 I am saying that any man will see the moon.   18. I see (am seeing) that you are very good.   19. Will a blind man hear music ?   20. A blind man will hear music though he will not see the musician.   21. If I will hear music I will be happy.   22. Did you give the book to the boy ?   23. No.   24. Did the other boys come ? 25 No, but they are coming in the evening.   26. Will you not come to the big town ?   27. Did the men go to the town ?   28. No, but they will go to the wood to-day.   29. If they will not go to the wood to-day they will not go there to-night.   30 If I will arrive in the morning will you give me a drink of milk ?   31. I am going to make shoes.   32. I will do that and we will not be long in reaching it. 33. Are you going fishing to-night ?   34. Yes, if we reach the river before five o'clock we will do good fishing.   35. I will do that and we will not be long in reaching it.   36. Will you do this ?   37. Yes. 38. Who is it who did this ?   39 I did it and I will do it again.

553.   Read in Gaelic and translate into English :—

1. Cha d' fhuair se e an de ach fhuair se e an diugh.   2. De a gheibh e am maireach ?   3. Tha am bàta air a faighinn (Fhuaradh am bàta). 4. Chaidh mi dachaidh agus chunnaic mi m' athair.   5. Nuair a theid mi dachaidh chi mi an duthaich anns an do rugadh mi,   6. Biodh e air a dheanadh a nis.   7. Cha do rinn se e ach na'n d' iarr thu air e dheanadh se e.   8. Cha teid e air falbh fathast.   9. Nach deachaidh e dachaidh an de ?   10. Cha deachaidh, ach theid e dachaidh am maireach.   11. Thoir dhomh-sa sin agus bheir mise dhuit-sa so.   12. C'aite an d'fhuair thu e ?   13. Ma bheireas thu air bheir mi dhuit tasdan.   14. Cha bheirinn air cat dubh air airgiod sam bith.   15. Rug a' bho bhan an de   16.

Chuala mi thu anns an tigh an raoir. 17. Am faic thu an tuathanach an diugh ? 18. Mur faic, chi mi e am maireach. 19. Na'm faicinn e an nochd, gheibhinn bainne bhuaithe. 20. Faiceam (Stad ort) tha an oidhche gle dhorcha, agus cha tig e. 21. Cuin a thig e do'n bhaile? 22. Theid e do'n bhaile am maireach. 23. Fag sin agus dean so. 24. Cuin a rainig i an tigh an raoir ? 25. Thainig an duine sin do'n tigh againn an diugh agus thig e am maireach a rithist. 26. Cha deach e a dh'iasgach an de. 27. Is e so an duine a rinn am bàta. 28. Rachamaid agus faiceamaid i. 29. Gheibh thu leabhar aig an tigh againn mu theid thu (ann). 30. Am faigh mi e ? 31. Thoir domh an leabhar sin. 32. Chualas fuaim an so an raoir. 33. C'aite an do rugadh thu ? 34. Rugadh mi an Glascho ach tha Gaidhlig agam. 35. An do rinn e sin ? 36. An dean e dhomhsa e ? 37. Ni.

LESSON XLVIII.

583. Translate into Gaelic :—

1. What is he doing ? 2. He is singing now. 3. What was he doing ? 4. He was fishing in the stream. 5. What were they building ? 6. They were building a house. 7. Where is he going ? 8. He is going to strike you. 9. He lifted a foot to kick him. 10. He came to see my sister. 11. I am going to strike him. 12. He asked me to shut the door. 13. What will he be doing ? 14. He will be running home. 15. I am coming home now. 16. What are you asking ? 17. Is your father going fishing ? 18. The little girl came to open the door. 19. The big boy is gathering the stones. 20. The men were speaking to one another. 21. The shepherd is going home in the morning. 22. The men were sitting. 23. He is sitting. 24. I am standing here. 25. He lifted a hand to strike us. 26. He is lifting the big hammer. 27. The boy is breaking the stone.

584. Read in Gaelic and translate into English :—

1. Bithidh a' chaileag bheag a' fosgladh an doruis. 2. De tha e a' deanamh a nis ? 3. Tha e ag iasgach anns an t-sruth. 4. De tha an duine sin a' deanamh ? 5. Tha e a' dol a bhualadh a' ghille. 6. De tha an duine eile a' deanamh ? 7. Tha e a' tighinn a bhreabadh a' choin. 8. Togaidh mi mo lamh chli g'a bhualadh. 9. Tha e a' briseadh mo mhaide. 10. Bha e ag itheadh arain a' mhaduinn so. 11. Bithidh e a' dol dachaidh a nis. 12. Am bi an gille a' ruith air falbh ? 13. Bha na fir 'nan suidhe aig an dorus. 14. De bha thu ag radh ? 15. Bha an gille beag a' trusadh chlach. 16. De bha thu a' feoraich ? 17. Am bi t' athair a' dol a dh' iasgach am feasgair so ? 18. Tha an gille a' briseadh chlach le ord. 19. Bithidh e 'gar bualadh leis na clachan. 20. Bha sinn 'gam briseadh. 21. Tha Seumas a' cur arain air a' bhord. 22. Bha iad a' ruith dhachaidh. 23. De tha thu a' togail ? 24. Tha mi a' togail tighe bhig. 25. Tha Iain a' bualadh an doruis. 26. Thainig e a dh' fhaicinn mo pheathar an raoir. 27. Bithidh mi 'ga bhualadh. 28. Cha'n eil e air bhi ag ol uisge. 29. Co tha ag radh sin ?

LESSON XLIX.

585. Synopsis of a Gaelic Verb :—

INDICATIVE ACTIVE.

Pres. Prog.	Tha mi ag ol,	I am drinking.	Tha mi a' fagail,	I am leaving.
,, Perf.	Tha mi air ol,	I have drank.	Tha mi air fagail,	I have left.
,, Perf. (contin.)	Tha mi air bhi ag ol,	I have been drinking.	Tha mi air bhi a' fagail.	I have been leaving.
Fut. Indef.	Olaidh mi,	I shall drink.	Fagaidh mi,	I shall leave.
,, Prog.	Bithidh mi ag ol,	I shall be drinking.	Bithidh mi a' fagail,	I shall be leaving.
,, Perf.	Bithidh mi air ol,	I shall have drank.	Bithidh mi air fagail,	I shall have left.
,, Perf. (contin.)	Bithidh mi air bhi ag ol,	I shall have been drinking.	Bithidh mi air bhi a' fagail,	I shall have been leaving.
Past Indef.	Dh' ol mi,	I drank.	Dh' fhag mi,	I left.
,, Prog.	Bha mi ag ol,	I was drinking.	Bha mi a' fagail,	I was leaving.
,, Perf.	Bha mi air ol,	I had drank.	Bha mi air fagail,	I had left.
,, Perf. (contin.)	Bha mi air bhi ag ol,	I had been drinking.	Bha mi air bhi a' fagail.	I had been leaving.

INDICATIVE PASSIVE.

Pres. Defin.	Tha mi olte,	I am drank	Tha mi fagte,	I am left.
,, Prog.	Tha mi 'gam ol,	I am being drank.	Tha mi 'gam fhagail,	I am being left.
,, Perf.	Tha mi air m'ol,	I have been drank.	Tha mi air m' fhagail,	I have been left.
Fut. Indef.	Bithidh mi olte,	I shall be drank.	Bithidh mi fagte,	I shall be left.
	Olar mi,	I shall be drank.	Fagar mi,	I shall be left.
,, Perf.	Bithidh mi air m' ol,	I shall have been drank	Bithidh mi air m' fhagail.	I shall have been left.
Past Indef.	Dh' oladh mi,	I was drank.	Dh' fhagadh mi,	I was left.
	Bha mi olte,	I was drank.	Bha mi fagte,	I was left.
,, Prog.	Bha mi 'gam ol,	I was being drank.	Bha mi 'gam fhagail,	I was being left.
,, Perf.	Bha mi air m' ol.	I had been drank.	Bha mi air m' fhagail,	I had been left.
Subjun. Act.	Bhithinn ag ol,	I would be drinking.	Bhithinn a' fagail,	I would be leaving.
	Dh' olainn,	I would drink.	Dh' fhagainn,	I would leave.
	Bhithinn air ol,	I would have drank.	Bhithinn air fagail,	I would have left.
,, Passive	Bhithinn 'gam ol,	I would be drank.	Bhithinn 'gam fhagail,	I would be left.
	Bhithinn olte,	I would be drank.	Bhithinn fagte,	I would be left.
	Dh' oltadh mi,	I would be drank.	Dh' fhagadh mi,	I would be left.
	Bhithinn air m' ol.	I would have been drank.	Bhithinn air m' fhagail.	I would have been left.

LESSON L

592. Translate into Gaelic :—

1. You may sit but you may not stand. 2. May I stand on the floor ? 3. Must I go back ? 4. You must. 5. If I must go home I will not return. 6. Who may come ? 7. If you must come, you must. 8. We cannot return. 9. You ought to come. 10. I know that we ought to come but we cannot. 11. I had almost fallen just now—I nearly fell just now. 12. You cannot get it now. 13 I cannot know what will happen.. 14. We must be quiet. 15. You must be standing. 16. The girls ought to be quiet. 17. Let him do what he can (is able for). 18. Could you not see the house ? 19. They could not be there at 7 o'clock. 20. Rise and let us come away, said he.

593. Read in Gaelic and translate into English :—

1. Feumaidh mi falbh mur urrainn domh fuireach. 2. Nach faod mi fuireach na's fhaide ? 3. Cha'n fhaod. Feumaidh tu falbh 4. Cha bu choir duibh sin a radh. 5. Is aithne dhomh nach coir dhomh. 6. An aithne dhuibh ciod e ? 7. Cha'n aithne. Is coir fios a bhi agaibh. 8. An toil leat bainne no an annsa leat lionn ? 9. Cha toil leam lionn. 10. Faodaidh thu falbh a nis. 11. Am feum mi falbh a nis ? 12. Feumaidh. 13. Dh' fheum e (B'eudar dha) fuireach gù maduinn. 14. Na'm b' eudar dha falbh bu choir dha innseadh dhuinn. 15. Faodaidh thu fuireach ma's miann leat, ach tha fios agam gur coir dhuit falbh. 16. Cha do rinn e na b'urrainn dha. 17. Bu choir dha na b'urrainn dha a dheanamh. 18. Mur dean e na's urrainn dha cha choir dha a bhi an so. 19. Cha b'urrainn dha faicinn ach b' urrainn dha labhairt. 20. Is coir dhuit na tha fios agad innseadh. 21. Dh' fhaodainn t' fhaicinn anns an fheasgar.

The following examples of the translation of " have " will be useful :—

As described in Lesson XII., the verb " have," expressing " possession," has no actual translation in Gaelic, and' we make up an idiomatic expression with **tha + ag**. The direct object of the verb " to have " in English becomes the subject of the verb **tha** in Gaelic ; thus **tha leabhar agam** I have a book, *lit.* : a book is at me. A similar idiom is used when speaking of physical sensations and emotions **tha fiabhras ort.** You have a fever.

The English phrase " have to " usually means " must " and is translated in Gaelic as such : I have to go home now. **Feumaidh mi dol dachaidh a nis.**

The English verb " must " has no past tense of its own to express " duty " or " necessity." The English past tense would have the force of " had to," and in Gaelic we use the past of **feum.**

I had to go home, **Dh' fheum mi dol dachaidh.**
I would need have gone home, **Dh' fheumainn dol dachaidh.**

The English phrase " must have " always expresses " supposition," and is best translated by the verb **feum** in the present (or future) tense and the verb " to be " in the past.

You must have been tired, **Feumaidh gu'n robh thu sgith.**
He must have gone away, **Feumaidh gu'n d' fhalbh e.**

Compare also the following : We ought to go home **is coir dhuinn dol dachaidh.** But in English the verb " ought " has no inflection for past tense, and we have to use the *past infinitive* in English to express past time. In Gaelic we have a *past* of **is coir** in **bu choir,** and observe that we use the simple verbal noun only, no infinitive sign being required. (579 G.S.T.).

Ought you to have gone to Glasgow ? **Am bu choir dhuit dol do Ghlascho ?**

He ought not to have gone. **Cha bu choir dha dol.**

Examples of the verb " have " in other positions :—

I have written a letter, **Tha mi air litir a sgriobhadh.**
I have struck him, **Tha mi air a bhualadh.**
I have broken the stick. **Tha mi air am bata a bhriseadh.**
Have you done it ? **An do rinn thu e ?**
I shall have finished before you. **Bithidh mi air bhi deas romhad.**
I had written the letter to him. **Bha mi air an litir a sgriobhadh chuige.**

LESSON LI.

611. Translate into Gaelic :—

1 What is the price for the fish ? 2. John got the two fish for a shilling. 3. What came between you, James ? 4. I and the shepherd were on the hill, but the river was between us. 5. Where were you in the morning ? 6. I was fishing. 7. Who was with you ? 8. Malcolm, the joiner's son, was with me. 9. You ought to be in the field. 10. Yes, but I promised a trout or two to Malcolm's mother. 11. The small boy took the black cat from the table. 12. I found the knife between the tree and the house. 13. We went through the town about evening and we reached our home before morning. 14. That man struck me with a stone on the cheek. 15. I will be at the door with a stick at 5 o'clock. 16. The man went past the door just now. 17. I threw the stone across the street. 18. The mouse went through the hole when the cat was after it. 19. That man is without care (careless).

612. Read in Gaelic and translate into English :—

1 Cait' an robh thu a' mhaduinn so ? 2. Bha mi ag iasgach. 3. Co bha leat ? 4. Bha Iain mac an iasgair leam. 5. Nach robh an duine sin leotha ? 6. Tha an tigh eadar an abhainn agus a' mhuir. 7. Theid na gillean dachaidh re an t-samhraidh. 8. Is maith (toil) leinn a bhi ag iasgach anns an abhainn anns an fheasgar. 9. Chaidh

mi mu'n cuairt air an tigh mu choig uairean.   10. Fhuair mi duine
aig an uinneig.   11. Co aca is fearr leat a thighinn leat an uair so ?
12. Feumaidh mi dol gus a' bhaile a nis.   13. Cha choir duit a dhol
'nad aonar.   14. Thig mi leat an diugh.   15. Tha mi a' dol gus a'
bhaile 'nam aonar.   16. Is urrainn duit dol (ann) a nis agus faodaidh
thu a bhi ann romham.   17. Bha mise romhad-sa aig an drochaid an
diugh ach bha esan ann romham-sa.*   18. Bha thu romham aig a'
bhaile an raoir.   19. Tha am balla so ard ach tha mi a' dol thairis air.
20. Tha an t-uisge trom ach tha e a' dol tharainn.   21. Tha an duine
sin a' dol thairis air an abhainn ann am bàta.   22. Na seas eadar
mi agus an teine.   23. Tha e fuar agus tha a' ghaoth a' dol tromham.
24. Bha Iain eadarainn a' mhaduinn so ach tha Seumas eadar thu-sa
agus mise a nis.   25. Tha e so ro mhor domh a nis.   26. Theid a'
ghaoth troimhe.   27. Bha e gun airgiod gun chiall.   28. Tha thu
a' labhairt air a bhi gun chiall.   29. Is fear e is mo ciall.   30. Is
fheudar gur duine foghlumte e.   31. Tha e air tighinn an aite athar.
32. Thuit mi ann an toll agus theab mi mo chas a bhriseadh.   33.
Tha sinn air tighinn troimh thir gun chraobhan.

* The emphatic forms should be used here.

LESSON LII.

617. Translate into Gaelic :—

1. The brown dog is at your back.   2. I saw the man at the front
of the house.   3. He was standing against her.   4. When we were
sitting at the door the little boy threw stones among us.   5. The man
bought the books in my presence.   6. I was amongst the woods in
the morning and I found a small lamb at the head of the road.   7.
I went round about the garden and I found big stones in the place
of the trees.   8. He went inside (of) the house.   9. He put his hand
on my head and I sat in front of him.   10. I came towards the river
and I saw a sheep along with the lamb.   11. I left the dog along with
the horses.   12. Is the black dog along with them ?   13. No.   14.
We went round about the park.

618. Read in Gaelic and translate into English :—

1. Chunnaic mi duine air beulaobh an tighe.   2. Ruith mo chu dileas
air thoiseach orm chuige.   3. Bha sinn 'nar seasamh aig an dorus
agus thilg balach mor clachan 'nar measg.   4. Tha cat dubh air do
chulaobh.   5. Buail e le maide air mo shon.   6. Theid sinn mu'n
cuairt air an tigh a nis.   7. An cuala thu mu dheighinn an duine
sin fathast ?   8. Tha mi air tighinn a los labhairt mu dheighinn sin.
9. An tig thu comhla rium a steach do'n tigh ?   10. Ciod sin os ar
cionn ?   11. Tha a' ghaoth nar n-aghaidh ; an gabh sinn fasgadh
air cul a' bhalla so ?   12. Is leam-sa an tigh sin mu'r coinneamh.
13. Tha e agam an aite aoin a chaill mi le teine.   14. Thainig e 'nar
measg. 15. Chaidh sinn (ann) air son 'na caileige.   16. Chuir mi mo
lamh air a ceann agus shuidh i air mo bheulaobh.   17. An uair a

bha sinn 'nar suidhe aig an uinneig thilg droch ghille clachan 'nar measg. 18. Chuir sinn an cu 'na dheidh agus ruith e air beulaobh duine. 19. Bha am ministear 'na sheasamh an sin an lathair an t-sluaigh. 20. Bha sinn aig muir agus chiall sinn na raimh troimh 'n oidhche.

* **fasgadh** (*fashg ü*) *m*, a shelter.

LESSON LIII.

629. Translate into Gaelic :—

1. The dogs were running here and there. 2. They went out together 3. Is the man at work ? 4. He is down in the pit. 5. He went down last night. 6. He will come up to-morrow. 7. The shepherd went up yesterday. 8. The boys went a quarrelling.* 9. I was never in a boat. 10. I was in a boat yesterday and I will be in another boat to-morrow. 11. Where is the boat ? 12. It is down on the shore. 13. Who is up at the house ? 14. It is that man. 15. He is very good certainly. 16. I heard that John was sick. 17. When did he come ? 18. Is he inside = within ? 19. No, he has gone out with difficulty. 20. Who is with him ? 21. It is James who is there. 22. He has enough Gaelic. 23. Up with the Gaelic. 24. He came over to the door just now 25. He is now here at the end of the house. 26. I was south and north, west and east, but I am now in Scotland. 27. She will never leave it till the western ocean ebbs (goes dry). 28. My excellent dog went in front of me and he made on her (attacked her).

* **thar a cheile** *phr.* at variance (*lit.* over each other).

630. Read in Gaelic and translate into English :—

1. Chaidh an ciobair a suas am monadh anns a' mhaduinn ach thainig e a nuas an deidh mheadhon la. 2. Chaidh e o'n bhaile. 3. An robh e riamh roimhe o'n tigh ? 4. Bha e o'n tigh an uiridh. 5. Cuin a thig e dachaidh ? 6. C'aite am bheil do mhac ? 7. Tha e anns an tigh aig taobh na h-aibhne. 8. An teid e tarsainn an abhainn ? 9. Cha teid e tarsainn gus an taobh eile an diugh. 10. Dh' eirich an abhainn uidh air n-uidh. 11. Tha a chu a' ruith thall 's a bhos. 12. Tha e air bhi ann mo thigh, ach cha bhi e ann gu brath tuille. 13. Am bheil Gaidhlig agad ? 14. Tha Gaidhlig gu leoir agam. 15. Tha sinn daonnan a' labhairt Gaidhlig anns an aite so. 16. C'aite am bheil do mhac eile an nochd ? 17. Chaidh iad a mach le cheile. 18. Th'ainig mi a nuas o Ghlascho a' mhaduinn so agus theid mi a sios a ris an earar. 19. A reir Iain bu choir dhomh dol na bu mhinige. 20. Is fearr a dhol na's minige gu cinnteach. 21. Cha'n urrainn domh dol an ceart-uair. 22. Chunnaic mi e air taobh thall na h-aibhne am measg nan craobhan. 23. Tha e a' tighinn gu minig ach cha'n fhan e fada. 24. Cuin a bhios e air ais a ris ? 25. Abramaid gach aon fa leth ' Suas leis a' Ghaidhlig.' 26. Tha mi a' dol thar a' chuain gu tir mhor (na h-airde) n-iar agus cha docha leam (cha duth dhomh) tighinn sear a ris. 27. Faodaidh mi dol (gun teid mi) gu deas an ath bhliadhna.

LESSON LIV.

638. Translate into Gaelic :—

1. I have a house and a garden. 2. It is a man or woman. 3. (It is) Not you but James. 4. Mary and her brother. 5. As big as a rock. 6. The shepherd's dogs were hunting the deer on that hill. 7. I enjoyed peace and pleasure. 8. The sun is brighter than the moon (brighter is the sun than the moon). 9. He was so certain as that of (= as to) when he came home, James ! 10. I am as strong as I will be. 11. Those were the laws according to the opinion of John. 12. Well, well ! 13. Farewell.

639. Read in Gaelic and translate into English :—

1. An e fear no bean ? 2. Mo thigh agus mo gharradh. 3. Tha Mairi agus a piuthar an so. 4. Tha a piuthar cho ard agus a bhitheas i (a chaoidh). 5. Bha i cho cinnteach gun robh i a' tighinn an so. 6. Cha bhi sith no solas agam a nis. 7. Bi cho math agus an dorus a dhruidteadh agus an uinneag fhosgladh. 8. Tha Iain cho glic ri Mairi. 9. Am bheil sin a reir Iain ? 10. Theid mi no cha teid mi a reir an ama (na h-uine). 11. Gidheadh, is e do dhleasnas (is coir dhuit) dol. 12. Oidhche mhath leat (*or* leibh). 13. Slan ieat (*or* leibh).

THE GOVERNMENT OF NOUNS.

Compound nouns have the first consonant of the second word of the compound aspirated whether noun or adjective in agreement as an adjective with the gender of the first element. If the second element is a noun in the genitive plural it is aspirated in all cases—

Noun.		*Adjective.*	
Sing.	*Plur.*	*Sing:*	*Plur.*
òr-chèard, *a goldsmith:*		crom-chas, *a bandy-leg.*	
N. òr-chèard	òr-chiuird	N. crom-chas	crom-chasan
G. òr-chiuird	òr-cheard	G. crom-choise	chrom-chas
D. òr-cheard	òr-chiuird	D. crom-chois	crom-chasan
V. òr-chiuird	òr-chearda	V. chrom-chas	chrom-chasan

Masculine.		*Feminine.*	
Maor-fuinn, *a ground-officer.*		Cearc-fhraoich, *a moor-hen.*	
N. maor-fuinn	maoir-fhuinn	N. cearc-fhraoich	cearcan-fraoich
G. maoir-fhuinn	mhaor-fuinn	G. circe-fraoich	chearc-fraoich
D. maor-fuinn	maoir-fhuinn	D. circ-fhraoich	cearcan-fraoich
V. mhaoir-fhuinn	mhaora-fuinn	V. chearc-fhraoich	chearcan-fraoich

Pàiste giullain, *a chit of a boy.*		Clach mhine, *a stone of meal.*	
N. pàiste giullain,	pàistean ghiullan.	N. clach mhine,	clachan mine.
G. pàiste ghiullain,	phàistean ghiullain.	G. cloiche mine,	chlach*an* mine.
D. pàiste giullain,	pàistean ghiullan.	D. cloich mhine,	clachan mine.
V. phàiste ghiullain	phàistean ghiullain!	V. chlach mhine,	chlachan mine!